LEARNING SYSTEM DESIGN

An Approach to the Improvement of Instruction

• LEARNING SYSTEM DESIGN •

AN APPROACH TO
THE IMPROVEMENT OF INSTRUCTION

ROBERT H. DAVIS
LAWRENCE T. ALEXANDER
STEPHEN L. YELON

MICHIGAN STATE UNIVERSITY

WITHDRAWN

Theodore Lownik Library
Illinois Benedictine College
Lisle, Illinois 60532

McGraw-Hill Book Company

New York   St. Louis   San Francisco   Düsseldorf   Johannesburg   Kuala Lumpur   London   Paris
Mexico   Montreal   New Delhi   Panama   Sao Paulo   Singapore   Sydney   Toronto   Tokyo

LB
1027
.D32
1974

LEARNING SYSTEM DESIGN

An Approach to the Improvement of Instruction

Copyright © 1974 by McGraw-Hill, Inc. All rights reserved.
Printed in the United States of America. No part of this publication
may be reproduced, stored in a retrieval system, or transmitted, in any
form or by any means, electronic, mechanical, photocopying, recording, or
otherwise, without the prior written permission of the publisher.

1 2 3 4 5 6 7 8 9 0 VH VH 7 9 8 7 6 5 4 3

This book was set in Univers by Publications Development Corporation.
The editors were Robert C. Morgan and Deborah Batterman; the designer
was Maxine Olman; and the production supervisor was Judi Frey.
Von Hoffman Press, Inc. was printer and binder.

Library of Congress Cataloging in Publications Data

Davis, Robert Harlan, 1974
  Learning system design.

  1. Lesson planning. 2. Learning, Psychology of.
3. Behaviorism (Psychology) I. Alexander, Lawrence
T., joint author. II. Yelon, Stephen L., joint
author. III. Title.
LB1027.D32   371.3   73-14918
ISBN 0-07-074334-7

TO OUR WIVES AND DAUGHTERS

A series of twelve film strip-tape presentations, a student workbook, and an instructor's manual are available to enable students to practice the skills discussed in this book. These supplementary materials may be purchased directly from:

Instructional Media Center
Michigan State University
East Lansing, Michigan 48824

Contents

Preface

Most human learning does not occur by design. The classroom is unique because it is a designed educational experience. We have written this text to help teachers develop a clear understanding of the ways in which people learn and to prepare them to use this knowledge to design effective learning experiences for their students.

Learning System Design is the outgrowth of the authors' combined experience as learning system designers and training consultants for educationa, industry, and the military. In the course of working with teachers, military instructors, and industrial trainers, it became clear to us that basic principles of learning and instruction are essentially the same for all learners. The examples in the text apply to all levels of instruction. The principles described apply to a wide range of instructional modes including the traditional lecture, independent study, and the newest forms of instructional technology.

Preliminary versions of the manuscript have been used for in-service and pre-service training programs to help teachers develop a more systematic approach to instruction and to acquaint them with instructional principles derived from modern psychology. The text has been class tested at Michigan State for three years and for shorter periods at other schools in the United States and Europe.

The book is designed to enable the reader to participate actively in the learning process in addition to reading about it. As a guide, we have included: (1) an outline at the start of each chapter; (2) a carefully developed set of objectives; (3) response frames, which provide feedback and enable the reader to gauge his own learning; and (4) a posttest for each chapter.

We would like to express our appreciation to the many instructors who have reviewed these materials in preliminary versions and from whom we have learned so much about the learning system design process. In particular, we want to thank Dr. Allan J. Abedor, who gave us the benefit of his insights, background, and experience throughout the writing of this book. We would also like to express our appreciation to Dr. Ernest Tiemann of the University of Texas, who encouraged us to test the first draft of the book at his annual institute for community college teachers. We appreciate his sound advice about content, format, and method. Our debt to teachers who have served as "experimental subjects" is substantial and it would take a book to list them all. Our gratitude goes to those colleagues who have read and reacted to the chapters, including Dr. M. Ray Denny, Dr. Henry Foth, Dr. S. Liebskind, and Dr. Robert N. Singer. Dr. Donald M. Johnson suggested a number of ideas which were incorporated into the chapter on Problem Solving. To our secretaries, Marjorie Burzych, Traute Reimer, Mary Terry, and Carol Vedders, we want to express our thanks for their help; and of course to our wives, Marilyn Davis, Carryl Alexander, and Fran Yelon, for their patience and understanding. Without all of these people and the team at McGraw-Hill, the project would not have been possible.

Robert H. Davis
Lawrence T. Alexander
Stephen L. Yelon

OVERVIEW OF LEARNING SYSTEM DESIGN • REC OGNIZING WELL-FORMULATED OBJECTIVES • DERIVING AND WRITING LEARNING OBJECTIVES • EVALUATING LEARNING SYSTEMS • TASK DE SCRIPTIONS•TYPES OF LEARNING • ANALYZING TASKS, OBJECTIVES, AND LEARNER CHARAC TERISTICS • GENERAL PRINCIPLES OF LEARNING AND MOTIVATION • THE LEARNING AND TEACH ING OF CONCEPTS AND PRINCIPLES • THE LEARN ING AND TEACHING OF PROBLEM SOLVING • PERCEPTUAL-MOTOR SKILLS • THE SYSTEM APPROACH TO INSTRUCTION • **OVERVIEW OF LEARNING SYSTEM DESIGN** • RECOGNIZING WELL-FORMULATED OBJECTIVES • DERIVING AND WRITING LEARNING OBJECTIVES • EVALUAT ING LEARNING SYSTEMS • TASK DESCRIPTIONS • TYPES OF LEARNING ANALYZING TASKS, OBJEC TIVES, AND LEARNER CHARACTERISTICS • GEN ERAL PRINCIPLES OF LEARNING AND MOTIVA TION • THE LEARNING AND TEACHING OF CON CEPTS AND PRINCIPLES • THE LEARNING AND TEACHING OF PROBLEM SOLVING • PERCEPTUAL- MOTOR SKILLS • THE SYSTEM APPROACH TO INSTRUCTION • **OVERVIEW OF LEARNING SYS TEM DESIGN**•RECOGNIZING WELL-FORMULATED OBJECTIVES•DERIVING AND WRITING LEARNING OBJECTIVES • EVALUATING LEARNING SYSTEMS • TASK DESCRIPTIONS•TYPES OF LEARNING • ANALYZING TASKS, OBJECTIVES, AND LEARNER

1

NOTE: An outline precedes each chapter. The topics and subtopics are presented in sequence. Use the outline to organize your study of the chapter.

CHAPTER OBJECTIVES

After reading the chapter, you should be able to:

- Match instructional problems with their causes.
- List components of the learning system design process.
- Given a list of assumptions about teaching and learning skills, correctly identify those that underlie the learning system design process as described in this chapter.

INTRODUCTION

A primary task of professional educators and industrial or military trainers is the design of learning systems. Depending upon the objectives, the interests, and the responsibilities of its designers, a learning system may be as large as the biggest school system or as small a unit as the individual student and a carrel. Learning system boundaries, in this sense, are arbitrary. In this book, the word **design** is used when referring to learning systems, in precisely the same sense as it is used when one speaks of **designing** an information processing system. Good system design implies the careful specification of requirements and objectives, the systematic analysis of these objectives to specify alternative approaches to achieving them, the development of a system to meet the objectives, and the evaluation of its performance.

Students are not infinitely adaptable and their capacities for learning are limited. It has been widely observed that there is an information explosion and that the student is at ground zero; he cannot learn all there is to know or even a substantial part of the knowledge in one field. With so much to be learned, the student must depend on greater selectivity in regard to what he learns and greater control over how material to be learned is presented.

A fundamental, almost trivial, premise underlies this notion of improving the effectiveness of learning through careful system design: there are alternate ways of presenting materials to different students—some of which are better than others and will therefore hold a student's attention better. There are ways of dealing with subject matter that will encourage, and not discourage, further learning. A learning system can be designed to maximize student performance along prescribed dimensions, or performance may change along unknown and perhaps undesirable dimensions. There are ways to design a learning system that takes account of the fact that individuals differ from one another in their abilities, backgrounds, and "styles of learning," or one can refuse to take note of these differences and hope for the best. No responsible educator can ignore these options. His fundamental responsibility is the design, development, and evaluation of learning systems that will maximize student performance on specific criteria at a minimum cost in time, effort, and money.

Whenever one approaches the problem of designing a complex system, there is always the temptation to assume that a fixed sequence of steps will invariably produce the one best solution to the problem. Unfortunately, this is seldom true. There may be an idealized or model solution to particular design problems; but in practice, the optimal approach generally involves deviating from the model in numerous ways. The skilled designer, in fact, has at his disposal both a strategy and a set of principles, procedures, and techniques which he uses as they are needed; consequently, he does not obstinately treat the system design process as if there were only one approach to it, in a fixed and established sequence of formal steps. The designer should recognize that he has a "tool kit" of techniques from which he must select those that are most appropriate to a given situation. Indeed, in large part, his skill is knowing when to apply what tools.

There is an apocryphal story which illustrates this point. It concerns a consultant who was called to General Motors during World War II and asked to advise the management on the repair of a giant press urgently needed for the war effort. The consultant asked for a hammer and ladder; he then climbed to the top of the press, carefully selected a point on the press, and hit it with the hammer. Immediately, the press started working again. Later, the management was concerned when a bill arrived from the consultant for $500. They wrote the consultant a letter demanding to know why he had charged $500 for climbing to the top of a ladder and hitting a press with a hammer. The consultant responded that the $500 was not for climbing to the top of the ladder, nor was it for hitting the press with a hammer. It was for knowing **where** to hit it!

The learning system designer is often in an analogous position to the GM consultant. Frequently, his most critical decision concerns what technique to use and when to use it; however, such expertise is attained only after one has had experience in analyzing and designing many learning systems.

The approach to system design developed in this book is to view the process as an idealized flow of events. In doing so, we have tried to provide the designer with a set of tools which he can use under a wide variety of circumstances. Not all of the tools are appropriate to all situations, and they should be applied selectively. After the reader has mastered the approach described and has had some experience in applying it, he will appreciate the need to deviate from it, selecting those techniques which best fit each particular design problem.

In this chapter, you will learn about the learning system design approach and its uses. The various techniques of learning system design are described in general terms in this chapter; each technique will receive detailed treatment in later chapters.

PROBLEMS IN LEARNING SYSTEMS

Teachers face many problems in attempting to help students learn. There are five major kinds of instructional problems that teachers should try to avoid. They are problems of direction, evaluation, content and sequence, method, and constraints. (See Table 1.1.) The five types are not entirely independent; they overlap somewhat. Tools, techniques, and methods for solving these five types of problems will be covered the chapters that follow.

TABLE 1.1   TYPES OF INSTRUCTIONAL PROBLEMS

Type of Problem	Description of the Problem	Some Consequences
Direction	Goals or objectives are not known by students.	Students try to outguess the teacher.
Evaluation	Evaluation procedures are not known by students.	Unfair testing and grading procedures are used; students dissatisfied.
Content and Sequence	Content is missing. There's no attempt at logical sequence or structure.	Course is perceived as trivial, irrelevant, or disorganized.
Method	Poor conditions to motivate and promote learning.	Students are not motivated and are not learning.
Constraints	Resources such as instructor skill, student abilities, and school's resources are ignored.	Excess demands made of own abilities, and students' abilities; failure to utilize available resources.

DIRECTION PROBLEMS

Students indicate lack of direction by asking such questions as: "What are we learning?" "What are we supposed to study?" "What should we pay attention to in class?" Students may also signal insufficient direction by complaining that the objectives they were given are irrelevant or ambiguous.

EVALUATION PROBLEMS

Teachers reveal evaluation problems by asking: "How do I know my students are learning?" "How do I know the course is working?" "What parts of my course should be changed and in what ways?" "How do I assign fair grades?" "How can I create an exam that will tell me how much the students have learned?" Students express the same problems differently. They ask: "Have I learned anything in this course?" "What does a C+ mean?" "These test questions are ambiguous!" "This test is too hard!"

CONTENT AND SEQUENCE PROBLEMS

When teachers fail to take into account the structure of the knowledge they are trying to teach, they are apt to have content and sequence problems, revealed by glaring omissions in the subject matter they teach or the failure to present prerequisite concepts early in learning. One teacher, for example, complained that his students were handing in unsatisfactory term papers. Although the students were supposed to analyze specific political issues in the paper, what they analyzed were not the issues. After some investigation, it became apparent that the students had not been taught what an issue is. An essential portion of course content had been omitted from the sequence of instruction.

Students signal possible content and sequence problems by statements such as: "You never taught us that." "I don't understand what the teacher is saying!" "The instructor teaches us all kinds of irrelevant garbage." "We never had that before!" "He's talking over our heads!" "I don't understand!" These indicate content which is irrelevant, erroneous, or missing from the course.

METHOD PROBLEMS

Method problems generally become most apparent in student attitudes. If students are bored, complain about their courses, and tend to avoid coming to class and studying, the problem is probably one of method.

In order to determine where the method problem lies, unsatisfactory student performance must be analyzed. One science teacher who consistently gave detailed lectures, complained that students were cutting class and doing poorly on exams. After reviewing his lecture notes and exam questions, it became clear that the students needed a laboratory experience to augment the lecture. The lecture alone was an inappropriate method for the students to acquire the capabilities expected of them. By including a laboratory in conjunction with his lecture, student exam performance improved and class attendance increased.

CONSTRAINT PROBLEMS

Three major resources are needed in designing a learning system: human, institutional, and instructional; however, the availability of these resources is usually limited. Every teacher is limited in what he can accomplish by a set of constraints. His own capabilities and interests automatically restrict him. Student differences in preparation for the course and in ability to learn further limit his procedures. There may be insufficient classroom space, or labs may be too old and poorly lighted. Finally, the supply of instructional resources, such as projectors, film strips, and workbooks may also be limited. In designing a learning system, one must take these constraints into account or else the resulting system will be less effective.

NOTE: *Frames such as the one which follows are an important part of your learning experience. Each chapter contains exercises of this kind. The frames differ in format, but all of them provide you with an opportunity to actively practice the information you have read. Feedback to the frames, or knowledge of results, will be found at the bottom of the page. Such feedback is critical to your learning. You will learn more from each chapter if you respond to the questions by writing your answers and then checking them.*

F R A M E

1.1

Imagine that you are helping teachers identify kinds of problems they have so that they can use the proper tools and techniques to remedy them. Label the problems given here with the letter associated with the type of problem.

_____ 1. Student: *What am I supposed to be studying?*

_____ 2. Teacher: *How can I teach this course without chemicals (or films or slides, etc.)?*

_____ 3. Student: *We learn everything in the same way—lecture.*

_____ 4. Student: *The teacher never tells me exactly how I'm doing on my homework.*

_____ 5. Student: *I can't follow his presentation—he skips around too much.*

a. Direction
b. Evaluation
c. Content and Sequence
d. Method
e. Constraints

LEARNING SYSTEM DESIGN

The origins of learning system design are rooted in the education and training procedure developed intensively in recent years in industrial and military settings. The system approach has two aspects. On one hand, it is a philisophy that conditions the attitude of the system designer towards reality; on the other hand, it is a process and set of conceptual tools.

The central idea in the system's philosophy is very old. There are elements of the system approach in the writings of philosophers from Plato to Whitehead and of many psychologists as well. To see a collection of elements as a system is to recognize that it is made up of interacting and interdependent parts. If we wish to create or improve a system, we must understand its components and the ways in which they interact with one another, as well as the context within which the system is embedded. It is critical to recognize that we cannot change a component of a system without changing the system. Put a computer in a classroom and we do not have the old classroom plus a computer; we have an entirely new system.

FEEDBACK:

1.1   1 a
       2 e   4 b or d
       3 d   5 c

While it is possible to improve and optimize the performance of system components, the greatest improvement will result from attention to the interaction of components with one another.

The system philosophy tends to condition a particular approach to problems by shaping attitudes and perceptions. The system attitude, or "state of mind," consists primarily of a sensitivity to the systemic nature of reality as it is outlined in the above paragraph. The point may be illustrated by using an example from system training. Over two decades ago, the RAND Corporation in California began a series of studies of radar sites operated in the United States about the possibility of a surprise attack by air and there was serious concern that the United States air defense system could not deal with the threat. Because many of the men assigned to study this problem at RAND were social scientists, they set out to solve it by traditional social science methods such as better human engineering, improved operator training, and organizational change. In other words, they focused their attention on improving the components of the air defense system rather than the system as a whole. They developed ways and means of studying the information processing behavior and organization of radar sites, but the more they studied these sites, the more convinced they became that the problem would not be solved using traditional techniques. The order of magnitude of improved performance needed was 100 to 200 percent. Conventional methods might yield 5 or 10 percent improvement in performance, but that is about all.

Working with different groups of officers and airmen, these social scientists slowly evolved a set of procedures which led to startling improvements in the performance of air defense crews. The procedures were remarkably simple in concept; present the system as a whole with a controlled situation, take data on the system's performance, provide the men in the system with information regarding the results of their efforts, and encourage the entire group—officers and airmen—to engage in problem-solving behavior. The principles were these: train the system as a whole, give it feedback, and encourage discussion.

Why was this method so successful?

The secret lay in the fact that this approach improved interacting skills which had not been improved through training up to that time. Prior to this, men had been trained outside the system to read radarscopes, to plot tracks on plexiglass boards, to identify aircraft, and so on. But other necessary skills associated with these tasks had been ignored. If a man were to be trained to read a radarscope and report his observations to another individual who plots them on a vertical board, a great deal of procedural learning that cannot be taught outside of the system complex would take place between these two individuals. The radarscope operator learns something about the speed with which the plotter can handle traffic called to him. He also learns about the plotter's idiosyncrasies and weaknesses, and, knowing these, he may be able to adjust his reporting speed or format to insure accurate and timely transmission of information.

One important aspect of the system approach or philosophy, then, is this sensitivity to system variables, or interactions which are not immediately apparent. We do not wish to suggest that there is nothing more to a system approach than this sensitivity to interactions between components of a system, but that it is a crucial part of the attitude or state of mind of the system designer.

The system designer is generally a pragmatist. He is concerned with questions of cost and questions of effectiveness. He is not content merely to build a better mousetrap; he would like to build it for less.

As we have already observed, the system approach also consists of a set of tools or techniques. Some of these tools include the ability to: (1) write carefully developed and operational learning objectives; (2) develop complete and accurate task descriptions; and (3) conduct task analyses. Task analysis is particularly important because it involves the application of scientifically validated principles of human learning to the teaching of concepts, principles, and skills identified as a result of writing the objectives and doing a task description. These tools and the instructional system design approach require that the teacher view instruction as setting up the conditions for learning. The principles of learning act as a guide for teachers in arranging the most effective learning conditions possible.

F R A M E

1.2

1. A course of learning system may be seen as a set of _____ components functioning to encourage student learning.

2. Learning system design requires the application of scientifically validated principles of human _____ .

3. Learning system design includes a philosophy and a set of conceptual _____ .

Having defined the attitude of the system designer, let us now turn to a description of the steps in system design and attempt to interpret the implications of the process in structuring improved learning environments.

FEEDBACK:

1.2   1 interacting   2 learning   3 tools

SYSTEM DESIGN TECHNIQUES

DESCRIBING THE CURRENT STATUS OF THE LEARNING SYSTEM

All efforts at system design begin with defining a system as it exists, its inputs, outputs, and present mode of operation, then proceeding with its design or redesign. Many of the new utopians in education talk as if the first step in the process of designing instructional systems is always to specify detailed objectives. This is not necessarily true.

Think for a moment about a course which is taught by several instructors who must share instructional aids and materials and in which students must take common exams. A first step in designing such a course may be to arrive at some agreement regarding broad subject areas to be developed, rather than to write detailed and operational objectives. This stage of coordinating materials and ideas among different individuals and groups frequently requires a great deal of time and effort.

Indeed, there are whole series of questions to be answered before we can intelligently proceed with the design of an existing course. How many students are involved? What are their backgrounds? In what ways do they differ from one another and in what ways are they alike? How many sections are taught? What are the strengths and weaknesses of those responsible for the course? How is the course currently handled? Are there special problems? Establishing the answer to questions of this kind by means of a system operating description is essential to good learning system design.

The system approach admonishes us to beware of proceeding with the design of the system until after we have fully described its current state, including all of its relevant dimensions. The description of the current status is done with recognition of the fact that the design process seldom really begins from scratch, and that the environment surrounding the system is rich with resources (and constraints) which should be inventoried. A total survey of the educational environment would include extracurricular activities, courses other than the one being taught, and teacher surrogates such as films, books, and programed materials, many of which lie outside the immediate bounds of the system to be designed. The description of the current status provides the information and data needed to insure that design decisions will consider all of the relevant variables, facts, and problems before proceeding with the design.

Frequently, those directly responsible for an area of educational development already have a relatively complete system operating description before they begin to design or redesign a learning system. But generally, it has not been formalized or written down and the information is scattered through various files and documents. Whenever learning system development involves enlisting the support of others who lack this privileged information, it will be necessary to provide them with a system operating description in one form or another, as the first step in the design process.

When a learning system designer describes the current status of a system, he seeks to answer questions like these:

- What are the important characteristics of the instructional system in which I have to work? What is its purpose? What means are advocated to accomplish these purposes?

- What resources will I have? Space? Media? Books? Articles? Equipment? What limits and constraints are there?

- Who are the students? What are their skills and expectancies? What do they need to learn? How many of them are there?

- What do I do particularly well that will contribute to the course?

The answers to these questions provide the basis for many of the decisions to be made in the later stages of the design process. Chapter 12 tells how a system description is developed and used.

The reader may wonder why we discuss the first step in the learning system design process, that is, "describing the current status of the system," in the last chapter of the book. The answer is that in order to perform an accurate system description, the designer must be able to anticipate many of the design decisions he will have to make later in the design process and, in making these decisions, he must apply many of the design concepts and principles covered in later chapters. Consequently, we first teach you the concepts and principles that apply to system design decision making and then show you how these concepts and principles are integrated into a description of the current state of the system.

Why should an instructor bother with a system description? Some of the reasons are:

- A teacher is more likely to use available resources if he is aware of their existence.

- If a teacher possesses data about students, he is more likely to help these students learn what they need to know, what they are capable of learning, and what they want to learn.

- If a teacher takes stock of his own capabilities, he is more likely to make the best use of his skills and is likely to continue to develop other skills rather than trying to do things he is not prepared to do.

Imagine talking with one of your colleagues in the lounge in a new school.

You: *You look worried.*

New Colleague: *I am. I've never taught this course before. I don't know what to to do first. I don't know what the purpose of the course should be. I'm not sure what the department thinks it should be. I'm not sure what kind of help I will have. No one has said who the interested students are. I'm not even sure I know what I can contribute.*

You: *Well, don't just sit there looking worried. What you have to do, according to the learning system design process, is:*

   a.   Start teaching and these things will work themselves out.
   b.   State your objectives.
   c.   Describe the current status of the instructional system.
   d.   Use a computer to teach the course.
   e.   Select a good programed textbook.

DERIVING AND WRITING LEARNING OBJECTIVES

Whatever the nature of the system to be designed, an early step in the process is the specification of objectives. Decisions about sequence, method of instruction, and evaluation inevitably depend upon a precise, operational and unambiguous statement of learning objectives.

The process of specifying learning objectives involves selecting what will be taught from all that might be taught in a given area. Every good teacher realizes that a student can only learn a small part of the material to which he is exposed, and that most of what is learned today is forgotten almost immediately. This common sense observation made by the average teacher is supported by overwhelming evidence from the psychological laboratory. Therefore, the first responsibility of the teacher is to decide what to teach. Deciding what is to be taught is an extremely difficult and painstaking process because the criteria for choosing are not always clear. Indeed, it is probably always easier to simply bundle up a more or less random assortment of "goodies" and dump them on the student, in effect, leaving the selection process to him; but this vastly overrates his capacity to select intelligently from among the alternatives and learn them.

To say that the teacher is responsible for defining learning objectives does not mean that the students' needs and opinions should be ignored. It is important for the teacher to establish what the student wants to know so that his concerns can be taken into account throughout the design process. Student learning objectives are important because they provide the

FEEDBACK:

1.3   c

teacher with clues regarding the motivation and reinforcement of a student's behavior—two factors which the teacher can ignore only at his own peril. When the teacher states his objectives, taking into account student learning objectives, he is in a far better position to generate student interest and exercise some control over student behavior.

Obviously, the process of selection which we have just described has distinct advantages for both the student and the teacher. It narrows the range of material the teacher must consider, allowing him to focus his attention on selected elements; it helps the teacher decide on such subsequent steps as the sequence and method of instruction; and it provides a means of communicating to the student the critical elements to be learned.

There is more to defining instructional objectives, however, than selecting the elements which are to be taught. A well-stated objective must be unambiguous. This means that it should not be possible to interpret the objective in more than one way. Chapters 2 and 3 deal with the general problem of how to recognize unambiguous objectives and how to write them.

Why should a teacher derive and write objectives?

- Most course design decisions are based on objectives. Course content and instructional procedures are chosen to help the student in meeting the objectives.
- Objectives play a critical role in instructional evaluation. They lay a foundation for the evaluation and provide the primary criteria used to judge both student achievement and the success of the instructor.
- Gaps and overlap in the curriculum may be eliminated when objectives are used as a communication vehicle among different instructors.
- Objectives tell students how to guide their own study and evaluate their own progress.

PLANNING AND IMPLEMENTING EVALUATION

Assume that a teacher has derived and written objectives for his new course. He now has statements that describe what the student will be able to do as the result of taking the course. Given a set of objectives, he should begin to think about questions like these:

- How will I know if my students reached the course objectives?
- How can I tell that I have done a good job of arranging conditions for learning?
- How will I know which instructional procedures worked best?
- How will I know which instructional procedures to revise?

All of these questions are evaluation questions. Although we generally think of evaluation as coming at the end of a process, planning for evaluation should coincide with writing course objectives. There are two reasons for this. First, plans for evaluation grow directly out of course objectives. Second, an evaluation plan provides a check on how precisely and clearly objectives have been written.

Why should a teacher make a special effort to plan his evaluation carefully?

- With an adequate evaluation program, the teacher and his students will be able to find evidence that learning has or has not occurred. Without an evaluation program, he cannot show that anything happened. With an inadequate program, he is likely to be misinformed.

- So what if the teacher can't show any learning? What are the consequences of evaluation? If the teacher uses the data he collects when he evaluates the course, his instruction is more likely to improve and less likely to remain stagnant. In other words, the evaluation is just as important to the teacher as it is to the student. If a large number of well-qualified students fail a course, for example, that says something very important about the quality of the teaching.

You are a learning system designer consulting with a teacher in a community college. He says:

I may be thinking too far ahead, but I have described in detail what I want my students to do by the time they are finished with their on-the-job training in computer programing. How will I know they can do these things when their on-the-job training is finished? How will I know if the on-the-job experience was a good one? How will I know what we might change in the on-the-job experience?

What learning system design step should he carry out?

a. System description   d. Task description
b. Deriving and writing objectives   e. Figuring out and carrying
c. System design step 2   out evaluation plans

FRAME 1.4

You are at a faculty meeting. One of your colleagues is explaining one of his problems:

Colleague: *As you know, I teach the general course in our area; however, many students outside our area are required to take this course. Lately, I have been getting many requests from both students and teachers to spell out exactly what we have to offer. It seems that students have been claiming that most of the course content and exams are inappropriate for them. Is there a systematic way that I can explain what the course is?*

FRAME 1.5

(Continued on next page)

FEEDBACK:
1.4   e

You: *I know what you need. You have to:*

    a. Make a list of readings and references.
    b. Write out a course description.
    c. Derive a method such as lecture or lab.
    d. Figure out and record the course objectives.
    e. Ask your colleagues what they teach.

PERFORMING A TASK DESCRIPTION AND TASK ANALYSIS

In the early stages of the design process, we are normally trying to identify the concepts, principles, and perceptual-motor skills which must be learned by the students. One approach to this overall goal, as we have already observed, is to specify the instructional objectives. Another approach, particularly useful for some types of learning, is the **task description.** The task description is used to answer these questions:

- What are the most efficient and effective ways that experts perform the behavior that the students will learn?

- What steps are involved in the performance of a task?

A task description is undertaken in order to identify the steps an expert goes through when he performs a task. In the chapter on task descriptions (Chapter 5), we will distinguish between two broad classes of tasks: **action tasks** and **cognitive tasks.** Action tasks generally involve a clearly defined, observable set of steps and can, therefore, be broken down into subtasks and sequenced. Examples of action tasks are the steps in driving a car, flying an airplane, or operating a lathe, all of which can be defined and generally agreed upon.

Cognitive tasks are performed mentally, so that the activity is generally not observable. They involve such activities as deciding, evaluating, and discriminating. Sometimes experts can describe how cognitive tasks are performed, in which case it is useful to list the steps or describe them in narrative form.

There is a third class of tasks which involve a heavy element of creativity. Even an expert in doing the task may not be able to describe how such a task is performed. If an expert can't tell how it is done, then you would not undertake a task description of such purely creative-type activities. It is always appropriate to write objectives, but a task description is only done when the detailed steps in the task are known and follow a logical and relatively fixed sequence, or when a cognitive task can be broken down by an expert.

Given a task description or set of objectives, the learning system design-

FEEDBACK:
1.5   d

er next analyzes these for the types of learning involved. The output is called the **task analysis.** The task analysis seeks to answer the following question:

- What types of learning are involved in a task or a set of objectives, i.e., concepts, principles, and/or perceptual-motor skills.

The task description explains step-by-step how a task is performed. A task analysis involves a careful examination of the task description and/or a set of behavioral objectives to identify the knowledge and skills required to perform the task described. For example, ideas such as random assignment, control group, and skills needed to operate delicate apparatus may be prerequisites for the task of "setting up an experiment." These are the things that must be taught to the student.

It is important to specify the various types of learning involved in performing a task because different types of learning require different instructional procedures. For many years, many experts believed that all learning took place in the same way. Now there is considerable evidence to show that different conditions are needed for learning concepts, principles, perceptual-motor skills, and other types of learning. Three chapters in this book will enable you to learn how to do a task description and task anallysis: Task Descriptions (Chapter 5). Types of Learning (Chapter 6), and Analyzing Tasks, Objectives, and Learner Characteristics (Chapter 7).

Task description, task analysis, and the objectives all interact. Take, for example, the task of driving an automobile. An analysis of that task might indicate that in order to drive a car, a student should be able to read a map (a new objective). If we undertake a detailed task description of how to read a map (a new task), we may discover that in order to read a map, students will have to be taught points on a compass (another new objective), and so on. In this way, new tasks and objectives emerge from the analysis of original tasks and objectives. The relationship between a task description, objectives, and the task analysis is illustrated in Fig. 1.1. The given task is sharpening a pencil. A simple outline task description is developed in the figure along with a statement of the objective. These are then analyzed to identify the concepts, principles, and perceptual-motor skills to be taught.

Should a teacher always go to the trouble of doing a task description? No. A task description should only be undertaken where knowledge is highly structured or when a cognitive task can be broken into clearly defined subtasks. Some sort of task analysis (or analysis of objectives) is always needed, however. These are the advantages of the task description and task analysis:

- When instruction is based upon a task description and task analysis, students are taught the best procedures for doing things. Nothing irrelevant or erroneous is taught; no gaps are present.

- Analyzing complex objectives to identify component knowledge and skills is more likely to result in well-organized instructional units incorporating the most effective conditions for students to learn under.

- Students are more likely to learn if the material is presented in the correct sequence.

OBJECTIVE	TASK ANALYSIS	
Given a dull pencil and a pencil sharpener, the student will be able to sharpen the pencil to a fine point without breaking the lead.	Concepts	
	1. Dull	5. Break
	2. Point	6. Press
	3. Sharp	7. Gently
	4. Fine	8. Crank
TASK DESCRIPTION	Principle	
1. Inspect point.	Press gently so as not to break point and turn crank.	
2. Decide whether to sharpen.		
3. Locate pencil sharpener.	Perceptual-Motor Skills	
4. Place pencil in sharpener.	1. Turning crank.	
5. Press gently.	2. Pressing gently.	
6. Turn crank.		
7. Remove pencil.		

Figure 1.1 An illustration of the way in which a simple task (sharpening a pencil) can be analyzed into component concepts, principles, and perceptual-motor skills.

APPLYING PRINCIPLES OF HUMAN LEARNING

Many instructors begin to plan to teach by suggesting methods. "I'd like to use a computer to teach _____." "I think I'll look for a programed text." "My students need a laboratory." In the learning system design process, instructors consider such alternatives near the end of their planning, rather than at the outset. First, the instructor should determine what he wants to teach, and then he may consider the best method of teaching.

Initially the instructor should give careful consideration to the following questions:

- How should conditions be arranged so that sutdents will learn best?

- What perceptual-motor skills are involved in the performance of the task or meeting the objectives? How are they learned?

- What concepts are involved in performing the task or meeting the objectives? How are they learned?

- What principles are involved in performing the task or meeting the objectives? How are they learned?
- Are there any general principles of learning that can be applied?
- How does one apply these principles?
- How can a teacher arrange conditions so that students will be motivated to learn?

There are four chapters on principles of human learning which provide answers to the above questions. These chapters are: General Principles of Learning and Motivation (Chapter 8), The Learning and Teaching of Concepts and Principles (Chapter 9), The Learning and Teaching of Problem Solving (Chapter 10), and The Learning and Teaching of Perceptual-Motor Skills (Chapter 11). They will help the instructor make decisions regarding the design of learning systems. The principles contained in these chapters should also help instructors organize learning conditions so that their students learn faster and better.

Why should an instructor study principles of learning and apply them to teaching? If he knows the principles of learning, he can help to insure student learning by arranging the appropriate conditions in his course of instructions. Principles of learning provide a set of criteria for selecting effective instructional procedures and, in effect, help in the solution of methods problems.

The training program for the astronauts' first moon landing was planned according to the system approach. The objective was to get men to the moon, have them collect rock samples, perform certain experiments and return safely. At a certain point in planning, the astronauts' instructors had to describe the most effective and efficient way to do all these tasks. They had to find the ideas and skills that had to be taught to the astronauts so they could carry out the mission. If you were an advisor to the training group, what steps from the learning system design process would you advise at this point?

F R A M E

1.6

     a.   System description
     b.   Task description
     c.   Deriving goals and objectives
     d.   Choosing textbooks
     e.   Goal formation

FEEDBACK:

1.6   b

F
R   A high school teacher said:
A
M   *I'm planning a physics course. I have certain information students must know;*
E   *several skills are required and some scientific principles are necessary. I think I'll*
             do it by computer. I plan on some three hour study units where students must
1.7   *solve problem after problem. All they have to do is turn the computer on and it*
             does the rest.

Another science teacher challenged him saying:

> *How do you know that stands any chance of working? What are your criteria for*
> *deciding to do it that way?*

What steps in the learning system design approach provides the basis for decisions of this type?

    a. Applying principles of human learning
    b. Applying experimental principles
    c. Experimenting with human beings
    d. Being human in our applications
    e. Applying common sense to humans

Now let's summarize the more or less idealized approach to learning system design which we have just described. The time line graph (Fig. 1.2) illustrates the design process. Note how the various components of the learning system design process (describing the current system status, planning the evaluation, etc.) overlap. Where the components of the process overlap, they also interact. As we have already emphasized, objectives may be derived from the task description and vice versa. Note also that the entire process is divided into three loosely defined phases which overlap: the analysis phase, the design phase, and the evaluation phase. The boxes within each of these three phases are tasks of the learning system designer. The components generally include specific learning system design techniques and procedures. The various chapters which describe how to use these techniques and procedures are listed in the column on the left, headed **Related Chapter(s).**

Consider the problem of a teacher of an entirely new course. His first step would be to describe the learning system, its purpose, resources and constraints, the students entering the program, their skills, expectations and needs, and his own capabilities. He would, in other words, want to describe the current status of the system (Chapter 12). As the description of the current status of the system proceeds, the teacher would want to find out in what way students will use their knowledge in the real world, so that as teacher, he can determine his course outcomes and state them in the form

FEEDBACK:
1.7   a

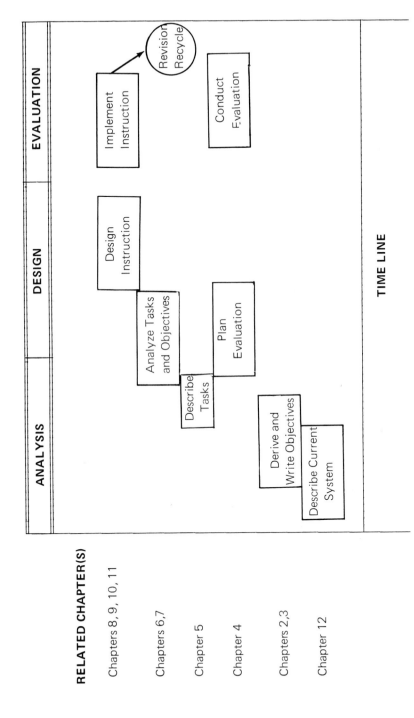

Figure 1.2   A time-line graph illustrating in a somewhat idealized way the learning system design process.

of objectives (Chapters 2 and 3). Based on the objectives, he would plan an evaluation program (Chapter 4). He would be sure to include evaluation methods to assess the students' achievements as well as his own instruction. In some cases, the objectives selected may include tasks which need to be described (Chapter 5), and describing a task may result in the identification of new objectives.

By analyzing the objectives and the tasks, the teacher is able to identify the prerequisite concepts, principles, and skills to be taught (Chapters 6 and 7). He applies the principles of learning to the design of the course (Chapters 8, 9, 10, and 11). He then creates the materials and presentations for the students. During and following instruction, the teacher carries out his evaluation program and considers revisions of the course based on the data he has collected.

ASSUMPTIONS UNDERLYING THE LEARNING SYSTEM DESIGN APPROACH

Sometimes, when people study new subjects, they find themselves spending more time in conflict over what is being learned rather than just learning it. This often happens because of differences between the student and teacher over basic assumptions about the material being taught and how it should be presented.

The authors believe a teacher is a person who knows how to set up the environmental conditions so that his students can learn. He's not necessarily a great speaker or a great actor, nor is he an authority figure who thrives on obedient students. He attempts not only to teach knowledge and skills to his students, but also to teach them how to learn on their own.

Regardless of what some authorities say, we believe that there is no one correct way to teach. There are many ways to teach well and still use the best learning principles. One of our goals in this text is to demonstrate that the skills a teacher possesses are learned; hence, we believe it is possible for the reader to continually learn more teaching skills. Two of the most critical teaching skills are careful planning and flexibility, or the ability to react quickly and appropriately to unpredicted contingencies.

F R A M E

1.8

Based on your reading so far, see if you can answer the following questions as if you were the authors of this book. First put a check (√) mark next to those assumptions you believe are true. Second put an X next to those assumptions you think the authors believe.

_____ 1. A teacher is a person who can present information well.

_____ 2. A teacher is a person who arranges environmentai conditions so that a student will learn.

_____ 3. A teacher should arrange conditions so that students must always seek advice from the teacher.

_____ 4. Teaching is an inborn trait or talent.

_____ 5. The skills that teachers need are learned.

_____ 6. Teaching, like learning, takes a good deal of effort and planning.

_____ 7. Good planning has flexibility built in.

_____ 8. Teaching is a relatively easy task.

_____ 9. Planning should be minimal so as not to inhibit flexibility.

_____ 10. There is one correct way to teach.

_____ 11. There is no one correct way to teach, yet there are valid principles and techniques that work well under specified conditions.

_____ 12. Only the latest scientific principles and techniques are appropriate for learning system design.

_____ 13. Principles and techniques are suggested, not because they are old or new, but because they are effective.

_____ 14. Once a course of instruction is planned by this approach, an instructor's planning work is done for a number of years.

_____ 15. A course of instruction planned by the learning system design approach has adaptive change built in.

_____ 16. Teachers can improve.

_____ 17. Teachers have learned all they are going to learn about teaching by the time they are given the responsibility to teach.

_____ 18. Student learning should be evaluated.

_____ 19. Student learning is too complex to be evaluated.

_____ 20. Teaching should be evaluated.

SUMMARY

Professional educators, teachers, and military and industrial trainers are primarily learning system designers. In approaching the design task, they commonly encounter five types of problems discussed in this chapter. They are problems of: (1) direction; (2) evaluation; (3) content and sequence; (4) method; and (5) constraints. The approach developed in the subsequent chapters of this book attempts to help learning system designers solve these five kinds of problems. Learning system design is both a de-

---

FEEDBACK:

1.8   The authors check: 2, 5, 6, 7, 11, 13, 15, 16, 18, and 20.

sign philosophy and a set of tools. The basic objective of learning system design is to identify the concepts, principles, and skills to be taught so that scientifically validated information about human learning can be applied in the creation of a system to teach them.

SUGGESTED READINGS

Banathy, Bela H.: *Instructional Systems,* (Belmont, California: Fearon/Lear Siegler, Inc., 1968).

Carter, Launor F.: "The Systems Approach to Education: Mystique and Reality," *Educational Technology,* April, 1969, pp. 22-31.

Churchman, C. West: *The Systems Approach,* (New York: Dell, 1968).

Davis, R. H.: "Zur Design-Problematik von Lernsystemen," *Lehr-und Lernmittelforschung,* (Berlin: Verlag Julius Beltz, 1971). Also in *Programmiertes Lernen und Programmiertes Unterricht,* April, 1968.

Gagné, R. M. (Ed.): *Psychological Principles in System Development,* (New York: Holt, Rinehart and Winston, 1962).

Goodwin, W. R.: "The System Development Corporation and System Training," *American Psychologist, 12:* 524-528, 1957.

Hamreus, D. G.: "The Systems Approach to Instructional Development," *The Contribution of Behavioral Science to Instructional Technology,* (Monmouth: Teaching Research Division of Oregon State System of Higher Education, 1968).

Heinich, Robert: "The Teacher in an Instructional System," In Knirk, F. G., and Childs, J. W. (Eds.) *Instructional Technology: A Book of Readings,* (New York: Holt, Rinehart and Winston, 1968), pp. 45-60.

Homme, Lloyd: "A Behavior Technology Exists—Here and Now," In F. A. Praeger (Ed.), *Technology and Innovation in Education,* (New York: F. A. Praeger, 1968), pp. 17-28.

MacKenzie, N., Eraut, M., and Jones, H. C.: *Teaching and Learning: An Introduction to New Methods and Resources in Higher Education,* (Paris: UNESCO-IAU, 1970).

Mauch, James: "A Systems Analysis Approach to Education," *Phi Delta Kappan, 43:* 158-162, June, 1962.

Smith, R. G.: "The Design of Instructional Systems," *Technical Reports,* No. 66-18, (Washington, D.C.: Human Resources Research Office, The George Washington University, 1966).

Smith, Robert G.: "An Annotated Bibliography on the Design of Instructional Systems," *Technical Reports,* No. 67-5, (Washington, D.C.: Human Resources Research Office, The George Washington University, 1967).

Tracey, Wm. R., Flynn, E. B., Jr., & Legere, C.: "Systems Thinking for Vocational Education," *Educate, 3:* 18-24, November, 1968.

DECISION AID

NOTE: *A decision aid, or checklist, is used to summarize the essential information in a chapter. It is designed so that the reader will be able to use it to carry out his own instruction long after he has read the chapter. The decision aid which follows refers the reader to particular procedures and chapters in this book which have been designed to answer specific instructional questions.*

Instructional Questions	Learning System Design Procedure	Chapters
1. What resources are available?		
2. What is the nature of the students?		
3. What is the scope of my abilities?	Describe	The System Approach to
4. What are the existing characteristics of the instructional system?	Current System	Instruction (Chapter 12)
5. What are the existing purposes of the instructional system?	Status	
1. What should students learn?		
2. What do students have to know outside of the classroom?		Recognizing Well-Formulated Objectives (Chapter 2)
3. What requirements are my responsibility?	Deriving Objectives	
4. How do I plan well?		
5. How do I communicate goals to students?	Writing Objectives	Deriving and Writing Learning Objectives
6. How do I communicate goals to colleagues?		(Chapter 3)
1. How do I check student achievement?		
2. How do I check the quality of my instruction?	Evaluation	Evaluating Learning Systems (Chapter 4)
3. How do I check my methods?		
4. How do I revise my course?		
1. How are the required actions done best?	Task Description	Task Descriptions (Chapter 5)
2. What must students learn to achieve the objectives in the course?	Task Analysis	Types of Learning (Chapter 6) Analyzing Tasks, Objectives, and Learner Characteristics (Chapter 7)

1. How do I arrange conditions for learning?		General Principles of Learning and Motivation (Chapter 8)
2. How do I arrange conditions for motivation?	Application of Psychological Principles of Human Learning	The Learning and Teaching of Concepts and Principles (Chapter 9)
3. How do I arrange conditions for learning concepts?		
4. How do I arrange conditions for learning skills?		The Learning and Teaching of Problem Solving (Chapter 10)
5. How do I arrange conditions for learning principles and problem solving?		The Learning and Teaching of Perceptual-Motor Skills (Chapter 11)

POSTTEST

NOTE: *The posttest will help you judge whether you have attained the objectives stated at the beginning of the chapter.*

1. Which of these assumptions underly the approach used in this book:

	T	F
a. An instructor's job is to set up the environment so that a student will learn.	___	___
b. Teachers are born, not made.	___	___
c. Teaching is a set of complex, learned skills.	___	___
d. There is one right way to teach.	___	___
e. Student learning is far too complex to be measured.	___	___
f. Learning system designers should follow all the steps described in this chapter in every case.	___	___

2. Match the problem statement to the appropriate category.

   a. "I wish the teacher would do something besides talk!"   Direction _____

   b. "What's he trying to say? What will I know when I've finished this course?"   Method _____

   c. "Wow! Does he jump from topic to topic!"   Content and Sequence _____

   d. "I wish some of us didn't have to sit on the floor!"   Evaluation _____

   e. "I'd sure like to know how well I'm doing. I don't know whether I've learned anything or not."   Constraints _____

3. Which of the following are the five major components of the learning system process as described in this chapter? Check "T."

	T	F
a. Selecting students	____	____
b. Describing the current status of the system	____	____
c. Developing a "lesson plan"	____	____
d. Preparing a list of assigned readings	____	____
e. Deriving and writing learning objectives	____	____
f. Doing a task description and task analysis	____	____
g. Tutoring students	____	____
h. Applying principles of human learning	____	____
i. Planning and implementing evaluation	____	____
j. Independent study	____	____

Answers to this posttest can be found on page 335.

OVERVIEW OF LEARNING SYSTEM DESIGN • **REC OGNIZING WELL-FORMULATED OBJECTIVES** • DERIVING AND WRITING LEARNING OBJECTIVES • EVALUATING LEARNING SYSTEMS • TASK DE SCRIPTIONS•TYPES OF LEARNING • ANALYZING TASKS, OBJECTIVES, AND LEARNER CHARAC TERISTICS • GENERAL PRINCIPLES OF LEARNING AND MOTIVATION • THE LEARNING AND TEACH ING OF CONCEPTS AND PRINCIPLES •THE LEARN ING AND TEACHING OF PROBLEM SOLVING • PERCEPTUAL-MOTOR SKILLS • THE SYSTEM APPROACH TO INSTRUCTION • OVERVIEW OF LEARNING SYSTEM DESIGN • **RECOGNIZING WELL-FORMULATED OBJECTIVES** • DERIVING AND WRITING LEARNING OBJECTIVES • EVALUAT ING LEARNING SYSTEMS •TASK DESCRIPTIONS • TYPES OF LEARNING • ANALYZING TASKS, OBJEC TIVES, AND LEARNER CHARACTERISTICS • GEN ERAL PRINCIPLES OF LEARNING AND MOTIVA TION • THE LEARNING AND TEACHING OF CON CEPTS AND PRINCIPLES • THE LEARNING AND TEACHING OF PROBLEM SOLVING • PERCEPTUAL- MOTOR SKILLS • THE SYSTEM APPROACH TO INSTRUCTION • OVERVIEW OF LEARNING SYS TEM DESIGN•**RECOGNIZING WELL-FORMULATED OBJECTIVES**•DERIVING AND WRITING LEARNING OBJECTIVES • EVALUATING LEARNING SYSTEMS • TASK DESCRIPTIONS•TYPES OF LEARNING • ANALYZING TASKS, OBJECTIVES, AND LEARNER

2

I CHAPTER OBJECTIVES

II INTRODUCTION

III WHAT LEARNING OBJECTIVES ARE (AND WHAT THEY ARE NOT)
    A Definition of a Learning Objective
    B Learning Objectives Are Not a Substitute for a Philosophy of Instruction
    C Learning Objectives Are Not Course Descriptions

IV COMPONENTS OF A LEARNING OBJECTIVE
    A Terminal Behavior
        1 Action Verbs
    B Conditions of Demonstration or Test
        1 Types of Conditions
    C Performance Standards
        1 Types of Standards
    D Performance Stability

V DESCRIBING OBJECTIVES IN NONVERBAL TERMS

VI TERMINAL AND ENABLING OBJECTIVES

VII THE UTILITY OF OBJECTIVES

VIII SUMMARY

IX SUGGESTED READINGS

X POSTTEST

CHAPTER OBJECTIVES

- Given several examples of learning objectives, you should be able to select those stated in behavioral terms according to the definition learned in this chapter.

- Given several examples of objectives, you should be able to correctly identify the words that describe: (1) terminal behavior; (2) conditions of demonstration or test; and (3) the standards of acceptable performance, according to the definitions in this chapter.

- Given several examples of learning system design procedures, such as sequencing subject matter topics, guiding student learning, evaluating student learning, and evaluting instructional effectiveness, you should be able to state whether or not learning objectives are useful for each procedure.

INTRODUCTION

In the first chapter we surveyed a problem-solving approach to instruction called **learning system design.** The learning system design process was described as a set of procedures for systematically applying learning principles to instruction. The various kinds of problems that usually arise when learning principles are ignored or inappropriately applied to teaching were discussed. We indicated, in a general way, how an instructor can employ learning system design procedures to anticipate and avoid these problems. In this and in the following chapter you will learn one of the basic procedures in designing learning systems—how to formulate and write learning objectives.

Learning objectives are essential in all phases of the instructional design process. In planning for teaching, they provide a guide for choosing subject matter content, for sequencing topics, and for allocating teaching time. Learning objectives also guide the selection of materials and procedures to be employed in the actual teaching process. In addition, they provide standards for measuring student achievement. Finally, objectives act as criteria for evaluating the quality and efficiency of the instruction. Without well-formulated objectives, instruction often tends to be poorly organized and student learning difficult to assess.

Is it possible to teach at all without having objectives? Most teachers have some goals in mind when they plan their courses. However, these goals are often so vague and ambiguous that they become quite worthless for planning or evaluation purposes. A learning objective, on the other hand, is a clear and precise description of an instructional goal. In comparison to vaguely stated goals, learning objectives are written to serve as guides for instructional planning and evaluation.

Because learning objectives are so important for learning system design, we have prepared two chapters on how to write them. In this chapter, you will learn how to identify the component parts of a learning objective and how to recognize a well-formulated objective when you see one. In the next chapter, you will learn a step-by-step procedure for writing objectives for your own instructional purposes.

WHAT LEARNING OBJECTIVES ARE (AND WHAT THEY ARE NOT)

Let us begin by clarifying what we mean by instructional goals. If we can agree on what goals are, we will be in a better position to understand why learning objectives are needed and how they should be written.

By an instructional goal, we mean some outcome of instruction, expressed in terms of student learning. An instructional goal describes, in general terms, the new knowledge, skills, abilities, and attitudes that the teacher expects the student to acquire as a result of his instruction. Some examples of instructional goals are:

> To understand the theory of evolution
> To know the principles of administration
> To affirm democratic principles
> To have a feeling for mathematics
> To operate a turret lathe
> To appreciate Hellenic sculpture

Our instructional goal for this book is that the reader will be able to use learning system design procedures in his own teaching. Simply stated, an instructional goal is a general description of what the student is expected to learn as a result of instruction.

DEFINITION OF A LEARNING OBJECTIVE

We have said that a learning objective is a precise way of stating an instructional goal. Thus, we would expect a learning objective to be an accurate way of describing an outcome of instruction, or in other words what the student learns as a result of instruction.

**DEFINITION:
A LEARNING OBJECTIVE IS A DESCRIP-
TION OF THE BEHAVIOR EXPECTED OF A
LEARNER AFTER INSTRUCTION.**

Later in this chapter we will explain why an instructional outcome should be described in terms of learner behavior. Let us look at some examples of instructional goals and corresponding learning objectives. As you consider these examples, study the words (italicized) that express the performance expected of the learner after instruction.

1. Goal: To know the characteristics of air masses.

   Objective: On a map of the Northern Hemisphere, the student will be able to *mark the source regions* of at least three air masses and *indicate their direction of movement in summer and winter.* The answer must conform to the text.

2. Goal: To be familiar with Gothic architecture.

   Objective: The student should be able to *identify* on a diagram or photograph the significant parts of a cathedral (for example, the nave, arch, transept).

3. Goal: To demonstrate empathy in a counseling interview.

   Objective: With a simulated client, the student *will conduct* an interview lasting from 15 to 30 minutes and *react correctly* to all emotional disturbances expressed by the patient. A correct reaction is one that applies the principles of psychological interaction given in the text.

4. Goal: To apply principles of expository writing.

   Objective: Given any topic sentence (for example, "It was a dark and stormy night."), the student will *write a relevant paragraph* that exhibits the structure presented in lecture.

5. Goal: To understand the concept of the derivative in mathematics.

   Objective: (a) The student will apply principles, formulas, or theorems to new situations *by solving given problems* involving derivatives, differentiation, increasing and decreasing functions, and extrema, with 75 percent accuracy on each problem; and he will graph 8 out of 10 functions correctly.

   (b) Given four theorems that he has never seen, the student will *formulate a proof* for each theorem by drawing on elements from previous sources, and *he will rate* them together to form a pattern proof—with 80 percent accuracy

In the previous examples, the words describing the performance expected of the student are italicized. In every case, the objective is a more precise and unambiguous description of an instructional outcome than the goal.

The fifth example includes two objectives for a single goal. The objectives were written by different instructors who interpreted the meaning of the goal differently. The objectives and the italicized performance verbs show that the two instructors had different outcomes in mind for the goal of understanding the concept of the derivative.

Mark each of the following statements frue or false.

1. Writing learning objectives is a basic procedure in learning system design. T F

2. Goals do not describe instructional outcomes. T F

3. Learning objectives describe student performance. T F

4. Only one learning objective can be derived from an instructional goal. T F

LEARNING OBJECTIVES ARE NOT A SUBSTITUTE FOR A PHILOSOPHY OF INSTRUCTION

Learning objectives do not spell out what should be taught nor what the larger goal of education should be. These judgments must be made by the teacher. Once they are made, objectives assist in expressing them as learning outcomes.

Learning objectives may be written for any unit of instruction, from a single lesson to an entire course. The subject matter may deal with a single concept, a skill, a set of principles, or a complex body of knowledge. But whatever the content, the objective describes the learning outcome that the teacher intends to produce as a result of his instruction. The objective states what the student will be able to do after instruction that, presumably, he was not able to do before.

LEARNING OBJECTIVES ARE NOT COURSE DESCRIPTIONS

A course description provides information about course content or course procedures. It does not describe course outcomes. A typical course description might include the following information:

> Essential points of grammar will be reviewed; written and oral reports will be required, and students will be encouraged to participate actively in class discussions.

A course description indicates what topics will be covered in the course and what class activities might be expected. In short, it provides information about requirements and ways and means, but does not specify outcomes.

Learning objectives are often confused with what the teacher hopes to accomplish in class. For example, when asked what his course objectives were, one teacher gave the following list:

> To encourage discussion
> To meet the class regularly

FEEDBACK:

2.1 1 T   3 T
     2 F   4 F

To maintain a democratic atmosphere

Not to lose my temper when students give stupid answers

These items may express good intentions and are undoubtedly good teaching practices. In fact, we might label them "instructor objectives." Instructor objectives are not learning objectives because they do not describe a student behavioral outcome.

In the following exercise, see if you can distinguish learning objectives from course descriptions.

F R A M E

2.2

Suppose you are the Dean of Instruction of a newly organized community college. You ask instructors to submit learning objectives for courses they are planning to teach. You receive the following list. Check which of the following are learning objectives.

Check Here

1. Students will be able to solve equations involving the multiplication and division of whole numbers having positive, negative, and zero exponents. ☐

2. Several field trips are planned in which effects of urban pollution will be studied. ☐

3. To assemble and install an automobile carburetor. ☐

4. To demonstrate to the students how principles of psychology can be applied to their own life situations. ☐

Items 1 and 3 are objectives since they describe instructional outcomes in terms of student behavior. Item 1, "to solve equations" clearly indicates what the student is expected to be able to do. It is clear from Item 3 that the outcome of instruction is to assemble and install.

Items 2 and 4 do not describe outcomes of instruction. Item 2 describes an instructional activity. Item 4 describes what the teacher intends to do. This kind of information may be appropriate and useful in a course catalog, but it is not of use in designing learning systems.

For a learning objective to be useful in designing learning systems, it must perform three functions: (1) it must serve as a guide for planning instruction; (2) it must provide a standard for assessing student achievement; and (3) it must provide a criterion for evaluating instruction itself. How does a description of the behavior expected of a student after instruction perform these three functions?

First, when a teacher chooses an objective, he is committing himself to

---

FEEDBACK:

2.2   1, 3

plan his teaching so that his students will be able to achieve the objective. Consequently, a clear description of what the student will be able to do as a result of instruction that he could not do before, guides the teacher in selecting content materials, and instructional procedures.

Second, since a learning objective describes the behavior expected of the student, it is also a description of expected student achievement. The teacher need only devise a test to measure whether or not the student achieved the objective.

Third, the major criterion of teaching effectiveness is student achievement. Consequently, the instructor need only determine how many students achieved the objective to get a pretty good idea of how effective his instruction was.

In the next section of this chapter we shall describe the three component parts of a learning objective and show how each component contributes to learning system design.

COMPONENTS OF A LEARNING OBJECTIVE

A learning objective consists of three components: (1) terminal behavior; (2) test conditions; and (3) standards.

TERMINAL BEHAVIOR

DEFINITION:
TERMINAL BEHAVIOR IS THE COMPONENT OF A LEARNING OBJECTIVE THAT DESCRIBES THE BEHAVIOR OF A STUDENT AFTER INSTRUCTION.

Terminal behavior is the part of an objective we have been referring to as the intended outcome of instruction. It describes what the student will be able to do in order to demonstrate that he has achieved the objective. It is the behavior that will be accepted as evidence that the student has learned.

By behavior, we mean any performance or activity that can be observed or recorded. In the following examples, the terminal behavior is in bold type.

1. **Identify** by underlining positive and negative examples of participative management.
2. **Draw** a diagram of each of the three classes of levers.
3. **Present** an impromptu speech.
4. Given an hypothesis derived from the principles of operant condi-

tioning, the student will **design** an experiment that . . .

5. From several examples of French Impressionist art, the student will **select** those that exemplify . . .

An objective that describes student behavior so that it can be observed or recorded has been written in behavioral terms.

FRAME 2.3

For each of the following pairs of statements, check the one tnat is stated in behavioral terms:

Check Here

1. a. Knows how to operate a desk calculator. ☐
   b. Can state the function of the operation keys of a desk calculator. ☐

2. a. Appreciates the value of democracy. ☐
   b. Votes ☐

3. a. Can predict the effect on the price (of beans) of the following events . . . ☐
   b. Grasps the significance of the concept of supply and demand. ☐

4. a. Can state the feelings of a patient. ☐
   b. Has acquired the ability to empathize with a patient. ☐

5. a. Has achieved skill in the following poetic meters: ☐
   b. Can compose three poems in each of the following meters: ☐

6. a. Has a positive attitude toward mathematics. ☐
   b. Elects to take a nonrequired mathematics course. ☐

ACTION VERBS Terminal behavior should be described using **action verbs.** Words such as "select," "assemble," "measure" describe actions that can be observed or recorded. Using action verbs you can communicate clearly what you expect the student to be able to do. However, words such as

---

FEEDBACK:

2.3	1	b	4	a
	2	b	5	b
	3	a	6	b

"understand," "appreciate," "know" are so vague as to be almost meaning-less.

Table 2.1 contains two lists of words that express instructional out-comes. The words on the left are ambiguous and can be interpreted in a variety of ways. The words on the right are action verbs.

TABLE 2.1   INSTRUCTIONAL OUTCOMES EXPRESSED BOTH AMBIGUOUSLY
            AND BY ACTION VERBS

Ambiguous Words	Action Verbs
know	discriminate (or distinguish between)
understand (or really understand)	choose (or select)
determine	assemble
appreciate (the value of)	adjust
grasp (the significance of)	identify (the ones which _____)
become familiar with	solve
	apply
	align
	list (the properties of _____)

The ambiguous words are what we have labeled instructional goals. They certainly describe desirable outcomes of instruction. Indeed, these are the words we usually use to describe the purposes of educa-tion. We cannot measure a person's achievement of instructional goals because they refer to states or qualities that are wtihin him; to measure student achievement of an objective, we must state the ob-jective in behavioral terms.

Terminal behavior can be thought of as an external manifestation of an internal state. As teachers, we certainly want the outcomes of our instruction to be increased knowledge, understanding, apprecia-tion, etc., on the part of the student. But if we wish to assess these outputs, we must express them so that they can be observed. The ter-minal behavior component of a learning objective describes an observable outcome.

When an instructor writes the terminal behavior component of an objective, he should try to answer the following questions:

- What do I expect a student to be able to do?
- In what way should the student demonstrate that he has learned?
- What student performance will I accept as evidence that he has learned?

A good procedure for determining whether or not an objective clearly describes an instructional outcome is to write a test item to assess student achievement of the terminal behavior. This procedure is illustrated in the following exercise.

F R A M E 2.4

You are teaching a course which has as one of its goals that the students will be able to critically evaluate the concept of utopianism. You want to write a learning objective in behavioral terms that expresses what you mean by "critically evaluate." Which of the following objectives are stated in behavioral terms (more than one answer is possible). Underline the words that describe the behavior.

Check Here

1. Will be able to state the social, economic, and political characteristics of utopian communities. ☐

2. Will apply principles learned in the course to account for why particular utopian communities lasted longer than others. ☐

3. Will name a historical utopian community that failed and indicate how it might have been designed to last longer. ☐

4. Will design a hypothetical utopian community having characteristics that exemplify the following principles discussed in the course: (principles listed here). ☐

All four objectives are stated in behavioral terms. Any one of them could be accepted as evidence that the student could "critically evaluate" the concept of utopianism.

1. If a student can "state the . . .characteristics," he knows the defining properties of utopian communities.

2. If the student can "apply principles" to account for a given phenomenon (i.e., that some lasted longer than others) he presumably can apply these principles to account for other related social phenomena.

3. If the student can "indicate" how a utopian community (that failed) might have been designed to last longer, he can apply the principles learned.

4. If the student can "design" a utopian community, he can apply the principles to solve problems.

FEEDBACK:
2.4   All

    1 state   3 name
    2 apply   4 design

Note that the four statements describe different levels of accomplishment. The first requires the student to convey factual information. The last requires the student to identify the essential components of a problem and then solve the problem. Terminal behavior should describe the level of accomplishment that the instructor intends the student to achieve.

CONDITIONS OF DEMONSTRATION OR TEST

The **conditions** component of a learning objective describes the situation in which the student will be required to demonstrate the terminal behavior. It is the component that describes the test conditions.

Students sometimes complain that examinations are unrelated to the course material or that they are taught one thing and tested on another. One reason for these complaints is that the instructor often has no clear idea about how he expects to assess student achievement before he begins teaching. For example, some mathematics teachers provide intensive instruction on how to solve equations and then test their students' ability to translate word problems into equations. Consequently, students may be asked to demonstrate what they have learned under conditions for which they have not been prepared.

The conditions conponent of a learning objective describes the _____
situation in which students will be required to demonstrate the terminal behavior.

FRAME 2.5

TYPES OF CONDITIONS   There are three general types of conditions that affect performance on a test. First, the aids or tools that the student will be permitted to use in the test situation, such as reference books, notes, a slide rule. Second, the kinds of restrictions that will be placed on a student, such as completing a test within a limited time period. Restrictions may also be placed on the use of the senses as with some physicians who must be able to tie surgical knots blindfolded. Third, how information will be presented; for instance, in writing or by other media, such as videotape recording; or perhaps, as an essay test. Complete learning objectives specify all of the conditions under which performance will be tested.

Which of the following objectives include conditions? Underline the words that state the conditions.

1. Without referring to a wiring diagram, the student will be able to trace the following circuits: . . .   _____

2. The student will write an essay in the expository form. The

FRAME 2.6

(continued on next page)

FEEDBACK:

2.5   test

essay must be at least 400 words long and be written in class within one-half hour.

_____

3.   Given a videotape recording of a classroom situation, the student will be able to identify and name examples of nonverbal cues employed by the instructor.

_____

4.   The student will be able to tune an automobile engine.

_____

PERFORMANCE STANDARDS

The third component of a learning objective is a statement of the standards by which the learner's performance will be judged. A **standard** describes the minimal level of performance that will be accepted as evidence that the learner has achieved the objective.

The following are typical ways of stating performance standards. The student must:

Answer nine of the ten questions correctly.
Solve the problem within ten minutes.
Be accurate to within plus or minus 0.05 inches.
Perform the procedures in the same order as in the text.

The performance standard provides a criterion for judging the effectiveness of the terminal behavior. Consider the following objective:

Using a 35-pound longbow, the student will shoot ten arrows at a target at a distance of 50 yards.

In this objective, the terminal behavior and conditions of test are clearly stated. However, there is no indication of how well the student must shoot. As stated, it would be impossible to score the student's performance or assign a grade.

Adding a standard completes the objective.

Using a 35-pound longbow, the student will shoot ten arrows at a target and, at a distance of 50 yards, will hit the bullseye eight times.

F R A M E

2.7

For the following objectives, check the ones that include a performance standard. Underline the words that describe the standard.

_____

FEEDBACK:

2.6   1   Without referring to a wiring diagram
      2   400 words; written in class; one-half hour
      3   Videotape recording of a classroom situation
      4   None

Check Here

1. The teacher will reinforce the question-asking behavior   ☐
   of a shy student so that the number of questions asked
   will increase over the term.

2. Given four syllogisms, the student will identify the   ☐
   "middle term" in each.

3. The student will be able to conduct a fluent conversation   ☐
   in French.

4. The student will type 1000 words at a rate of 75 words   ☐
   per minute without committing any spelling errors.

TYPES OF STANDARDS The particular performance standard chosen depends upon the nature of the terminal behavior and the dimension along which improvement occurs. Here are some examples.

1. When mere OCCURRENCE of the behavior is sufficient, describe
   the behavior.
   Examples: The student (driver) will use hand signals before all turns,
              i.e., for a left turn, extend the left arm straight out through
              the left window.
              The knot will be tied loosely as in the photograph.

2. Where ACCURACY is important, provide a statement of acceptable
   range or deviation.
   Examples: The estimate must be correct within plus or minus 15
              percent.
              The answer must be correct to the nearest whole number.
              All positive and negative instances of the concept must be
              identified.

3. If number of ERRORS is important, state the number.
   Example: with a maximum of one error

4. If TIME or SPEED is important, state the minimal level.
   Examples: within five seconds
              five units per minute

5. If a KNOWN REFERENCE provides the standard, state the reference.
   Example: Perform the sequence of steps in the same order as
              given in the text.

6. If the CONSEQUENCES of the behavior are important, describe them
   or provide a model.

FEEDBACK:
2.7   1   The number of questions will increase.
       4   75 words per minute with no spelling errors.

Examples: Block the offensive tackle long enough so that the quarter back has at least three seconds to throw the pass.

Conduct a model so that it does not disintegrate in a pressure of two atmospheres.

Conduct the class so that all students participate in the discussion.

The standard should provide an objective criterion for judging the adequacy of the student's performance. The statement should leave no room for subjective opinion. A good test of objectivity is if several competent people can observe a student's performance and all agree whether or not he had performed at or above the standard.

Use this test in Frame 2.8.

You are stricken with severe abdominal pains and are rushed to the hospital. As you are being wheeled through the emergency ward, you notice a sign on the wall which says:

LEARNING OBJECTIVE FOR EMERGENCY WARD INTERNS: *THE INTERN WILL BE ABLE TO DIAGNOSE EMERGENCY CASES AND PRESCRIBE TREATMENT.*

This sign was an attempt to state an objective, but it does not include a performance standard. Write below performance standard(s) that might have been included.

PERFORMANCE STABILITY

A learning objective is a description of a test of student performance where the test measures whether or not a student has achieved the objective. To ensure that the test does indeed measure this achievement, it should include a sufficient number of opportunities for the student to demonstrate that he can perform the terminal behavior. Otherwise-one might suspect that his performance may be due to chance. If a teacher is concerned about this possibility, he should decide what

---

FEEDBACK:

2.8 Any of the following:

1 The diagnosis should be completed within some specified time limit.

2 All diagnoses should be correct.

3 All prescribed treatments should be appropriate.

4 Bad side effects should be minimized.

proportion of successes will convince him otherwise. Then he should include in his learning objective a statement of the number of opportunities the student will be given on the test and the number of times he must succeed. This statement is a description of performance stability.

Here are two examples of learning objectives that include a statement of performance stability:

1. The student will prepare and present three persuasive speeches (eight to ten minutes) on topics of his own choosing, using the Dewey Problem-Solving Format. He must change the attitude of at least 25 percent of the audience in two of the speeches.

2. Given a list of twenty-five accounting terms and a list of definitions taken from the glossaries of the unit chapters, the student will match at least twenty of them correctly.

The stability criterion in the first example is two out of three speeches; in the second example, it is twenty out of twenty-five.

The stability criterion is different from the standards component of the objective. The standards component describes how well the student must perform the terminal behavior. The stability criterion states how many times he must perform the terminal behavior at or above the standard.

In the first example, the student must present three persuasive speeches. The standard of a successful speech is an attitude change in at least 25 percent of the audience. The stability criterion is that he must give a successful speech twice.

In the second example, the student must match terms and definitions. The standard of matching is only that the matching be correct. Presumably, the definitions are sufficiently simple that their degree of correctness is not a matter of subjective opinion. The stability criterion is clear. Twenty of the twenty-five matches must be correct.

The instructor himself should decide what stability criterion will convince him that the student has indeed achieved the objective and that the student's performance was not due to chance.

In the following objectives, circle the words describing the performance standards and underline the words describing the stability criterion.

1. The student will run the 100-yard dash in 15 seconds, three out of five times.

2. Without using references, the student will list the steps involved in making a blueprint. The description and sequence of steps must conform to the lab manual.

**F
R
A
M
E
2.9**

(continued on next page)

3. The student-teacher will prepare an objective and a lesson plan. She will teach four different classes so that in three classes at least 90 percent of the students achieve the objective.

4. Given ten photographs of biological cells, the student will identify nine correctly as either plant or animal cells.

DESCRIBING OBJECTIVES IN NONVERBAL TERMS

Some outcomes of instruction cannot be described either verbally or in writing. For example, it is impossible to describe in words how a passage of music should be played, or how a dramatic line in a play should be intoned. These kinds of instructional outcomes can only be described and conveyed by demonstration.

An art instructor was teaching her students how to design a "visual metaphor." She asked the authors to help her write an objective for this unit of her course. It was impossible to describe a visual metaphor verbally. However, when the instructor showed us examples of visual metaphors, we immediately understood what she wanted her students to learn to do. We advised her to show her students the examples just as she had shown them to us. She did so and found that this demonstration method of describing terminal behavior was quite effective.

Artistic learning is not the only domain in which objectives must be described by demonstration. Most complex perceptual-motor learning falls in this category also. The surgical amphitheater was devised so that medical students could observe advanced surgical techniques. Athletic coaches know that showing students how to perform the desired art or skill is the most effective method of conveying the required action. Airplane instructors must demonstrate complex procedures such as how to land an aircraft in a severe crosswind.

Instructors who teach complex artistic or perceptual-motor skills should attempt to describe the behavioral component of an objective. The standards component may only be describable by demonstration. The instructor should describe the behavior expected of the student by modeling the terminal behavior himself or by showing the student a product that results from correct performance of the terminal behavior.

FEEDBACK:

2.9	1	Standard: 15 seconds Stability: three out of five times	3	Standard: 90 percent achieve Stability: three-fourths
	2	Standard: conform to lab manual Stability: not given	4	Standard: correctly Stability: nine-tenths

TERMINAL AND ENABLING OBJECTIVES

Most units of instruction may be broken down into smaller units. To illustrate, a course may be composed of several topics and each topic may be further subdivided into facts, concepts, and principles. Learning objectives may be written for any unit of instruction and for every one of its subunits. The objectives for a given instructional unit are called **terminal objectives**; the objectives for the subunits of instruction are called **enabling objectives.**

Enabling objectives may be thought of as prerequisites for terminal objectives. Enabling objectives describe the knowledge or skills that contribute to or facilitate achieving the terminal objective. The following example, from a course in obedience training for dogs, illustrates this point.

One unit of the course has the following objective:

> The dog is in the sitting-heel position. When a stick is thrown the dog does not move. At the command "fetch", the dog retrieves the stick, sits before the trainer, drops the stick, and returns to the sitting-heel position.

Let us call this statement the terminal objective for the unit of instruction with which we are concerned. The unit consists of several component skills which must be taught before the terminal objective can be achieved. An objective can be stated for each one and, as a group, they comprise the enabling objectives.

The enabling objectives (identified by the associated commands) are sit, heel, automatic heel-sit (without command), come, fetch, drop, and delayed fetch (without command). The sequence of objectives is diagramed below.

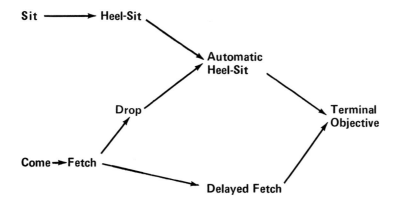

Enabling objectives are the milestones along the path from the beginning to the end of a unit of instruction. Terminal objectives describe the learning outcomes of the whole unit; enabling objectives describe the specific behaviors that have to be learned in order to achieve the terminal objectives.

In Chapter 5, you will learn a system design procedure called task description which will help you identify the components of instructional units and the related terminal and enabling objectives. Once you have described the terminal and enabling objectives for all units of your course, you will have a plan for designing the course and presenting the units in a systematic manner.

FRAME 2.10

A terminal learning objective describes the instructional outcomes of a unit of instruction. The objectives of subunits of instruction are called (1) _____ _____. Enabling objectives contribute to the learning of (2) _____ _____.
A teacher should arrange his instructional units so that students achieve all the enabling objectives necessary to achieve (3) _____ objectives.

Each chapter in this book contains behavioral learning objectives for the student. The chapter objectives, stated at the beginning of each chapter, contain a terminal behavior and sometimes include a statement of conditions. The conditions, when not included in the objective, are generally implicit in the chapter or the posttest. The performance standard, if omitted from the objective, will also be found in the chapter. It is not always necessary to write complete behavioral objectives except for design purposes. When giving objectives to help guide a student in his learning, it is often preferable to state only the terminal behavior to avoid overwhelming him with information; however, a learning system designer should always be prepared to give complete objectives to students, if asked.

Some educators reject the entire approach of writing behavioral learning objectives. This is unfortunate since learning objectives serve several essential functions which will be summarized in the next section. Even a teacher who rejects the writing of behavioral objectives completely, must somehow identify the concepts, principles, and skills to be taught. The techniques and criteria developed in subsequent chaters can still be used to help design the teaching strategy, even if the teacher has failed to state objectives.

FEEDBACK:

2.10 1 enabling objectives
      2 terminal objectives
      3 terminal

THE UTILITY OF OBJECTIVES

At the beginning of this chapter, we said that writing learning objectives is one of the important procedures for designing learning systems. Throughout the chapter we have given several examples of how objectives are used in learning system design. In this final section, the uses of objectives will be summarized.

TO EVALUATE INSTRUCTION

The criterion of good instruction is student learning. Objectives state what the student is expected to be able to do as a result of instruction. If an objective includes terminal behavior, conditions of test and criterion standards, it can easily be translated into a test of student achievement and, from this, the quality of instruction can be inferred.

TO GUIDE STUDENT LEARNING

It is generally agreed that students should share responsiblity for their own learning. The ultimate goal of education is to produce a student who can continue to learn independently of the teacher. However, proficiency in learning is a skill which must itself be learned. The student must learn how to learn, and it is the responsibility of the teacher to facilitate the process. One obvious method is to provide cues that the student can use to guide himself.

Enabling and terminal objectives provide these cues. They tell the student what the outcome of his learning should be and provide criteria he can use to judge his own learning progress. When objectives are not provided, the student is faced with an uncertain situation. He must guess what the instructor considers important, what the instructor expects of him, and whether his progress is satisfactory. Typically, when objectives are not provided, the student uses other means to reduce his uncertainty. Instead of learning the course material, he hearns to "psych-out" the instructor.

TO PROVIDE CRITERIA FOR COURSE DESIGN

An instructor must make many decisions in designing a learning system. Some of these are: what content to include, how to sequence the content, how to present material, what aids to use. Objectives provide criteria for making these decisions.

TO COMMUNICATE TO COLLEAGUES

Few courses are taught in isolation. Most are components of a curriculum. Objectives are an effective means for specifying course outcomes so that they can be sequenced with minimum redundancy and maximum coverage. Objectives also enable different instructors to communicate with one another in unambiguous terms the expected outcomes of the courses they teach.

F R A M E

2.11

The following is a list of instructional problems that teachers occasionally encounter. Check those for which instructional objectives are useful.

		Check Here
1.	Students complain that tests are unfair.	☐
2.	Students do not perceive the relevancy of course material.	☐
3.	How to get students to learn concepts and principles rather than merely memorizing facts.	☐
4.	How to determine whether a TV lecture is effective.	☐
5.	How to determine whether or not a student has learned the course material.	☐
6.	How to determine whether several graduate teaching assistants are covering the same course materials.	☐

SUMMARY

A learning objective is a description of the behavior expected of a learner after instruction. It has three component parts: (1) terminal behavior; (2) conditions; (3) standards. Terminal behavior describes what the student will be able to do as a result of what he has learned. Conditions describe the aids or restrictions of the test in which the student demonstrates the terminal behavior. Standards describe the minimal acceptable performance the student must demonstrate.

Terminal objectives describe the expected outcomes of a given unit of instruction. Enabling objectives describe the subtasks or subunits of instruction that are prerequisite to achieving a terminal objective.

Learning objectives are instruments or tools for clearly describing instructional outcomes. They assist the teacher in designing instructional systems by guiding the selection and sequencing of subject matter content and the choice of instructional materials and procedures. Learning objectives enable a student to guide and manage his own learning. They serve as criteria for assessing student achievement and for evaluating the quality of instruction.

FEEDBACK:
2.11 All

SUGGESTED READINGS

Ammerman, H. L. and Melching, W. H.: "The Derivation, Analysis, and Classi-
fication of Instructional Objectives," *Hum RRo Technical Report, 66-74,
(Alexandria, Virginia:* Human Resources Research Office, the George
Washington University, 1966).

Boutwell, Richard C., and Tennyson, Robert D.: "Instructional Objectives—
Different by Design," *National Society for Programed Instruction
Journal,* Vol. 10, No. 7, (1971), pp. 7-14.

Burns, R. W.: "The Theory of Expressing Objectives," *Educational Technology,* October 30, 1967.

Eisner, Elliot W.: "Instructional and Expressive Educational Objectives: Their
Formulation and Use in Curriculum," in W. J. Popham (ed.), *AERA Monograph Series on Curriculum Evaluation, No. 3.* (Chicago: Rand McNally,
1969), pp. 1-19.

Gagné, R. M.: "Learning Hierarchies," *Educational Psychologist,* Vol. 6, No. 1,
1968, pp. 1-9.

Krathwohl, D. R., Bloom, B. B., and Masia, B. B.: *Taxonomy of Educational
Objectives: 11. Affective Domain.* (New York: David McKay, 1956).

Merrill, M.D., "Necessary Psychological Conditions for Defining Instructional
Outcomes," in M.D. Merrill (ed.): *Instructional Design: Readings.*
(Englewood Cliffs, New Jersey: Prentice Hall, Inc., 1971), pp. 173-184.

POSTTEST

1. Each of the following statements indicates a possible use for objectives in
   designing an instructional system. Which of the statements are true or
   false.

	T	F
a. To choose instructional materials and procedures.	___	___
b. As a guide for test design.	___	___
c. To provide a criterion for evaluating student perfor-mance.	___	___
d. As a learning guide for students.	___	___
e. To plan a lecture.	___	___
f. To sequence courses in a curriculum.	___	___
g. To inform colleagues what is to be taught in a course.	___	___
h. To provide a criterion for evaluating instruction.	___	___

2. Which of the following statements describes an outcome of instruction?

_____

    a. The political, social, and economic developments in Europe after 1789 will be surveyed.

    b. To state and give examples of the causes of the Franco-Prussian War of the nineteenth century.

3. Which of the following statements is in behavioral terms?

_____

    a. To be familiar with three types of composition.

    b. To list three elements of each of the following types of composition: narration, description, exposition.

4. Which of the following statements is in behavioral terms?

_____

    a. To develop a positive attitude toward mathematics.

    b. To elect nonrequired mathematics courses.

5. Label the parts of the following objective.

    a. Ten second-degree equations will be given the form $Ax^2 + Bxy + Cy^2 + Dx + Ey + F = 0$, where $B \neq 0$ _____

    b. Assuming the equation represents a nondegenerative conic, _____

    c. The student will identify and sketch the curve. _____

    d. To receive credit, nine out of ten equations must be identified and sketched correctly. _____

Answers to this posttest can be found on page 335.

OVERVIEW OF LEARNING SYSTEM DESIGN • REC
OGNIZING WELL-FORMULATED OBJECTIVES •
DERIVING AND WRITING LEARNING OBJECTIVES
• EVALUATING LEARNING SYSTEMS • TASK DE
SCRIPTIONS•TYPES OF LEARNING • ANALYZING
TASKS, OBJECTIVES, AND LEARNER CHARAC
TERISTICS • GENERAL PRINCIPLES OF LEARNING
AND MOTIVATION • THE LEARNING AND TEACH
ING OF CONCEPTS AND PRINCIPLES •THE LEARN
ING AND TEACHING OF PROBLEM SOLVING •
PERCEPTUAL-MOTOR SKILLS • THE SYSTEM
APPROACH TO INSTRUCTION • OVERVIEW OF
LEARNING SYSTEM DESIGN • RECOGNIZING
WELL-FORMULATED OBJECTIVES • **DERIVING
AND WRITING LEARNING OBJECTIVES** • EVALUAT
ING LEARNING SYSTEMS •TASK DESCRIPTIONS •
TYPES OF LEARNING • ANALYZING TASKS, OBJEC
TIVES, AND LEARNER CHARACTERISTICS • GEN
ERAL PRINCIPLES OF LEARNING AND MOTIVA
TION • THE LEARNING AND TEACHING OF CON
CEPTS AND PRINCIPLES • THE LEARNING AND
TEACHING OF PROBLEM SOLVING • PERCEPTUAL-
MOTOR SKILLS • THE SYSTEM APPROACH TO
INSTRUCTION • OVERVIEW OF LEARNING SYS
TEM DESIGN•RECOGNIZING WELL-FORMULATED
OBJECTIVES•**DERIVING AND WRITING LEARNING
OBJECTIVES** • EVALUATING LEARNING SYSTEMS
• TASK DESCRIPTIONS•TYPES OF LEARNING •
ANALYZING TASKS, OBJECTIVES, AND LEARNER

3

CHAPTER OBJECTIVE

● Given a general goal and an objective derived from it, you should be able to correctly apply procedures in the Guide for Deriving and Writing Learning Objectives on page 73.

INTRODUCTION

One of the most serious obstacles for a teacher who wishes to improve his instruction is the lack of an adequate instrument or tool to help set up clear and unambiguous instructional outcomes. Learning objectives provide such an instrument.

Writing well-formulated objectives is an essential initial step in planning and carrying out instruction in a systematic manner. Objectives provide criteria for judging the relevance of course content, for choosing and organizing effective teaching methods and materials, and for evaluating student achievement. By analyzing student achievement of learning objectives, an instructor can obtain valuable information about the effectiveness of his instruction in addition to cues about where improvements are needed.

REVIEW OF THE CHARACTERISTICS OF A WELL-FORMULATED LEARNING OBJECTIVE

In the previous chapter, you learned how to recognize a learning objective stated in behavioral terms and how to identify the three properties of a learning objective. Use the following two frames as a review.

F R A M E 3.1

Which of the following objectives is stated in behavioral terms?

_____ 1. The learner will thoroughly understand the properties of well-formulated objectives and the use of objectives in planning instruction.

_____ 2. A series of lectures will be given regarding the latest methods of applying learning principles to instruction.

_____ 3. The participant in the seminar will learn to write objectives in his own subject matter area.

_____ 4. The learner will write an objective for a course of his own choosing. The objective will conform to all of the criteria listed in the Guide for Deriving and Writing Instructional Objectives.

FEEDBACK:

3.1   4

In the following objective, write the words that describe the component parts.

Objective: Given a simulated patient, the student will conduct an interview lasting from 15 to 30 minutes and react "correctly" to 90 percent of the emotional disturbances expressed by the patient. A correct reaction is one that, in the judgment of the instructor, applies the principles of psychological interaction stated in the textbook, *The Dynamics of Interviewing.*

Behavior: _____

_____

Conditions: _____

_____

Standards: _____

_____

Performance
Stability: _____

_____

STRATEGY OF DERIVING OBJECTIVES

In the previous chapter, we discussed the relationship between instructional goals and learning objectives. Instructional goals and learning objectives both describe instructional outcomes. However, goals are general descriptions and objectives are precise and unambiguous statements; goals are easily stated and objectives require careful formulation.

The process of deriving learning objectives consists of transforming a general description of an instructional outcome into a precise one. In this chapter, you will learn all of the steps required to derive learning objectives from instructional goals.

In deriving a learning objective, start with a general description of what is to be achieved by the instruction. Then, by progressive steps, make this description more and more precise until it satisfies the requirements of a well-formulated objective.

The procedure may be summarized as follows:

1. Write a general instructional goal.

FEEDBACK:
3.2   Behavior: Conduct (an interview); react
       Conditions: A simulated patient; 15 to 30 minutes
       Standards: Applies principles in Wiley's book;   Performance
                     instructor's judgment   Stability: 90 percent

2. Select a situation outside of the course, in which achieving the goal is important to students (for example, another course, a job, an avocation). We call this a **referent situation.**

3. Describe the behavior a student must exhibit to succeed in the referent situation.

4. Write an objective for the course that is the closest possible copy of the conditions and performance requirements of the referent situation.

DERIVING LEARNING OBJECTIVES

STEP I: WRITE A GENERAL GOAL

The first step in deriving a learning objective for a course is to write an instructional goal. An instructional goal is some outcome of instruction that is of value to the students. Some examples of instructional goals are:

- Know the laws of fluid mechanics

- Appreciate nonrepresentational art

- Be able to write effectively

Contrast the above examples of goals with the following examples which are descriptions of instructional procedures rather than instructional outcomes:

- Student will conduct lab experiments in fluid mechanics

- Student will examine and compare a wide variety of art

- Student will be required to write ten essays throughout the term

---

F R A M E 3.3

1. Which of the following is a general goal?

    a. Practice writing instructional objectives.   ____

    b. Know how to write objectives.   ____

2. Which of the following is a general goal?

    a. The students will conduct experiments using the following laboratory equipment . . . .   ____

    b. The students will be able to criticize erroneous application of learning principles . . . .   ____

SOURCE OF INSTRUCTIONAL GOALS   Goals are derived from three sources: the subject matter; the educational philosophy of the instructor; and the characteristics of his students.

FEEDBACK:

3.3   1   b   2   b

Subject Matter   The most obvious source of instructional goals is the subject matter being taught. Most subjects are divided into units, either by tradition or for convenience, and a course is composed of one or more of these units. At least one general goal should be written for each unit of a course and for the course as a whole.

Instructional Philosophy   The instructor's attitudes toward the subject matter, or his philosophy of education often influence the instructional goals he selects. Many instructors consider it their obligation to teach students more than the subject matter of the course. Some instructors feel responsible for leaving their students with a positive attitude toward the subject matter. Others feel obliged to teach students how to learn.

The following is a list of goals that one instructor developed to supplement his subject matter goals:

1.   Know how to acquire knowledge (in the subject matter) and how to use it.
2.   Master the skills of communication.
3.   Be aware of your own values and the contrasting values of other individuals and cultures.
4.   Be able to cooperate and collaborate with others in studying, analyzing, and formulating solutions to problems, and taking action on them.
5.   Have awareness, concern, and a sense of responsibility regarding contemporary events, issues, and problems.

The instructor who wrote these goals obligated himself to design his course so that the students could achieve these goals in addition to those derived from the subject matter.

Student Characteristics   An instructor should consider the level of knowledge and skill of the students entering his course and select goals that can be attained within the available time. In addition, he should take account of student goals in the design of the instructional system. If an instructor does these things, he is more likely to increase student interest and motivation in the course which, in turn, will lead to better learning.

What are the three sources of general goals?

      1._____

      2._____

      3._____

F
R
A
M
E

3.4

FEEDBACK:

3.4   1   Subject matter   2   Instructor's educational philosophy   3   Students' characteristics

You have just finished Step I in deriving and writing an objective. Following the discussion of each of the steps, the important points are summarized. Each summary includes three parts: (1) the name of the step; (2) notes: a list of the questions you should answer in performing the step; (3) check: a list of questions you should use to check your work. The summaries are repeated in abbreviated form on page 73 of this chapter.

SUMMARY OF STEP I: WRITE A GENERAL GOAL

Notes: Answer the questions. What is an important outcome of my course? Is achieving the goal of value to my students? What does a student have to know, or be able to do, in order to succeed in this subject?

Check: Is the goal stated in terms of outcomes of instruction (as opposed to procedures, media, equipment to be used)?

If either answer is "no," rewrite your general goal.

STEP II: STATE A REFERENT SITUATION

When an instructor designs a course, he hopes that the knowledge and skills students learn will be useful to them at some later time, that is, in some situation external to the course. We call this a **referent situation**. Examples of referent situations are: the next course in a curriculum, a job or profession, an avocation, or any of the many situations which students may encounter in later life.

In designing a course of instruction, it is important for the teacher to identify at least one referent situation. If he fails to do so, or fails to communicate the referent situation he has in mind to his students, he runs the risk of students not perceiving the relevance of what he is trying to teach. Teachers should encourage students to describe referent situations that are important to them.

In choosing a referent situation, the instructor should ask himself the following question:

In what kinds of situations will my students use what I expect them to learn?

For some courses the answer may be obvious. The referent situation for a course in educational psychology for student teachers is the classroom in which they will eventually teach. For a course in auto repair, the referent situation might be a commercial garage. For a two-course sequence in physics, the referent situation for the first course is the following course in the sequence, and so on.

Many courses, however, do not have referent situations which are immediately apparent. For example, what might the referent situation be for a course in world history or Latin, or for an elementary course in philosophy? These courses may have as many referent situations as there are students in the class. While it is not feasible to define a referent situation for all students, an instructor should attempt to identify groups of students with similar aspirations and identify at least one referent situation for each group. In college or university settings, majors and nonmajors in a particular discipline might be two such groups.

A referent situation is defined as a situation in which the student

_____.

F
R
A
M
E

3.5

After selecting a referent situation, the instructor should reconsider the goal he has selected from the standpoint of whether or not achieving the goal would be of use to his students in the given situation. If achieving the goal is important in the referent situation selected, the students will be more likely to perceive the relevance of the subject matter being taught, thus increasing their motivation to learn.

An example will illustrate this process. The teacher of a freshman college course in English composition began with the following goal:

> To be able to write creatively.

After considering several referent situations, she decided to change the goal. She realized that, although being able to write creatively might be important in a literary career, none of her students would be likely to embark on such a career. The most relevant situation for most of her students was the writing they would do in their subsequent college courses where being able to write clearly and precisely was more important than being able to write creatively. Consequently, she changed her goal to the following:

> To be able to choose the appropriate form of writing (narration, description, and exposition) and be able to write a paper demonstrating application of the elements of effective writing in each form.

SUMMARY OF STEP II: STATE A REFERENT SITUATION

Notes: Answer the question: Where might my students use what they have learned in my courses?

Check: Is achieving the goal useful in referent situation?

If answer is "no," select another referent situation.

FEEDBACK:

3.5   can use or apply what he learns in a course.

For each of the following courses, select the most appropriate referent situation(s):

1. Course in general psychology for college freshmen
   a.   The dormitory   _____
   b.   Academic appointment in psychology   _____
2. Course in driver education for high school students
   a.   City streets   _____
   b.   Superhighways   _____
   c.   Indianapolis speedway   _____
3. High school technical course in auto repair
   a.   Engineering school   _____
   b.   Commercial garage   _____
4. College course in music appreciation
   a.   Attending a concert   _____
   b.   Attending a Conservatory of Music   _____
5. Political science course in a community college
   a.   Graduate courses in political science   _____
   b.   The community   _____

STEP III: WRITE A REFERENT SITUATION TEST (RST)

The next step in deriving a learning objective is to devise a referent situation test. For convenience, we will, in some cases, abbreviate the term referent situation test (RST).

To understand the meaning and purpose of a referent situation test, we must first discuss the question of the relevance of instruction. What does relevant instruction mean? How can a teacher make what he teaches relevant? One concept of relevance is that students can transfer what they have learned in class to their lives outside of the classroom. In other words, relevant instruction can be thought of as teaching students knowledge and abilities that they can apply in referent situations.

To make his instruction more relevant, a teacher should endeavor to write learning objectives that are related to referent situations. Then, if students achieve the objectives, they will be able to perform successfully in referent situations. A referent situation test is a mechanism for relating objectives to referent situations.

A referent situation test describes a set of circumstances that the student might encounter in the referent situation. These include the conditions, the behavior he would have to exhibit, and the standards of successful perform-

FEEDBACK:
3.6   1 a   4 a
      2 a, b   5 b
      3 b

ance. In devising the referent situation test, the instructor should ask himself the question, "What would a student have to do in the referent situation to demonstrate that he had achieved the instructional goal?" The test should be so designed that only a student who has achieved the goal can pass the test.

The following are several examples of referent situation tests. Notice that each includes behavior, conditions, and standards.

- An English course for foreign students has as one of its goals "to attain language fluency in practical situations." The referent situation is a supermarket. A possible referent situation test would be:
  > While shopping for food, the student would be able to obtain what he asked for without having to repeat himself or asking the clerk to repeat himself.

- A humanities course in which the goal is "to appreciate art." A referent situation is the student's living quarters. One appropriate referent situation test would be:
  > The student selects and displays "good" pictures in his dorm room or home.

- The goal of a course in nursing is "the ability to sense problems." A referent situation is a hospital. An appropriate referent situation test would be:
  > In a hospital, when a patient displays unpredicted symptoms, the student will take appropriate action in time to prevent complications.

- A course in teacher training, in which the goal is "to demonstrate flexibility." A referent situation is the classroom. One appropriate referent situation test would be:
  > In a classroom, when the teacher realizes that students are having a learning problem, he identifies the problem and modifies his instructional procedures to remove it.

The referent situation test must be an accurate copy of the referent situation. The test conditions, the required performance, and the standards of success should all be similar to those expected in the referent situation.

If an instructor is not sure of the conditions, performance requirements, and standards in the referent situation, there are two things he can do:

- Consult a practitioner. Ask people who actually work in the referent situation to describe typical situations the student might encounter and standards of behavior that would be required in order for him to succeed. If the referent situation is another course of instruction, a discussion with the teacher of that course should provide the required information.

- Consult written descriptions of the referent situation. If no written descriptions can be found, the instructor may wish to write one of his own. A procedure for doing this is described in Chapter 5 on task descriptions.

FRAME 3.7

In each of the following examples, select the most appropriate referent situation test:

1. Course: General Psychology for College Freshmen
   Goal: Apply principles of interpersonal relations
   Referent situation: Residence dormitory
   RST A: Be able to define and give examples of defense mechanisms.   ____
   RST B: When approached by another person with an emotional conflict, the student will spend time listening.   ____

2. Course: Auto Repair
   Goal: Apply troubleshooting techniques
   Referent situation: Commercial garage
   RST A: Be able to state procedures for troubleshooting according to the repair manual.   ____
   RST B: Be able to diagnose and repair engine malfunctions according to the repair manual.   ____

3. Course: Political Science
   Goal: Understand principles of political dynamics
   Referent situation: An election campaign
   RST A: Be able to identify pressure groups in the community.   ____
   RST B: Be able to write an essay discussing the theory of political parties   ____

In example 1, RST A is not a good indicator of whether a student has achieved the goal, i.e., to apply principles of interpersonal relations in the dorm. It is difficult to conceive of a dorm situation in which being able to

---

FEEDBACK:
3.7   1   RST B
        2   RST B
        3   RST A

define and give examples of defense mechanisms would be necessary for good interpersonal relations. On the other hand, RST B is a much better indicator of goal achievement. Being willing and able to listen to another person almost always demonstrates interpersonal sensitivity.

In example 2, RST B is a more appropriate test of whether a student could apply troubleshooting techniques in a garage. A garage mechanic is not judged on the basis of whether he can state procedures but whether he can get the job done.

In example 3, RST A is the more appropriate test of whether a student understands how principles of political dynamics apply to an election campaign. Being able to identify community pressure groups is a better indicator of successful performance in an election campaign than being able to write an essay.

SUMMARY OF STEP III: WRITE A TEST OF GOAL ACHIEVEMENT IN THE REFERENT SITUATION (RST)

Notes: 1.   Answer the question: If I could observe a student in the referent situation, how would I know he had achieved the goal?

2.   State conditions, behavior, and standards.

Check: 1.   Is the test behavior of the type required in the referent situation?

2.   Are the test conditions similar to those encountered in the referent situation?

3.   Are the standards of performance similar to those required in the referent situation?

If any answer is "no," rewrite the test.

REVIEW

We have completed the first three steps in the process of deriving learning objectives. The first step consisted of writing an instructional goal which described some knowledge or skill that a student was to acquire as an outcome of instruction. The second step required identification of a referent situation in which a student could apply what he had learned. In the third step, a referent situation test was devised. The referent situation test described the conditions, behavior, and performance standards of the referent situation. The referent situation test was designed to measure whether or not a student who had achieved the goal could apply what he had learned in the referent situation.

In the next series of steps, the procedure for transforming the referent situation test into a learning objective will be discussed.

FRAME 3.8

The first three steps in the process of deriving learning objectives are:

1. Write an instructional _____.

2. Identify a _____ _____.

3. Devise a _____ _____ _____ (RST).

WRITING LEARNING OBJECTIVES

The referent situation test is a mechanism for relating a learning objective to a referent situation because both the test and the objective are criteria of achievement. The referent situation test describes successful performance in the referent situation; the objective describes successful performance at the end of instruction. Therefore, the learning objective should be the closest possible approximation of the referent situation test. The instructor should try to reproduce the same conditions, behavior, and standards in the objective as in the test. In this way, he can ensure that achieving the learning objective will transfer to the referent situation.

Because of practical considerations, it is sometimes not feasible for the objective to be an exact copy of the referent situation test. Physical restrictions of the classroom may make it impossible to create the same conditions or permit the student to perform the same behavior as in the referent situation. Nevertheless, taking all practical constraints into account, the instructor should attempt to write an objective that deviates as little as possible from the referent situation test.

If, in writing the objective, it is necessary to modify the behavior in the referent situation test, the behavior specified in the objective should at least be prerequisite to what is required in the referent situation test. For example, if the referent situation test requires the student to be able to solve problems, and conditions in the classroom cannot be arranged for him to demonstrate his problem-solving ability, the objective should state that he at least demonstrate knowledge of the principles that would be applied in solving the problem.

If it is necessary to deviate from the referent situation test conditions, the aids and restrictions in the course objective should be of the same type as those of the referent situation test. For instance, if, in the referent situation test, the student must be able to solve problems quickly,

FEEDBACK:
3.8   1   goal
       2   referent sitaution
       3   referent situation

the conditions of the objective should specify a time limit.

When the standards included in the learning objective deviate from those required in the referent situation test, objective standards should be set sufficiently high so that, if a student achieves them, he will be able to continue learning on his own. If, in achieving the objectives, a student reaches a level of learning that enables him to identify and correct his own mistakes, he will probably be able to continue learning to the level specified in the referent situation test.

To summarize the principle for translating a referent situation test into objectives:

- The instructor should write objectives that deviate as little as possible from the referent situation test.

- If classroom constraints require deviations, the instructor should select conditions, behavior, and standards for the objectives that result in maximum transfer to the referent situation.

---

1. A learning objective is similar to a referent situation test in two ways:

   a. They both have the same three _____.

   b. They both are criteria of successful _____,

2. Classroom _____ may cause a learning objective to deviate from a referent situation test.

3. If a learning objective deviates from a referent situation test, the instructor should attempt to make

   a. The behavior in the objective prerequisite to the behavior in the _____ _____ test.

   b. The aids and restrictions in the objective of the same type as those encountered in the _____ _____.

   c. The standards in the objective at a high enough level that the student can continue to _____ on his own or by himself.

FRAME 3.9

STEP IV: WRITE THE LEARNING OBJECTIVE

In this section, we will discuss the procedures for transforming a referent situation test into a learning objective. To follow the discussion, it is essential that you be able to recognize a well-formulated objective. If you are unable to do this, review Chapter 2 before proceeding.

FEEDBACK:

3.9 1 a component parts (or any equivalent words)   3 a referent situation
        b performance   b referent test
     2 constraints or restrictions   c learn

Let us begin by reviewing the component parts of a well-formulated objective. A well-formulated objective includes: (1) a description of the behavior expected of a student after instruction; (2) a description of the conditions in which the student will be required to demonstrate the behavior; and (3) the standards of minimal acceptable performance.

Ideally, the learning objective would be an exact replica of the referent situation test. However, practical constraints of the classroom setup make this difficult to achieve. In practice, therefore, the problem is to write an objective whose component parts deviate as little as possible from the components of the referent situation test. The following guidelines will help to minimize this deviation.

WRITING THE BEHAVIOR COMPONENT OF THE LEARNING OBJECTIVE

Referent situations refer to complex real-life circumstances. Consequently, a referent situation test frequently requires behavior at a higher level of competence than can be achieved in class. In such cases, the instructor can only hope to prepare his students for the real world by helping them acquire prerequisite knowledge and skills. In order to accomplish this, the instructor should identify these prerequisite abilities and specify them in the behavior portion of the objective.

To illustrate, the authors of this book expect readers to be able to apply concepts and principles of learning system design to their own instruction. We do not, however, expect readers to achieve this level of competence merely by reading the book. We do expect them to learn these concepts and principles as a result of reading and to understand that knowing them is prerequisite to being able to apply them.

The idea of prerequisite knowledge and skills gives us the first guide for writing a learning objective.

GUIDE 1

IDENTIFY AND SELECT THE HIGHEST PREREQUISITE ABILITY FOR THE BEHAVIOR COMPONENT OF THE OBJECTIVE.

In order to select the highest prerequisite ability, we need a method of classifying behavior that enables us to place behavioral skills in rank order from lowest to highest. Using this method, we could locate the behavior of the referent situation test and identify the abilities prerequisite to it. Then we could select the highest ability that we could expect to achieve in class.

Several methods of classifying behavior have been proposed by psychologists and educators. One such method lists the following categories for classifying cognitive abilities:

Lowest: Memory
             Translation
             Interpretation
             Application
             Analysis
Highest: Synthesis

We shall not attempt to develop any of these methods of classifying behavior in detail. Instead, we shall present, in behavioral terms, some examples of the abilities listed above in order to illustrate how a classification method may be used to identify the highest prerequisite ability. In
the classification scheme, illustrated in Table 3.1, each behavior is prerequisite to those above it. Study the table for a few minutes. Note how
the cognitive abilities are organized into a hierarchy from lowest (being
able to define or state) to the highest (produce creative solutions).

TABLE 3.1   SCALE FOR CLASSIFYING TYPES OF COGNITIVE ABILITIES
             (EXAMPLES OF EACH TYPE ARE GIVEN IN BEHAVIORAL TERMS)

Highest: PRODUCE A NEW, UNIQUE, OR CREATIVE SOLUTION TO A PROB-
LEM
            (Example: An original work of art or an original piece of research.)

RECOGNIZE A PROBLEM AND SOLVE IT
            (Example: State an hypothesis to account for contradictory data:)

APPLY PRINCIPLES TO SOLVE A GIVEN PROBLEM
            (Example: Diagnose a disease.)

PREDICT CORRECT APPLICATION OF A PRINCIPLE
            (Example: If a gas is compressed, it will _____.)

RECOGNIZE CORRECT AND INCORRECT APPLICATION OF A
PRINCIPLE
            (Example: If a gas is compressed, it will be hotter; true or false.)

GIVE EXAMPLES OF A CONCEPT
            (Example: Give an example of a one-cell organism.)

DISTINGUISH BETWEEN EXAMPLES AND NONEXAMPLES OF A
CONCEPT
            (Example: Which of the following are examples of one-cell
                      organisms?)

RECOGNIZE AN EXAMPLE OF A CONCEPT
            (Example: An amoeba is a one-cell organism; true or false.)

Lowest: DEFINE OR STATE A CONCEPT OR PRINCIPLE
            (Example: What is a semipermeable membrane? State the principle
                      of conservation of mass and energy.)

To use the classification scheme illustrated in Table 3.1:

1. Identify the level of behavior in the referent situation test.
2. Select the highest category of cognitive ability that can be achieved in class.
3. Describe the cognitive ability selected in behavioral terms.

Using an ordered scale of behaviorally stated abilities helps a teacher improve his instruction and makes it more relevant. Writing objectives calling for high prerequisite abilities requires him to design his instruction so that students will attain these abilities. Consequently, his students will be better prepared to cope with referent situations outside of class.

Instructors who write objectives at too low a level are shortchanging their students. Writing low-level objectives usually results in low-level tests which, in turn, result in low-level learning by the students. There is an all-too-common practice for instructors to devise tests that require students to merely reproduce information previously presented in the course. This practice encourages students to memorize facts instead of learning general principles and their application, since high grades can be attained merely by memorizing. Consequently, when they leave the course, students are not well-prepared to apply what they have learned.

Using a referent situation test described on page 59 of this chapter, and the classification scheme in Table 3.1, let us demonstrate how to specify an appropriate behavioral component in the learning objective. The reader may test his own ability to use the classification scheme.

One of the goals for a course in nursing was "the ability to sense problems." The referent situation was a hospital ward, and the referent situation test was stated as follows:

> When patients display unusual symptoms, the student takes appropriate action to relieve the symptoms in time to prevent complications.

To use the classification scheme in Table 3.1, first identify the level of behavior in the referent situation test.

F R A M E 3.10

In the example above, the level of behavior in the referent situation test is to:

1. Apply principles to solve a given problem.
2. Recognize a problem and solve it.
3. Produce a unique or creative solution to a problem.

The behavior in the referent situation test is "to recognize a problem

---

FEEDBACK:
3.10 2

and solve it." The student must recognize when a patient's symptoms are unusual. Then she must decide what the consequence might be and take appropriate action. The words, "in time to prevent complications," describe the standards of acceptable performance.

Choice number 1, "apply principles to solve problems," is not a correct answer because the problem is not given to the student. The student has to first recognize the problem, which is the unexpected nature of the patient's symptoms.

Choice number 3," produce a unique or creative solution," is incorrect. Hospitals are run according to standard procedures based on medical principles. A "unique" way of responding to a problem may produce confusion to the detriment of the patient's well-being.

After identifying the level of behavior in the referent situation test, select the highest category of cognitive ability that can be achieved in class (Table 3.1). In the nursing course from which this example was taken, the instructor selected the two categories immediately lower in the scale: "apply principles to solve a given problem" and "predict correct application of a principle."

These categories were selected because for a nurse to be able to recognize unusual symptoms and take appropriate actions, she must have already learned principles of nursing care for various pathologies and procedures for applying these principles. Only then can she apply her knowledge and skills to solving the problems she may face.

The next step is to describe the selected cognitive ability in behavioral terms. See if you can discover how these cognitive abilities have been described in behavioral terms in each of the following frames. Choose the alternative that corresponds to the cognitive ability level selected.

Which of the following objectives describes the ability to "apply principles to solve a given problem"?

1. The student will be able to list the symptomatology of the following pathology categories . . . (categories listed).

2. Given a selected nursing care problem (such as abdominal pain, urinary retention) and patient history (on Cardex file or patient chart), the student will state the nursing care actions indicated and explain the expected results within 10 minutes.

   Answers must be in accordance with nursing care principles given in the course and the manual of hospital procedures. No references or texts may be used.

F R A M E

3.11

FEEDBACK:
3.11 2

The first alternative is incorrect because "listing the symptomatology" does not represent the cognitive ability of applying principles. In the nursing example, the two cognitive abilities selected were: "apply principles . . ." and "predict correct application . . ."

FRAME 3.12

Which of the following objectives describes the ability to "predict correct application of a principle"?

1. Given several case histories, the student will prepare a nursing-care plan and give the reason for each step in the plan. No references may be used.
2. The student will be able to state the steps that should be included in a nursing-care plan. No references may be used.

The second alternative is incorrect in this frame because the ability to "state the steps" does not correspond to the "ability to predict."

WRITING THE CONDITIONS COMPONENT OF THE LEARNING OBJECTIVE

The conditions of an objective describe the aids the student may use and the restrictions that will be imposed on him. These conditions should correspond as closely as possible to the conditions in the referent situation test. If, because of classroom constraints, it is necessary to deviate from test conditions, the conditions in the objective should simulate the test conditions.

In the nursing example, the referent test conditions call for patients who display unusual symptoms. It is usually not feasible to arrange these conditions in the classroom. However, the symptoms can be represented by providing written case histories or by simulated role playing techniques.

GUIDE 2

INCLUDE IN THE LEARNING OBJECTIVE ALL AIDS AND RESTRICTIONS THAT INFLUENCE PERFORMANCE OF THE TASK IN THE REFERENT SITUATION TEST.

The instructor is normally familiar with the referent situation and he is in the best position to decide which conditions influence performance. If he is not sure, he should consider using the task description procedures described in Chapter 5.

Let us return to our nursing example to illustrate the use of Guide 2. The instructor of the nursing course knew the conditions that influence

---

FEEDBACK:
3.12   1

performance in the referent situation. She knew that in a hospital, a student would normally not have access to a textbook on nursing care principles, and even if a textbook were available, she would not have time to use it. Accordingly, this condition was included in the learning objective for the course.

WRITING THE STANDARDS COMPONENT OF THE LEARNING OBJECTIVE

The standards component of a learning objective describes the minimal level of acceptable performance. If possible, the standards included in the objective should be the same as those in the referent situation test. Because of classroom restrictions, it may be necessary to deviate from the test standards. In that case, two options are possible.

- If the behavior in the objectives is the same as the behavior in the referent situation test, use the same type of standard in the objective but reduce the minimal level of acceptable performance.

- If the behavior in the objective is different from the behavior in the referent situation test, use a standard appropriate to the behavior in the objective.

Some examples of types of standards are described in Chapter 2.

The instructor must decide how much to reduce the standards included in the objective. His decision should be determined by the entry skills of the student and how much instructional time he plans to allocate to achieving the objective. It will take students more time to achieve an objective at a highe level if their entry skills are sufficiently lower than the standard. However, the higher the standards, the more easily the students will be able to transfer what they have learned to the referent situation. On the other hand, if insufficient time is available to help students improve from their entry skill level to the level specified in the objective, there will, of course, be little or no transfer.

GUIDE 3

a. *IF BEHAVIOR IN THE OBJECTIVE IS THE SAME AS IN THE RST, WRITE THE SAME TYPE OF STANDARD IN THE OBJECTIVE, BUT REDUCE MINIMUM LEVEL OF ACCEPTABLE PERFORMANCE.*

b. *IF BEHAVIOR IN THE OBJECTIVE IS DIFFERENT FROM THAT IN THE RST, WRITE THE TYPE OF STANDARD APPROPRIATE TO BEHAVIOR IN THE OBJECTIVE.*

Let us consider again the referent situation test in our nursing example. In this test the standards of acceptable performance were, "take appropriate action to relieve symptoms in time to prevent com- lications." These are "consequence" types of standards. They signify that the consequences of appropriate action are the relief of symptoms and the prevention of complications.

In the objective, the behaviors required of the student were to "state the nursing care actions indicated and explain the expected results." These behaviors are different from the RST which require the nurse to relieve symptoms and predict complications. Since the behavior in the objective is different from the behavior in the RST, according to Guide 3, the type of standards chosen should be appropriate to the behavior in the objective. The appropriate standards for the behavior in the objective are two reference sources: the nursing principles given in the course and the manual of hospital procedures. The latter stan- dards were included in the objective. (See Frame 3.11, page 67.)

SUMMARY OF STEP IV: WRITE THE LEARNING OBJECTIVE

Notes: 1. If behavior in referent situation test cannot be included in the objective, identify the highest prerequisite ability.

2. If referent situation conditions cannot be replicated, include all aids and restrictions that influence performance in the referent situation test.

3. Write standards appropriate to the behavior in the objective.

Check: 1. Is the ability stated in behavioral terms?

2. Do conditions in objective closely approximate conditions in referent situation test?

3. Do standards closely approximate standards in referent situation test?

If any answer is "no," rewrite the objective.

STEP V: WRITING THE LOWER LIMIT OF PERFORMANCE STABILITY

The performance stability refers to the test used to measure student achievement of the objective. It is a statement of the number of oppor- tunities the student will have to perform the terminal behavior and the number of times his performance must reach or exceed the standard. An instructor includes a performance stability component in a learning objective to assure himself that the student's test performance is not due to chance.

The instructor himself must decide what proportion of successes will convince him that the student had indeed achieved the objective and that his performance was not due to chance. His decision should be based on two considerations, which we have stated in Guides 4 and 5.

GUIDE 4

THE PERFORMANCE STABILITY LIMIT SHOULD BE THE SAME RATIO OF SUCCESSES TO OPPORTUNITIES AS THE STUDENT IS LIKELY TO HAVE IN THE REFERENT SITUATION.

GUIDE 5

SET THE PERFORMANCE STABILITY HIGH IF THE STUDENT PERFORMANCE IS CRITICAL OR IF THE STUDENT MUST APPLY HIS LEARNING IN THE REFERENT SITUATION AFTER A LONG TIME INTERNAL.

Guide 5 applies a psychological principle which states that retention is increased by overlearning, that is, by requiring the learner to practice beyond the point at which he attains a minimal level of performance. An instructor should apply this principle when training students to perform critical skills. Whether he is training a surgeon or an airplane mechanic, the instructor should set extremely high criteria of satisfactory performance to stabilize performance at that level. A surgeon doesn't often get a second chance. A high stability level is also required if a long interval is expected to occur between completion of a course and the time when the student will encounter the referent situation in order to minimize forgetting.

SUMMARY OF STEP V: WRITE THE LOWER LIMIT OF PERFORMANCE STABILITY

Notes: 1. Write number of chances student will be given to demonstrate that he has achieved the objective.

2. Write proportion of times student must succeed.

Check: 1. Is this proportion of successes the same as the student is likely to encounter in referent situation?

2. Is this proportion of successes sufficiently high for retention of objective?

If either answer is "no," rewrite limit.

The procedure for deriving and writing an objective requires the system designer to use thought and judgment. He must have a thorough knowledge of the subject matter and must carefully consider situations in which his students will use what they have learned.

Many instructors mistakenly assume that writing well-formulated objectives means writing very detailed objectives. Objectives should be clear and precise descriptions of instructional outcomes; however, clarity and precision need not mean overly detailed specification of minutiae. The reader should recall the major functions of an objective: to guide the system designer and to provide direction to the student. Objectives should be written in sufficient, but not extensive, detail to serve these functions. Note the examples of objectives at the beginning of each chapter of this book. They are sufficiently clear to guide the authors in writing the chapters. Were they sufficiently clear to guide the reader?

SUMMARY

In this chapter, a series of steps for deriving and writing learning objectives has been outlined. The procedure for deriving and writing an objective is:

- Identify an instructional goal of value to students.
- Identify a referent situation in which students can apply what they have learned.
- Write a referent situation test that precisely describes the conditions, behavior, and standards of the referent situation.
- Write a learning objective that approximates the referent situation as closely as possible.

If, because of constraints imposed by the classroom, the objective must deviate from the referent situation test, the following guide should be used:

- Select the highest prerequisite ability for the behavior component of the objective.
- Include in the learning objective, all aids and restrictions that influence performance of the task in the referent situation test.
- Write the lower limit of performance using the same type of standard (time, errors, etc.) as the referent situation test.
- The performance stability limit should be the same ratio of successes to opportunities as the student is likely to have in the referent situation.
- Set the performance stability high if the student must apply his learning in the referent situation after a long time interval.

SUGGESTED READINGS

Bloom, B.B. (ed.): *Taxonomy of Educational Objectives: I. Cognitive Domain,* (New York: David McKay, 1956).

Gagné, R.M.: "An Analysis of Instructional Objectives for the Design of Instruction," in Robert Glaser (ed.): *Teaching Machines and Programed Learning II,* (Washington, D.C.: National Education Association, 1965), pp. 21-65.

Mager, Robert F.: *Developing Attitude Toward Learning,* (Belmont, California: Fearon/Lear Siegler, Inc., 1968).

Mager, Robert F.: *Preparing Instructional Objectives,* (Belmont, California: Fearon/Lear Siegler, Inc., 1962).

Tyler, Ralph W.: "Some Persistent Questions on the Defining of Objectives," in C. M. Lindwall (ed.): *Defining Educational Objectives,* (Pittsburgh: University of Pittsburgh Press, 1964), pp. 77-83.

DECISION AID

NOTE: *The procedures discussed in this chapter have been incorporated into the following Guide.*

GUIDE FOR DERIVING AND WRITING LEARNING OBJECTIVES

Step I: **Write a General Goal**

Part A. Notes: What should students get from my course?

They should _____

Part B. Check: Did you state an outcome (not how to achieve the outcome)? Yes_____ No_____

Step II: **State a Referent Situation**

Part A. Notes: Where will students use what they have learned?

_____

Part B. Check: Is the goal important to the student in the referent situation? Yes_____ No_____

Step III: **Write a Referent Situation Test**

Part A. Notes: If I could observe a student in the referent situation, how would I know whether he had achieved the goal?

Conditions: _____

Behavior: He would _____

Standards: So that _____

Part B. Checks: Do these conditions occur in the referent situation?

Yes_____ No_____

Is this behavior required in the referent situation?

Yes_____ No_____

Are these the standards used to judge performance in the referent situation? Yes_____ No_____

Step IV: **Write the Objective**

Part A. Notes: How will I test students at the end of instruction?

Conditions: Given_____

Such as:_____

Aids or restrictions:_____

Test Behavior:

The student will_____

Standards (Use one or more of the following):

Time limit:_____/Speed:_____Accuracy:_____

According to:_____

So well that:_____

Part B. Checks: Do the conditions closely approximate

conditions in Step III? Yes_____No_____

Do the conditions affect performance? Yes_____No_____

Is performance in behavioral terms? Yes_____No_____

Is behavior a close approximation of

behavior in Step III Yes_____No_____

Do standards closely approximate

standards in Step III? Yes_____No_____

Step V: Write Lower Limit of Performance Stability

Part A. Notes: On final test, how many chances will a student be
given to show that he has achieved the objective?

_____

What proportion of times must he succeed (e.g.,
9/10)? _____

Part B. Checks: Is this proportion of successes needed in

the referent situation? Yes_____No_____

Is this proportion of successes needed

for retention? Yes_____No_____

Step VI: Check Your Objective for Clarity

Part A. Notes: Rewrite your objective here:

Conditions: _____

_____

_____

Behavior: _____

_____

_____

Standards: _____

_____

_____

Limits: _____

_____

_____

Part B. Check: If two of your colleagues looked at the above objective and a student's performance, could they
agree whether or not the standards and limits had
been achieved?   Yes____ No____

POSTTEST

ITEM I

You are assisting a colleague to write objectives for a course he is preparing. As a
first draft, he shows you the following general goal, referent situation, and objective.

General Goal: To provide an opportunity for students to become
familiar with research methods.

Referent Situation Test: An industrial laboratory.

Objective: The student will demonstrate his familiarity with
research methods and principles. He will correctly
demonstrate this understanding in several real situations.

Answer the following questions with reference to the above statements. You are
permitted to use the Guide for Deriving and Writing Learning Objectives.

	T	F
1. The general goal states an outcome of instruction.	____	____
2. The general goal is stated in behavioral terms.	____	____
3. "An industrial laboratory" is *not* an example of a referent situation test.	____	____
4. The statement "in real situations" shows that the instructor was trying to write a standard of performance.	____	____
5. A major flaw in the objective is that it is not stated in behavioral terms.	____	____
6. The statement "will demonstrate familiarity" is an attempt to state a learning outcome.	____	____
7. The word "correctly" is an attempt to state a performance standard.	____	____

8. The phrase "several real situations" is an attempt to state a performance stability limit. _____

ITEM II

1. You are preparing a course learning system design. Which of the following meets the definition of a general goal?

   a. Knows how to apply system principles.
   b. Study each of the chapters in sequence. _____

2. For a general course in chemistry for college freshmen not majoring in chemistry, select the most appropriate referent situation(s).

   a. An industrial laboratory.
   b. The community.
   c. Honors course in chemistry. _____

3. The referent situation for a high school course in automobile mechanics is a commerical garage. Which of the following is the most appropriate test in the referent situation.

   a. State procedures for repairing a transmission according to the repair manual.
   b. Analyze and repair engine malfunctions according to the repair manual. _____

4. A learning objective has three components: conditions, behavior, standards (or criteria). Which of these is/are in the referent situation test?

   a. Conditions and behavior.
   b. Behavior and standards.
   c. Conditions and standards.
   d. All three. _____

5. An objective may differ from a referent situation test because of restrictions found in the classroom. Which of the following is an example of such a restriction?

   a. Entry skill level of students.
   b. Number of students in class
   c. Limited space or time.
   d. All of the above. _____

Answers to this posttest can be found on page 335.

OVERVIEW OF LEARNING SYSTEM DESIGN • REC
OGNIZING WELL-FORMULATED OBJECTIVES •
DERIVING AND WRITING LEARNING OBJECTIVES
• **EVALUATING LEARNING SYSTEMS** • TASK DE
SCRIPTIONS•TYPES OF LEARNING • ANALYZING
TASKS, OBJECTIVES, AND LEARNER CHARAC
TERISTICS • GENERAL PRINCIPLES OF LEARNING
AND MOTIVATION • THE LEARNING AND TEACH
ING OF CONCEPTS AND PRINCIPLES •THE LEARN
ING AND TEACHING OF PROBLEM SOLVING •
PERCEPTUAL-MOTOR SKILLS • THE SYSTEM
APPROACH TO INSTRUCTION • OVERVIEW OF
LEARNING SYSTEM DESIGN • RECOGNIZING
WELL-FORMULATED OBJECTIVES • DERIVING
AND WRITING LEARNING OBJECTIVES • **EVALUAT
ING LEARNING SYSTEMS** • TASK DESCRIPTIONS •
TYPES OF LEARNING • ANALYZING TASKS, OBJEC
TIVES, AND LEARNER CHARACTERISTICS • GEN
ERAL PRINCIPLES OF LEARNING AND MOTIVA
TION • THE LEARNING AND TEACHING OF CON
CEPTS AND PRINCIPLES • THE LEARNING AND
TEACHING OF PROBLEM SOLVING • PERCEPTUAL-
MOTOR SKILLS • THE SYSTEM APPROACH TO
INSTRUCTION • OVERVIEW OF LEARNING SYS
TEM DESIGN•RECOGNIZING WELL-FORMULATED
OBJECTIVES•DERIVING AND WRITING LEARNING
OBJECTIVES • **EVALUATING LEARNING SYSTEMS**
• TASK DESCRIPTIONS•TYPES OF LEARNING •
ANALYZING TASKS, OBJECTIVES, AND LEARNER

4

CHAPTER OBJECTIVES

- Given an objective and one or more test items, you should be able to select the items that are valid for determining achievement of the objective.

- Given one or more statements describing an evaluation method, you should be able to select the evaluation principle the method applies or the principle it violates.

- Given one or more statements describing an evaluation purpose (for example, to evaluate entry behavior of students or the adequacy of feedback provided to students), you should be able to select the evaluation method that accomplishes this purpose.

INTRODUCTION

Many teachers think of evaluation merely as assigning grades to students. While this is an important decision since it answers the question, "How well did the student do?" it is only one of the criteria involved in evaluating instruction. Evaluating a learning system properly involves finding answers to many other questions, such as "How well did the teacher do?" and "How well was the system designed?"

When you set out to design a learning system, there are many alternative options available and many decisions to be made. You must choose your objectives; you must select the topics to be covered, the sequence in which to present them, and how much time you will devote to each; you must select the media and procedures for presenting information in addition to the examples you will use to make your points clear; and, finally, you must decide on how and when practice will be provided, and how you will test student achievement.

On the other hand, there are factors which are not subject to your decision and about which you have no choice. Some of the things which teachers usually cannot select are the classroom they will use or whether the course they teach will extend for a period of four, ten, thirteen, or some other number of weeks. In some cases, teachers are not permitted to specify the prerequisites for entering a course.

However, for every option available to you, you must choose among given alternatives and come to some decision. Each decision and each choice you make should be to further the learning of your students. And for each decision you may ask: Did I choose correctly? How well did I succeed? What should I do next time? You need answers to these kinds of questions in order to properly evaluate a learning system and unless you obtain these answers, you cannot improve your instruction.

What is evaluation?

DEFINITION:
EVALUATION IS A CONTINUOUS PROCESS OF COLLECTING AND INTERPRETING INFORMATION IN ORDER TO ASSESS DECISIONS MADE IN DESIGNING A LEARNING SYSTEM.

This definition has three important implications. First, evaluation is an ongoing process, not something you do only at the end of a course. It is a process that starts even before instruction begins and continues until the end of instruction. Second, the evaluation process is not haphazard but instead, is directed toward a specific goal. It is directed at finding answers about how to improve instruction. Third, evaluation requires using accurate and appropriate measuring instruments to collect information needed for decision making. The evaluation process involves collecting information to enable you to decide how your instruction is progressing, how it turned out in the end, and how to do better next time.

In this chapter, you will learn how to plan an evaluation program to obtain information about your instruction and student learning. You will learn how to select or design tests and other measuring instruments to collect this information as well as how to analyze and interpret the information.

PLANNING FOR EVALUATION

In designing a learning system, one of the earliest steps is the preparation of a comprehensive evaluation plan, which should be developed soon after objectives have been formulated.

There are three advantages in early planning. First, the evaluation plans helps you to determine whether or not you have stated your objectives in behavioral terms. If the conditions, behavior, or standards or your objectives have been stated ambiguously, you will have difficulty designing a test to measure student achievement. Therefore, writing a test helps to check your objectives and enables you to revise them before you begin to design your instruction.

The second advantage of developing an evaluation plan early in the design process is that you will be prepared to collect the information you need when it is available. Often, evaluation information can only be obtained at particular times and, unless a test is designed and scheduled in advance, the opportunity to collect this information is lost. For example, when your students are told the objectives of the learning system, you should plan to test whether they understand them. At the end of instruction, if some students do not achieve the objectives, it is convenient to know whether their lack of understanding of the objectives may have been a contributing factor.

The third advantage of early development of an evaluation plan is that it provides sufficient time for test design. To design a good test requires careful preparation, and the quality of a test usually improves if it can be designed in a leisurely fashion.

FRAME 4.1

You are designing a learning system and have just written a first draft of your objectives. What do you do next?

1. Show the objectives to your students.   _____

2. Design instructional procedures.   _____

3. Design an achievement test for each objective. _____

4. Evaluate your objectives.   _____

In the remainder of this section, we shall discuss the kinds of questions that should be included in a comprehensive learning system evaluation plan. The properties of a good test will be described in the next section. The rest of the chapter will be a detailed discussion of the procedures for designing a test and how to interpret the results for decision making.

EVALUATION QUESTIONS

A learning system is designed to take students from one level of knowledge or skill to another. The purpose of evaluation is to assess the decisions made in the design process. One approach to the development of an evaluation plan is to identify critical evaluation questions. Let us examine a model of a generalized learning system to see how evaluation questions are derived.

The following diagram illustrates a model learning system that might result from following the design procedures outlined in Chapter 1.

LEARNING SYSTEM

Initial Conditions ⟶ Instructional Procedures ⟶ Terminal Objectives

---

Figure 4.1 A simplified representation of a learning system based on the design procedures discussed in Chapter 1.

FEEDBACK:

4.1   3

Initial conditions refer to the achievement level of students when they enter the learning system and the objectives refer to their terminal level of achievement. Instructional procedures refer to the means used to bridge the gap between the initial and terminal levels.

EVALUATION QUESTIONS DERIVED FROM INITIAL CONDITIONS Because of the limited amount of instructional time available to achieve objectives, a teacher must make certain decisions about the ability level of the students when they enter the system. It would be a waste of time to cover material students already know. On the other hand, if we assume students know more than they actually do, they will have great difficulty learning. Students must have attained a particular level of entry skills and knowledge so that they will be prepared for instruction. If the students do not have the necessary entry skills, the instructional procedures you have designed cannot be effectively implemented.

The first set of evaluation questions is derived from assumptions and decisions made about the entry skills of students. Some examples are:

- What proportion of students have the prerequisite entry skills?
- Which students do not have the entry skills?
- Which particular entry skills does a student lack?
- What modifications in instructional plans are required?

Procedures for evaluating student entry skills and for answering these questions will be described in the section of this chapter on evaluating entry skills.

EVALUATION QUESTIONS DERIVED FROM INSTRUCTIONAL PROCEDURES As we have already noted, decisions about instructional procedures are made as a result of: (1) analyzing the tasks and objectives to be learned; and (2) applying psychological principles of learning to the derived concepts, principles, and skills. Such instructional decisions include choosing and sequencing the conditions to facilitate learning, keeping track of student achievement, and providing feedback to students about their progress.

These design decisions give rise to the following kinds of evaluation questions:

- Have students achieved enabling objectives? Do they know the things they will need to know to achieve the terminal objectives?
- What problems are students having learning the material?
- How am I "coming across" to the students?

Procedures for evaluating instructional procedures to answer these questions are discussed in the section of this chapter on Continuous Evaluation.

EVALUATION QUESTIONS DERIVED FROM TERMINAL OBJECTIVES Terminal objectives describe the instructional outcomes of a learning system, and student achievement of these objectives represents one of the most important criteria for evaluating system design. However, a learning system is evaluated by other criteria as well. In designing the system, decisions are also made about how available resources can be used most efficiently. In some cases, the outcomes from two different learning systems, such as televised vs. regular classroom instruction, may be evaluated and compared.

These decisions produce the following kinds of evaluation questions:

- How many terminal objectives did each student achieve?
- What proportion of the students achieved each terminal objective?
- Which instructional procedures should be revised?
- Were student and instructor time used most efficiently?
- How does this system compare to some other system designed to achieve the same or similar objectives?

Procedures for evaluating these questions will be covered in the section of this chapter on Evaluating Instructional Outcomes.

UNITS AND SUBUNITS OF LEARNING SYSTEMS

The learning system diagrammed in Fig. 4.1 applies to an instructional unit of any size. The instructional procedures part of the learning system may be composed of several interrelated subunits, or subsystems (Fig. 4.2).

Initial Conditions for the Learning System	LEARNING SYSTEM INSTRUCTIONAL PROCEDURES			Terminal Objective for the Learning System
	First Unit	Second Unit	Last Unit	
	INITIAL OBJECTIVE	INITIAL OBJECTIVE	INITIAL OBJECTIVE	
	Instructional Procedures	Instructional Procedures	• • • • Instructional Procedures	

Figure 4.2 A learning system showing the breakdown of instructional procedures into subunits of instruction.

The evaluation questions we have listed above apply to each of the subunits of a learning system as well as to the system as a whole. For each unit, questions may be asked about student entry skills, instructional procedures, and instructional outcomes. Consequently, a comprehensive evaluation plan should include procedures for collecting pertinent information about each unit as it occurs.

Plans for evaluating student progress and identifying instructional problems should be based on the relationships that exist among the subunits of a learning system. For instance, if completing each unit is prerequisite to entering the next, then the terminal objectives for one unit constitute the entry skills of the following unit. In addition, the objectives for the subunits become the enabling objectives for the entire learning system. Thus, a comprehensive evaluation plan should be developed to provide information at every stage of the learning system about the effect of design decisions on student learning.

	T	F	
1. Instructional procedures are evaluated by testing student achievement of terminal objectives.	___	___	**F R A M E**
2. Instructional procedures are evaluated by testing student achievement of enabling objectives.	___	___	**4.2**
3. A learning system may be analyzed into component subsystems.	___	___	

In the remaining sections of this chapter you will learn how to collect and interpret evaluation information at each stage of a learning system; however, since the usefulness of evaluation information depends almost entirely upon the quality of the test by which the information is obtained, we shall begin, in the next section, by learning about the properties of a good test.

PROPERTIES OF A GOOD TESTING INSTRUMENT

Most instructors design their own tests of student achievement. Frequently, however, the tests they design are not accurate measuring instruments. As a result, the information provided by such tests is almost worthless. In this section of the chapter you will learn to recognize the properties a test should have in order to provide reliable and valid information about student achievement.

VALIDITY

The usual definition of test validity is that it measures what it is supposed to measure. Since tests used in learning systems are designed to measure student achievement of learning objectives, there is a close relationship

FEEDBACK:
4.2   1   T
      2   T
      3   T

between test validity and the learning objectives. This relationship provides a more useful definition of test validity.

DEFINITION:
A TEST IS VALID WHEN IT REQUIRES THE
LEARNER TO PERFORM THE SAME BEHAVIOR
UNDER THE SAME CONDITIONS SPECIFIED IN
A LEARNING OBJECTIVE.

A learning objective states the behavior the learner is expected to demonstrate as a result of instruction and the conditions under which he will perform that behavior. In effect, an objective describes the achievement test. Therefore, in order to obtain a valid measure of achievement, the test must be designed so that it presents the conditions and requires the behavior specified in the objective.

Here are several examples of valid and invalid tests.

1. Objective: Using standard laboratory equipment, the student will **design** and **conduct** an experiment to demonstrate the differential effect on learning rate of continuous and intermittent reinforcement. He will **interpret** the results by applying principles of operant conditioning.
Valid Test: Provide the student with laboratory space, equipment, and experimental subjects. Student must conduct an experiment, record and analyze data, and write a report.

Invalid Test: Give the student the results of an experiment and require him to interpret the results.

The objective calls for problem-solving behavior. It indicates that the student should be able to design and carry out an experiment in the laboratory and explain the outcome according to previously learned principles. The first test meets the objective. The second test is invalid because the problem is presented under different conditions from those specified in the objective. It requires only interpretation, not designing and conducting an experiment.

2. Objective: Given several pictorial examples of Renaissance art, the student will correctly **identify** the techniques employed using the criteria given in class.
Valid Test: In each of the five photographs of Renaissance paintings, state the technique employed.

Invalid Test: Name five Renaissance painters and the

techniques each of them used.

Invalid Test: Compare the techniques of Renaissance and modern painters.

The first test is the only valid one of the three since it requires that the student identify some Renaissance painting techniques.

3. Objective: Given a stripped-down carburetor, the student will **assemble** it.

Valid Test: Assemble stripped-down carburetor.

Invalid Test: Name the parts of a carburetor.

Invalid Test: Assemble and install a carburetor.

Invalid Test: Assemble a carburetor in ten minutes.

The first test is valid since it requires no more than the objective states. The second test is invalid because the ability to name the parts of a carburetor is not a test of ability to assemble it. The third test is invalid because it requires the student to do more than is stated in the objective. The fourth test is invalid because it imposes a time limit, a condition not specified in the objective. If it is important to be able to assemble a carburetor within a limited period of time, the time condition should be included in the objective.

4. Objective: The student will **understand** the concept of test validity.

Valid Test: Define test validity.

Valid test: Given an objective, write a valid test.

Valid test: Given an objective and a set of test items, choose the one(s) that are valid.

All of the tests are valid because the objective is so vague, ambiguous, and unsatisfactory that any one of the test items could be said to correspond. Unless objectives are written in behavioral terms, it is often impossible to measure student achievement.

The validity of tests can be increased by writing a sample test directly after writing an objective. This procedure has two advantages. First, it enables the instructor to compare the behavior and conditions of the learning objective with those of the test to make sure that they correspond. Second, since it is difficult to write a definitive test item for an ambiguous objective, the procedure helps the instructor to recognize an objective that is not written in behavioral terms.

The objection is often raised that if an instructor specifies learning objectives behaviorally and then designs his tests to measure student achievement of these objectives, he is "teaching for the test"; however, an alternative point of view suggests that an objective provides information which enables the student and the instructor to cooperate to facilitate learning. If an instructor expects his students to accept responsibility for their own learning, he must provide them with clear guides.

On the other hand, objectives are sometimes written in ways that neither facilitate the learning process nor contribute to valid testing. This often happens when an instructor writes objectives which are not broad enough for large classes of behavior. Consider the following objectives:

Objective 1: Be able to solve all quadratic equations of the form:
$$Ax^2 + Bx + C = 0$$

Objective 2: Be able to solve: $3x^2 + 4x - 20 = 0$

If an instructor designs a test to measure achievement of Objective 2, he might indeed be accused of teaching for the test. Objective 1 is not so constrained; it describes a general class of behavior. The key phrase in Objective 1 is "to solve all quadratic equations of the form. . ." The specific equation to be solved is not identified—only its general form; thus, the objective describes a class of behavior, not a particular one. A valid test of Objective 1 would measure the achievement of an important mathematical ability so that if students were given the objective in advance, the teacher could not be accused of teaching for the test.

THREE PRINCIPLES OF VALID TEST DESIGN

- *Design tests to require behavior specified in objectives.*
- *Design tests so that they include the same conditions specified in the objectives, and only those conditions.*
- *Design objectives requiring large classes of behavior.*

These three principles apply to all kinds of achievement tests.

FRAME 4.3

1. Which test is a more valid measure of the objective?

    Objective: The student will be given a list of topics dealing with campus affairs. For each topic he will *identify* the best expository form to use in writing an essay about the topic.

    a. Test 1: Write an essay on the topic, "Coeducational Dormitories," using the principles of exposition discussed in class. _____

    b. Test 2: Match the items in the following list of "Topics" with the correct item in the list of "Expository Forms." _____

2. Which of the following test conditions will provide a more valid measure of the objective?

Objective: The student will be able to apply psychological principles of personal interactions.

    a. Test 1: An encounter group. _____

    b. Test 2: An essay exam. _____

RELIABILITY

A reliable measuring instrument gives consistent values. To illustrate, if you were to measure the length of a table top several times using a wooden yardstick, you would obtain approximately the same result every time; however, if you were to use a rubber ruler or a piece of string, the results from one measurement to the next would differ widely. The wooden yardstick is a more reliable instrument for measuring length than one made of either rubber or string.

> **DEFINITION:**
> **A RELIABLE TEST PROVIDES A CONSISTENT MEASURE OF A LEARNER'S ABILITY TO DEMONSTRATE ACHIEVEMENT OF AN OBJECTIVE.**

Tests designed to assess student achievement must also be reliable measuring instruments. Unlike the table in the above example, the student is changing from one moment to the next. He is not apt to respond in precisely the same way if he takes the test a second time. Therefore, the teacher must test student achievement more than once in order to assess the consistency of his performance.

REPEATED TESTING A student demonstrates achievement of an objective by performing the behavior according to the standards specified. If the instructor provides several opportunities for the student to do this and the student performs at the minimum standard most of the time, then he can be reasonably confident that the student could perform at that level from that time on; thus, the test would provide a consistent measure of the student's ability to perform the objective.

You may recall that a well-formulated objective includes both a performance standard and a stability standard. The performance standard states the minimum level of performance required; the stability standard states what proportion of times he must demonstrate that minimum level. Consider the following objective:

> The student will run the 100-yard
> dash in 12 seconds, nine out of ten
> times.

In this objective the performance standard is 12 seconds, the stability standard is 90 percent. The test of achievement should include ten opportunities to run the 100-yard dash and the student should be able to run the dash in 12 seconds on nine of them. If he does, you can be reasonably sure that he has achieved the objective and that a consistent measure of his performance has been obtained.

How do you arrive at a stability criterion? There is a statistical procedure called **sequential sampling**, which provides a probability estimate of how many times a person must perform correctly for you to be convinced his performance is stable. However, you can rely on your experience to get a rough estimate of an adequate stability criterion. Ask yourself what the probability is of an untrained person achieving the objective by chance; then choose a higher probability. For example, if you believe that given ten trials, an untrained person would achieve the objective on five of them, the probability of success is five out of ten, or 50 percent. Therefore, if you choose a stability criterion of 80 percent, or eight out of ten, you can be reasonably sure of stable test performance.

REDUCE EXTRANEOUS FACTORS There are many other factors that affect a student's test performance other than his ability to perform the objective. Some of these, like fatigue, tension, or his love life, are beyond your control; however, the effect of other factors which are under your control should be reduced if you are to obtain a stable measure of performance. Some of these factors are:

- Unclear instructions
- Ambiguous test items
- Test conditions that are different from those stated in your objective
- Use of jargon words, the meaning of which has not been taught
- A new kind of test that the student has never experienced.
- Extreme levels of temperature and humidity in the testing room
- Raising student anxiety needlessly, e.g., "I don't expect many of you to pass this test!"

If such factors are allowed to operate, the test will not provide a reliable measure of student achievement.

Which of the following would increase the reliability of a test?

1. Increase the number of questions. _____

2. Try out your questions beforehand to see if they are clear. _____

3. Limit the time for taking the test. _____

4. Inform the students of the point value of each test item. _____

5. Make sure that information about the kind of test to be given
   does not leak out. _____

OBJECTIVITY

Have any of your students ever disputed the grade they received on a test?
Have you ever changed a grade because a student was able to convince you
that his answer was correct after you had previously marked it wrong? Such
situations occur when the criterion of successful performance on a test is a
matter of opinion, indicating that the test lacks objectivity.

> **DEFINITION:**
> **A TEST HAS OBJECTIVITY IF TWO OR MORE
> COMPETENT OBSERVERS CAN INDEPENDENTLY
> AGREE WHETHER OR NOT A LEARNER'S TEST
> PERFORMANCE MEETS THE CRITERIA STATED
> IN A LEARNING OBJECTIVE.**

The objectivity of a test is increased to the extent that the scorer is not
required to use subjective judgment to determine whether a student's performance corresponds to a learning objective. A teacher can increase the
objectivity of his tests by writing objectives in behavioral terms and by including a standard for judging the adequacy of student performance. Then,
by designing a test which requires a demonstration of that performance, he
will preclude subjective opinion regarding student achievement of the objective. Examine the following objectives:

1. The student will adjust the meter correctly.

2. The student will adjust the meter so that the needle registers
   at the null point plus or minus two degrees.

Little subjective judgment is required to determine whether or not the

FEEDBACK:
4.4 1, 2, 4

student has achieved Objective 2. However, in Objective 1, what constitutes "correct" adjustment is a matter of subjective judgment.

Short-answer tests, composed of true-false or multiple-choice questions, do not necessarily have objectivity. In fact, because of the necessity to create foil answers which are not obviously incorrect, it may sometimes be more difficult to write short-answer test items that do not require subjective judgment for scoring. The objectivity of a short-answer test may be estimated by having a colleague competent in the area take the test without referring to the scoring key. If the test has objectivity, the test designer and his colleague will agree on all the answers.

FRAME 4.5

The following test was designed for nurses training for a cardiac intensive care unit. Select the criterion (standard of judgment) that permits the most objective scoring of student performance; that is, select the criterion that requires the least subjective opinion.

1. Test: A patient has been admitted within the past 24 hours. When you first see him, he is showing anxiety symptoms. You will relieve the patient's anxiety:

   Criteria: a.   By following approved procedures.   _____

               b.   By applying the principles in the manual.   _____

               c.   So that the patient's blood pressure, pulse, and respiration are lowered.   _____

               d.   No criterion is needed.   _____

DIFFERENTIALITY

If you gave your final exam at the beginning of the course and discovered that the students answered all the items correctly, would you conclude that they had achieved the objectives? Your conclusion would not be warranted if the questions were asked in such a way that any naive person could answer them correctly. Such a test does not differentiate between the naive person and one who has achieved the objective.

We have all seen tests that are so simple that anyone could pass them. Some test questions give themselves away while others can be answered by information obtained from another question in the test. Multiple-choice questions are sometimes composed so that all options but the correct one are either obviously wrong or ridiculously out of context. Tests like these have low **differentiality**.

FEEDBACK:
4.5   c

DEFINITION:
A TEST HAS HIGH DIFFERENTIALITY IF IT IN-
CLUDES TASKS THAT ONLY LEARNERS WHO
HAVE ACHIEVED THE OBJECTIVE(S) CAN PER-
FORM.

One way of determining whether or not your test differentiates among students who have achieved the objectives from those who have not is to give the test at the beginning of the course. Assuming that the test is valid, reliable, and objective, you should look at those items which most students can answer before the course begins and either eliminate them or rewrite them.

Another method of determining the differentiality of a test is to give the test to advanced students who have already taken the course and done well. If the test items meet the requirements of validity, reliability, and objectivity, and the advanced students cannot answer them, these items should also be either rewritten or eliminated.

An instructor designed three tests. In order to test their differentiality, he gave them to a group of advanced students and also to his students on the first day of the course. He obtained the following results:

	Advanced students who passed (%)	Students who passed on first day of course (%)
Test 1	90	60
Test 2	30	10
Test 3	90	20

Which test had greatest differentiality?

F
R
A
M
E

4.6

In summary, a good test has properties that enable you to obtain accurate information about student achievement of objectives. If a test is valid, reliable, objective, and differentiating, you will be able to use the information it provides to evaluate your learning system.

EVALUATING ENTRY SKILLS

In the first section of this chapter, we pointed out that in order to evaluate a learning system properly, information about student performance should

---

FEEDBACK:
4.6   Test 3

be collected both at the beginning and at the end of each unit of learning. By gathering information at the beginning of a unit, the teacher obtains information about the student's prior learning. By measuring learning at the end of the unit, the teacher can see what students have learned from the instruction. The effectiveness of the learning system is determined by comparing these two types of information.

There are two reasons for measuring student entry skills. First, doing this helps to verify (or refute) design assumptions. A learning system is designed to advance students from one level of achievement to another. When instructional units are designed, the teacher always assumes that students possess some entry skills. If the student does not possess these assumed skills, the teacher may have to redesign his units taking this fact into account.

The second reason for measuring student entry skills is to provide a baseline for determining the adequacy of instruction. If, at the end of instruction, a teacher finds that many of his students have not achieved the terminal objectives, some indication of entry skills will help him decide whether this result was due to poor instruction or inadequate student preparation (entry skills).

DEFINITION:
PREREQUISITE ENTRY SKILLS ARE THE OB-
JECTIVES A STUDENT SHOULD HAVE ACHIEV-
ED BEFORE BEGINNING A UNIT OF INSTRUC-
TION.

If the learning objectives are sequenced, they can help the designer identify entry skills. The following illustration shows how objectives can be sequenced within an instructional unit to identify entry skills. The example is from a course in physiology and describes a laboratory unit which occurred near the end of the course. The lab unit was planned to take 60 minutes. In that time, students were to meet the terminal objectives and all enabling objectives.

Physiology 101

Terminal Objective:
The student will be able to measure human blood pressure with an accuracy of plus or minus 10 percent using a stethoscope and a sphygmomanometer.

Enabling Objectives:
The student will demonstrate that he can:

- Describe step-by-step procedure for measuring human blood pressure using stethoscope and sphygmomanometer

- Attach sphygmomanometer
- Describe how sphymomanometer operates in measuring human blood pressure
- Identify parts of sphygmomanometer
- Distinguish first and second heart sounds using stethoscope
- Describe how stethoscope is used in measuring human blood pressure
- Measure pulse rate using stethoscope
- Identify parts of stethoscope

Entry Skills:
The student will define:

- Blood pressure
- Systolic and diastolic blood pressure
- Ventricular systole and diastole

In planning the course, it was determined by pretesting that students were able to complete the lab unit and achieve the terminal objective within 60 minutes, providing they had the entry skills. If the duration of the lab session were decreased from 60 minutes, some of the enabling objectives might have to be included in the entry skills and taught to the students in a previous laboratory or lecture session. For instance, it might be necessary to teach students to distinguish first and second heart sounds, measure pulse rates, and identify the parts of a stethoscope in prior laboratory sessions.

	T	F
1. Grades earned by students in previous prerequisite courses provide an adequate measure of entry skills.	———	———
2. Enabling objectives may be considered as entry skills for an instructional unit.	———	———
3. If the amount of time planned for an instructional unit is decreased, the level of entry skills may have to be lowered.	———	———

FRAME 4.7

TESTING ENTRY SKILLS

Grades earned by students in previous courses generally do not provide a good measure of student entry skills. Therefore, it is usually necessary for each instructor to prepare his own tests of entry skills. If there are prerequisite courses for which terminal objectives have been specified, the final

FEEDBACK:
4.7   1   F (Grades do not necessarily reflect skills.)
      2   T
      3   F (Ther may have to be increased.)

examination from those courses may provide the basis for an entry skills test. If a course consists of a series of subunits, a test of terminal objectives for a given subunit can serve as the entry skills test for the next unit.

FRAME 4.8

You are preparing a course for education majors on how to diagnose reading problems. Which of the following will provide an accurate measure of the entry skills of students who have registered for the course?

1. Has received a grade "B" or better in a course on the Psychology of Reading   _____

2. Has had experience in the training of remedial reading   _____

3. Is familiar with the experimental literature on reading problems   _____

4. Can describe five procedures for measuring reading rate and comprehension   _____

HOW TO USE ENTRY SKILLS INFORMATION

There are three ways entry skills information is employed in learning system design:

1. For modifying design plans
2. For assessing the need for remedial instruction
3. For providing feedback to students

MODIFYING DESIGN PLANS Inflexibility is one distinguishing characteristic of the inexperienced teacher. After preparing a lesson, the novice often goes ahead despite indications that the plans he has prepared are not working. He may not even be aware of the fact that a problem exists. On the other hand, the skillful teacher tries alternative approaches when his original plans founder. A teacher who discovers that his students do not have the prerequisite entry skills and does not alter his instructional plans runs the risk that many students will fail to achieve the terminal objectives.

If an entry skills test shows that most students have not achieved the entry objectives for a unit of instruction, the following options are available:

- If there is evidence that entry skills have been learned previously and forgotten, a review can be conducted before regular instruction begins.
- If there is no evidence of previous learning, a special unit can be

---

FEEDBACK:
4.8   4

developed to train the prerequisite entry skills.

- If the instructor is operating on a tight time schedule and neither of the first two options is feasible, the number of terminal objectives can be reduced and the corresponding instructional units eliminated.

- If none of these options are feasible, only those students who have achieved the entry objectives should be permitted to enter the course.

Courses are now being designed in which students are not allowed to progress to a new learning unit until they demonstrate competency in the objectives of the previous unit. In these courses, the student may complete each unit at his own rate and may repeat a unit if he fails to achieve the terminal objectives the first time. The **competency** or **mastery instructional system**, as this system is called, has not as yet been employed widely. Where it has been used, the usual result is that students demonstrate superior achievement and greater personal satisfaction with the course than students enrolled in more "traditional" lecture-examination sections.

PROVIDING REMEDIAL INSTRUCTION Most teachers find that there is a wide range of entry skills among their students. Obviously, such variability among students presents the teacher with a serious problem. The best solution to this problem is to prepare remedial instructional units for each of the entry skill objectives and require students to study them independently.

FEEDBACK TO STUDENTS If students are to assume responsibility for their own learning, they must be provided with information about their learning progress. Terminal objectives help perform this function by describing expected learning outcomes. In the same manner, entry skill objectives describe the prerequisites needed to successfully learn the material in a unit. An entry skills test guides learning by providing a student with precise information about his readiness to begin a learning unit and by indicating where his deficiencies lie so that he may correct them.

An instructor should provide the student with entry and terminal performance information for every learning unit of the course. Such information will enable the student to evaluate his own learning progress and, if necessary, seek additional help before he falls too far behind.

EVALUATING TWO DIFFERENT LEARNING SYSTEMS

An entry skills test given before instruction begins, provides information about student achievement of entry objectives. This information enables an instructor to evaluate student preparation and make adjustments in his teaching plans. A test of student achievement of the terminal and enabling objectives in the course may also be given at the beginning of instruction as a baseline against which to evaluate the adequacy of instruction. Such a test provides useful additional information which enables an instructor to evaluate different learning systems.

Suppose you want to evaluate the effectiveness of large group lectures versus slide-tape independent study units. In comparing these learning systems, you would need to know the number of enabling and terminal objectives achieved by students at the end of instruction in each system. In addition, you would want to know if one system was more effective than the other for certain of the objectives.

In setting up an experiment to evaluate the two systems, you must obtain two equivalent groups of students. Unless the two groups are on an equal basis before instruction, you will not be able to compare the effectiveness of the two learning systems after instruction. Group equivalency may be obtained by giving a test that measures student achievement of the enabling and terminal objectives to be covered in the course. Students can then be paired according to their test scores and one member of each pair assigned to each system. By following this procedure the average level of achievement of the two groups will be equivalent. Scores on an entry skills test may be inadequate for obtaining equivalent groups, because an entry skills test measures only achievement of objectives that are prerequisite to instruction; thus, if an entry skills test is used to assign students to the two systems, the average entry skills scores may be equivalent, but the two groups may not be equivalent as regards the objectives to be covered in the course. A great deal of our research has demonstrated that the most critical factor in determining student achievement on an instructional unit is how much he knows about the material to be covered when he enters the unit. Consequently, it is absolutely essential to control for this factor when comparing two methods of instruction.

F R A M E 4.9

1. An instructor teaches a course in which majors and nonmajors are enrolled. At the beginning of the course he wants to identify students who require remedial instruction. What kind of test should he prepare?

   a. A test to measure student achievement of entry skills _____

   b. A test to measure achievement of enabling and terminal objectives _____

2. In the same course, the instructor wants to identify advanced students. What kind of test should he prepare?

   a. A test to measure student achievement of entry skills _____

   b. A test to measure achievement of enabling and terminal objectives _____

FEEDBACK:
4.9   1 a   2 b

CONTINUOUS EVALUATION

Continuous evaluation refers to procedures for collecting information about a learning system while it is in progress. In the preceding section of this chapter you learned how information obtained from an entry skills test given at the beginning of a course is used by an instructor to modify his instructional plans and by students to identify the material they do not know. Similar information collected while a course is in progress is used to provide feedback to students about their learning progress and to identify and correct instructional problems as they arise.

FEEDBACK FOR STUDENTS

Although we know that feedback is necessary for learning, we sometimes neglect to provide students with either sufficient or timely information about their learning progress. Students often report going through an entire course completely in the dark about what the instructor expects of them or whether they are progressing satisfactorily. To be most effective, feedback should inform a student of his progress toward objectives and should be made available during learning so that he can identify and correct his errors.

Tests should be planned to measure student achievement of all enabling objectives. Since such tests are for diagnostic purposes, formal exams are not necessary. Short quizzes provide sufficient information to identify the particular objectives with which a student is having difficulty, and results of these tests should be fed back to the student as soon as possible.

FEEDBACK MEDIA

Feedback information is more effective for guiding learning when it allows a student to identify his errors and compare his behavior with a standard. Therefore, feedback information should be presented in a medium appropriate to the skill being learned. Table 4.1 lists different kinds of media for providing feedback information.

TABLE 4.1   SOME MEDIA FOR PROVIDING CONTINUOUS FEEDBACK AS STUDENTS LEARN PARTICULAR SKILLS

Skills	Feedback Media
1. Knowledge of facts, concepts, principles.	1. Programed text, erasable cards, answers on back.
2. Complex motor skills.	2. Video recording, demonstration by expert.
3. Complex interpersonal behavior or complex problem solving.	3. Audio or video recording, debriefing, demonstration by expert.

When knowledge of facts, concepts, or principles is tested by means of a paper-and-pencil quiz, immediate feedback can be provided by specially prepared and commercially available answer sheets which indicate whether the student has chosen the correct alternative. Instead of checking an alternative, or filling in lines as with a machine-scored test, the student erases a printed dot. If his answer is correct, the erasure will disclose the letter "R" (right). Erasing any other alternative produces the letter "W" (wrong). This procedure provides immediate feedback for the students and enables the teacher to determine how many errors were made.

For complex motor skills, effective feedback can be provided by video tape recording. In a swimming course in which students learned several different swimming strokes, the instructor provided feedback information on two TV monitors. On the first monitor was a recording of an expert swimmer performing the stroke to be learned. The second monitor was used to play back a recording of the student himself performing the stroke. By comparing the two monitors, the student could see the errors he was making and where he needed further practice.

Another example of the use of video tape recording to provide feedback is in training school counselors. One of the skills that a counselor has to learn is to interpret the words and actions of a client. A skilled counselor uses subtle cues such as posture, hand movements, head position, in addition to verbal statements, to interpret a client's problems. The ability to notice and interpret subtle movements is a high-level skill. One method of testing a student's progress in achieving this skill is to record several practice counseling sessions on video tape and play back the tape with the student and instructor viewing it together. This method enables the instructor to point out cues that the student missed.

A third example illustrates the use of recorded material to provide feedback in complex problem solving. Graduate assistants participated as trainees in a program to improve their teaching. The graduate assistants taught a class of students while being video taped. Subsequently, all of the trainees met together with the instructor to review the video tapes. Instructional problems were identified and solutions suggested. Each trainee then practiced the suggested solution in his class and the subsequent TV tape provided precise feedback information to the trainee on how well he had done and the errors he had still to correct.

FRAME

4.10

You are teaching a course in meteorology in which one of the objectives is *to be able to recognize and name cloud formations.* Which of the following tests provides the best feedback information to guide student learning?

1. Short-answer questions about cloud characteristics   _____

2. Discussion about atmospheric conditions that produce
   various clouds   _____

3. Students name clouds seen in motion pictures.   _____

FEEDBACK FOR INSTRUCTORS

During the last 15 minutes of each class, a teacher asked his students
several questions about the material that had just been covered; however,
none of the students ever volunteered answers. Since the class was composed of honor students, he knew they were not lazy or disinterested in
the subject matter. The teacher set out to analyze his technique of formulating questions. A specialist in learning system design suggested that he
mention the problem to his students and ask them about it. He accepted
the suggestion and soon discovered that his students didn't attempt to
answer his questions because he always answered them himself. Whenever
he asked a question, he would immediately launch into an explanation of
the answer.

   This story illustrates that teachers also need feedback about their classroom behavior. As a teacher, you may find yourself wondering whether
you have gotten your point across to the students, or in doubt as to
whether they understand examples you give them. Are your students convinced that you really want them to express new and different ideas? Although we may attempt to achieve certain results or project a particular
image, we seldom have a clear picture of how we "come across" in class.
Students are the best source of feedback about the effects of our classroom behavior as teachers.

   A periodic postclass questionnaire (PCQ) is an excellent vehicle for obtaining student feedback. A PCQ consists of a few questions which the
students answer anonymously. The questions may be quite general or
they may be chosen to obtain specific information.

   The following is an example of five general questions that might be included in a postclass questionnaire. Each question is followed by some
actual examples of student answers.

   1. What did you like best about this class?

      Examples: Clearly stated objectives.
                  Informality of the class.
                  Opportunity to ask "stupid" questions.
                  The examples given.
                  The lectures are getting more relevant, or at

least I understand them better.
A chance to see alternative ways of solving
the problem.

2. What did you like least?

Examples: Please go slower on explantions.
Information was not clearly explained in proper
order.
Too much technical material at once.
Some people monopolize the discussion.
The room was too warm.
Too much jargon without explanation.

3. What did you accomplish?

Examples: I made up my "head" about my project.
The tension of waiting for a turn to report; of
finding out what you did wrong and have
to redo.
Verified that I was on the right track with my
project.
To be more specific in my approach.

4. What changes in class procedure would you suggest?

Examples: Confusion in class discussion could be cleared
up by explaining rules.
Give more examples.
Arrange time for students who are bogged down
with problems to come into your office for
help.
Work in smaller groups with the instructor.
More time to work independently.

5. What specific questions do you want answered?

Examples: What is a _____ _____ ?
Do we have to revise old material as we get new
ideas or make new decisions?
Is it possible to have class on a different night?
How do you account for the probabilities?

A postclass questionnaire may be given at preplanned times during the
course, or when the teacher has a feeling that something is going wrong.
Notice that general questions permit students to identify problems which
the teacher may not have suspected. In addition, the answers enable the
teacher to pinpoint differences in the reactions of individual students.

Students may also obtain feedback from a postclass questionnaire. To provide such feedback, the answers should be collated and handed back to the students. In addition, all practical suggestions should be implemented and explanations given regarding suggestions that are impractical. In this way, students receive satisfaction in knowing that the instructor is interested in and responsive to their needs, and they are therefore encouraged to present viable suggestions.

PROTOTYPE TESTING

Continuous evaluation procedures are also used to test a new learning system while it is being designed. By testing a prototype of the new system at an early stage of development, the designer may identify and correct deficiencies as they arise. The prototype should be evaluated using a representative group of students. Both achievement tests and measures of student attitudes should be incorporated into the evaluation plan.

The following is an account of how a prototype of "Sesame Street," the educational TV children's program, was tested. Before "Sesame Street" went on the air, prototype test studies were conducted throughout a six-month period. Information obtained from these tests guided the development of new production techniques, format procedures, and teaching strategies.

The prototype studies had two foci: the effectiveness of the educational content, and the holding power of the entertainment techniques. The educational impact was measured in field studies. These studies were conducted to determine the effects of several variables: repetition and spacing schedules providing the child with preliminary or follow-up explanations, presentation of different approaches separately or in combination, to a given objective and the relative effectiveness of adult versus child voices in narration. Extensive observation of children viewing the show provided information regarding their understanding of the material presented.

Appeal of the material and dramatic format was measured against the appeal of other movie and television shows. A child was placed in a room in which "Sesame Street" was shown on one TV set and another popular show on another set. The amount of time the child spent watching "Sesame Street" in comparison to the time spent watching the other show indicated its relative appeal.

Upon conclusion of the prototype test, the results were used to modify the show and to guide the production of subsequent programs.

The "Sesame Street" example illustrates four steps in conducting a prototype test. These are:

1. Select a set of entry and terminal objectives and design a unit of instruction to achieve the terminal objectives. The unit should include

the instructional procedures that will be used in the final system. If alternative procedures are being considered, they should be included in separate units.

2. Design a test for entry skills and a test for achievement of terminal objectives.

3. Design a test to measure student attitudes toward the new system. The questions should be directed at the specific instructional components or procedures of the system and should be formulated so that problems and deficiencies may be identified.

   Example: If the new system were an independent study unit incorporating photographic slides, audio tape, and a student workbook, the following kinds of questions should be included in the attitude questionnaire:

   - Was the unit too long? Was there too much redundancy? Did the students become bored?

   - Did the equipment break down? Was manipulating the equipment distracting?

   - Were the workbook instructions easy to follow? Were the objectives clearly stated? Was enough information provided to perform the exercises? Did the exercises provide sufficient feedback?

   - Were there a sufficient number of examples? Were the examples clear? Did they seem relevant?

   - Was the material well organized? Did the concepts fit together? Did the student know where he was going at every point in the lesson?

4. Analyze the prototype test data and make indicated changes. An effective method for analyzing these data is to ask students for their views. After completing an attitude survey about the prototype system, arrange to have students meet informally with you. At the meeting, permit the students to discuss in detail all aspects of the instructional system and encourage them to elaborate on the questionnaire. Students often suggest alternative approaches which result in improved instruction.

Continuous evaluation procedures can also be used to collect information about ongoing learning systems as well as instructional systems in the process of development. The information obtained during continuous evaluation can provide useful corrective feedback to both the instructor and the students.

The following is a list of instructional problems that often arise. For each problem, choose the best method of obtaining evaluative information.

1. An instructor is concerned whether his personal idiosyncracies, such as pacing in front of the class while lecturing, annoy the students, or interfere with their learning.

    a.   Paper-and-pencil test
    b.   Video recording
    c.   Opinion questinnaire

2. Before teaching about practical use of levers, the instructor wants to know whether every student can recognize various classes of levers.

    a.   Paper-and-pencil test
    b.   Class discussion
    c.   Opinion questionnaire

3. An instructor is trying a new instructional procedure. He divides his students into pairs and shows them how to tutor each other. The instructor wants to know how well the procedure is working.

    a.   Achievement test
    b.   Opinion questionnaire
    c.   Discussion

NOTE: *If you have been reading continuously from the start of this chapter, it's time to take a break. Before beginning the following section, review the objectives and the outline of the chapter.*

EVALUATING INSTRUCTIONAL OUTCOMES

In evaluating instructional outcomes, we seek answers to three questions:

*   How many terminal objectives did each student achieve?
*   What proportion of the students achieved each terminal objective?
*   Which instructional procedure should be retained and which should be modified?

This section describes: (1) how to design a test to measure student achievement of terminal objectives; and (2) how to translate test scores into grades.

TESTING ACHIEVEMENT OF TERMINAL OBJECTIVES

A terminal test should be designed to measure student achievement, not

FEEDBACK:

4.11   1   c
     2   a
     3   a, b, c

only of terminal objectives of the course as a whole but of the terminal objectives of course subunits as well. If a learning system is composed of several subunits, each covering a different aspect of the subject matter, terminal objectives for each unit should be included in the terminal test.

SUBJECT MATTER COVERAGE   To insure that all aspects of the subject matter are included in the terminal test, a chart showing the terminal objectives for each unit should be prepared. This chart may then be used to assign a weight to each objective according to its relative importance. Table 4.2 illustrates this procedure.

The table shows the distribution of 100 questions in a final examination covering the objectives of ten course units. The units are listed down the left-hand column of the table and the behavioral categories of the objectives are listed across the top. The number of questions to be included in the test are shown in the cells of the table.

Notice that for the units at the beginning of the course (which include material prerequisite to later units) objectives requiring definition and recognition of concepts and principles tend to receive heavier emphasis. Objectives calling for application and analysis are stressed in units at the end of the course.

A table of this kind can also be of assistance in designing a stable test of student achievement. A stable test includes a sufficient number of items for each objective to enable the instructor to decide whether the student has actually achieved the objective or whether his performance is due to chance. The number of questions in each cell of the table indicates the instructor's estimates of how many examples of student performance he needs to be assured of behavior stability. In Unit 10 on Electricity and the Nature of Matter, the instructor has decided that he needs six questions in order to be reasonably sure that the student has learned how to recognize and solve problems in that unit.

Each objective should be weighted according to its relative importance. The importance of an objective is determined by its contribution to successful performance in the referent situation. Increased weight may be given to an objective by assigning more questions to it or by assigning a greater number of points to the correct answer.

The totals in the row at the bottom of the table show the number of questions assigned to each of the types of behavioral objectives. This number indicates the instructor's estimate of the relative importance of each type of objective. Notice that the application of principles and the analysis and solution of problems are stressed more heavily than definitions or recognition of concepts. The totals in the column on the right indicate the instructor's estimate of the relative importance of each unit. You can see that the units in the latter part of the course are stressed more heavily since they require students to apply the knowledge and skills they had previously acquired.

TABLE 4.2   CHART SPECIFYING THE NUMBER OF QUESTIONS FOR VARIOUS BEHAVIORAL OBJECTIVES (FOR A FINAL EXAMINATION IN NATURAL SCIENCE)*

Objective Course Content	Define or State Concepts and Principles	Recognize Correct or Incorrect Application of Concepts and Principles	Apply Principles to Solve a Given Problem	Analyze a Problem and Solve It	Total
1. The Number Concept	2	4			6
2. Concepts of Arithmetic	3	2	2		7
3. Quantitative Descriptions	2	2	3	3	10
4. The Gas Laws	3	2	2	3	10
5. Air	1	2	3	4	10
6. The Kinetic Theory of Matter	4		5	4	13
7. The Atom	1	2	4	4	11
8. Electricity and Combustion	1		6	3	10
9. Static Electricity and Magnets	2	2	3	4	11
10. Electricity and the Nature of Matter	1	1	4	6	12
Total	20	17	32	31	100

*Based on Bloom, B. B., *Taxonomy of Educational Objectives,* (New York: Longmans, Green and Company, 1954). For a discussion of scheme for classifying cognitive ability, see Chapter 3, Table 3.1.

FRAME 4.12 An instructor teaches a course composed of three subject matter units. He designs a short-answer final exam to measure student achievement of six objectives, two for each of the units. Since the third unit is most important, he intends the objectives for that unit to contribute twice as much weight to the total test score as each of the other two units. In a 40-question test, does the following table represent his intentions?

Unit	Objective	No. of Questions
A	1	5
	2	5
B	1	5
	2	5
C	1	10
	2	10
	Total	40

Yes___ No___

SCORING THE TEST   The score a student receives on a test should reflect the relative importance of the objectives. The more important objectives should obviously contribute greater weight to the total score than the less important ones. If the test consists of a large number of short-answer questions and has been prepared by the tabular method just described, what each objective contributes to the total score will be determined by the number of questions assigned to it.

However, when terminal behavior is so complex that achievement cannot be tested by short-answer questions, another method of scoring must be employed. In this method, the instructor makes a subjective estimate of the relative importance of each objective and assigns a weight to it according to this estimate. One method of weighting is to rate each objective on a three-point scale. The objective is then assigned a number from one to three, which represents the instructor's estimate of its relative importance. This method is illustrated in the following example.

Suppose that five objectives are to be tested. In Table 4.3, the five objectives are listed in the first column. The second column, Importance Factor, shows the weight assigned to each objective. Objectives 1, 2, and 5 are considered most important and receive a weight of three, objective

FEEDBACK:
4.12   Yes; each of the first two units contributes only 10.

3 is less important, and objective 4 is least important of all. The instructor would be less concerned if a student did not achieve objective 4, but he would be quite concerned if he did not achieve objectives 1, 2, or 5.

TABLE 4.3   PROCEDURE FOR WEIGHTING AND SCORING OBJECTIVES

Objective	Importance Factor	Students						
		S-1	S-2	S-3	S-4	S-5	S-6	S-7
O-1	3	3	3	3	3	3	3	3
O-2	3	3	3	0	0	0	0	3
O-3	2	2	0	2	2	0	2	2
O-4	1	1	1	1	1	1	1	1
O-5	3	3	3	0	3	0	3	3
Totals	12	12	10	6	9	4	9	12

After the test has been administered, the next step is to record the objectives that each student achieved. For each objective achieved, the value of the importance factor in the table is recorded. If the student did not achieve an objective, a zero is recorded in the table. Take for example, the first student (S-1). Since he achieved objective 1, the importance factor 3, for that objective, is recorded in the proper cell of the table. Student 2 achieved all except objective 3. The importance factors for all the objectives he achieved are listed in his column, and a zero is placed in the column opposite objective 3.

The total score for each student is obtained by adding the numbers in his column, and then listed in the bottom row of the table. The total score for each student reflects both the number and importance of the objectives he has achieved. If there are many students in the class, the table can be produced by computer.

For a final exam in nursing, the weights assigned to three objectives are:

	Objective	Weight
A	Prepare and administer intravenous injection.	1
B	Prepare a nursing care plan.	2
C	Recognize changes in patient's condition and modify care plan accordingly.	3

Student a achieved objectives A and B
Student b achieved objectives A and C

(continued on next page)

FRAME

4.13

Student c achieved objectives B and C
Student d achieved objectives A, B and C

What total score did each student receive on the final exam? Use the following table to calculate scores.

Objective	Weight	Student a	b	c	d
A	1				
B	2				
C	3				
Total	6				

ASSIGNING GRADES

There are many methods of translating test scores to grades. Four examples are given here. Each of these examples is based on student achievement of a set of objectives for a course.

NUMERICAL SCALING   In this method, the total test score is merely translated into a standard letter grade along a commonly used scale, i.e., A, B, C, or 3.0, 2.0, 1.0. The instructor must decide which grades are to be assigned to each test score.

PASS-NO PASS   In this method students who achieve all, or some fixed percentage of the objectives, e.g., 90 percent, receive A's. Students who do not achieve this percentage of objectives either receive an incomplete grade or fail.

NUMBER OF OBJECTIVES ACHIEVED   This method assumes that each objective has equal weight. The instructor decides how many objectives a student must achieve to get each of the letter grades. For example, supposing there were five terminal objectives. The instructor might decide that those students who achieve five objectives would receive an A, those achieve four objectives would receive a B, those achieving three objectives would get C, and those who achieve fewer than three objectives fail or receive an incomplete grade.

LEVEL OF OBJECTIVES   In this method, objectives are ranked by level of difficulty and grades are assigned according to the level achieved. Examples of

FEEDBACK:
4.13 Student a: 3   Student c: 5
      Student b: 4   Student d: 6

higher-level objectives are those that require problem-solving behavior or the application of principles. A student achieving higher-level objectives would be given a higher grade. Examples of lower-level objectives are those that require recall of facts or definition of concepts. The instructor decides which objective must be achieved in order to receive each letter grade.

In all of the above methods of scoring and grading, the criterion for judging a student's performance is whether or not he achieved the learning objectives of the course. Thus, the grade a student receives reflects his actual degree of achievement. Contrast these methods of grading with the usual method of grading on the curve, where a student's grade is determined solely by how he performed in relation to other students in the class. A grade derived by the latter method has at least four disadvantages: (1) it provides no information about student achievement of course objectives; (2) it provides no information for evaluating instruction. Thirty percent of the class may receive a grade of A or B although they learned only half the material being taught. Since the grades students receive do not accurately reflect the amount learned, the teacher is unable to identify instructional deficiencies; (3) it gives ambiguous information regarding how well students are prepared for subsequent courses or for success in referent situations; and (4) it is unfair to the students since a student may achieve most of the objectives and still receive a low grade.

Two major disadvantages of grading on the curve are that:

1. A student may achieve most of the objectives and still receive an average grade.   _____

2. It provides no comparison of achievement among students.   _____

3. It provides unreliable information for evaluating instruction.   _____

F R A M E

4.14

INTERPRETING EVALUATION INFORMATION

Once having collected information about student performance, it becomes necessary to interpret that information and decide what steps should be taken to improve the effectiveness and efficiency of the instructional procedures used in the course. This section describes how data about student performance is interpreted.

INSTRUCTIONAL EFFECTIVENESS

The best measure of instructional effectiveness is the number of students

---

FEEDBACK:
4.14   1, 3

achieving the course objectives. Earlier in this chapter, we developed a procedure for weighing and scoring objectives (Table 4.3). Using the data in that table, we will now illustrate a procedure for evaluating instructional effectiveness.

TABLE 4.4 PROCEDURE FOR EVALUATING INSTRUCTIONAL EFFECTIVENESS

Objectives	Importance Factor	Students							Number of Students Achieving	Percent of Students Achieving
		S-1	S-2	S-3	S-4	S-5	S-6	S-7		
O-1	3	3	3	3	3	3	3	3	7	100
O-2	3	3	3	0	0	0	0	3	3	42
O-3	3	2	0	2	2	0	2	2	5	70
O-4	1	1	1	1	1	1	1	1	7	100
O-5	3	3	3	3	3	3	3	3	7	100

The first step is to count the number of students who achieved each objective and record this number in the column labeled Number of Students Achieving. Since all seven students achieved objective 1, a 7 is placed in the first row of the column. Similarly, three students achieved objective 2, five students achieved objective 3, and so on.

The next step is to record, in the last column of the table, the percentage of the students who achieved each objective. Of the seven students in this example, all, or 100 percent of them achieved the first objective; three out of seven, or 42 percent, achieved the second, and so on.

It can be seen from the table that relatively few students achieved objectives 2 and 3. There might be additional concern about objective 2 since the importance factor of 3 indicates that achieving this objective is quite important in the referent situation. Instructional procedures for objectives 2 and 3 should be reviewed and possible reasons for the low percentage of students achieving them should be considered. For each of these objectives, the following possibilities might be considered.

ORGANIZATION OF SUBJECT MATTER Was the objective clear to the students? Were the students tested to determine whether they understood the objective? Were any enabling objectives omitted? Was subject matter sequenced so that prerequisite enabling objectives were achieved before later ones?

INSTRUCTIONAL PROCEDURES Review the methods of presenting material to the students. Was adequate direction and context provided? Were a sufficient number of examples provided? Did students have sufficient opportunity to practice? Did students receive feedback so that they could tell how they were progressing?

STUDENTS WERE NOT ADEQUATELY PREPARED   Some students may have lacked the necessary entry skills needed to achieve the objective. To check this possibility, the teacher should compare the entry test scores of students who acieve the objective with those students who do not achieve it. This comparison should readily indicate whether or not a lack of entry skill accounts for the failure of some students to achieve the objective.

An instructor was analyzing final exam scores. He found that half of his students failed to achieve the objectives of one of his instructional units. He looked up the entry skill test scores for that unit and found that all of the students who failed to achieve the objective also failed the entry skills test. What should he do next?

FRAME

4.15

1. Check the organization of the subject matter for the instructional unit.   _____

2. Check his instructional procedures for the unit.   _____

3. Check scores on the entry skills test of students who achieved the objectives.   _____

4. Nothing.   _____

STUDENT OPINIONS

Student opinions offer another useful way of judging instructional effectiveness. All teachers are interested in knowing how they come across to the students. When preparing instruction, teachers have certain expectations about the results they want to produce and the effect they have on students. There is no better way of obtaining information to evaluate these expectations than to ask the students themselves. As we saw in the discussion of continuous evaluation, student ratings are an important source of information about instruction.

Student opinions are usually obtained by a questionnaire. In preparing a questionnaire, the first step is to identify general topics or areas within which questions will be developed. Given these broad general areas, questions should be written keeping in mind the following points. First, ask questions about how the instruction affected student achievement rather than questions about student achievement itself. "Was this course an effective learning experience?" is not a good question since the answer can

---

FEEDBACK:

4.15   3

best be obtained by an achievement test. However, a question such as, "Was the lecture material organized so that you could take notes easily?" is an appropriate question.

Second, include only questions that the students would be able to answer from their own experience. A question such as, "Was the subject matter covered adequately?" is inappropriate because presumably, the students' limited experience with the subject matter would not enable them to answer the question. On the other hand, "Were you able to see the relationship among the various topics of the course?" is a question students would be qualified to answer.

Third, ask questions in such a way that the answers will enable you to take some action. As an instance, suppose you are interested in whether the method you used to ask questions in class affected student participation in class discussions. Then the items, "I understood the questions asked in class," and "I had the opportunity to participate in class discussions," are better than an item such as, "I liked to participate in class discussion." Negative answers to the first two items would lead you to reexamine the questions you asked in class and whether you provide enough time or encouragement for students to ask questions. A negative or positive response to the third item, however, does not suggest any remedial action you could take.

Some topics suitable for inclusion in a student opinion questionnaire are presented in Table 4.5. Illustrative questions are given after each topic.

In addition to the types of questions just discussed, students should be given the opportunity to express other opinions that might be important to them. This can be accomplished by including open-ended questions such as: The primary objection I had to this course was _____.

The questionnaire should be presented to students in a nonthreatening manner so that they feel free to express their real opinions about each topic. Before the questionnaire is distributed, students should be told why their opinions are being sought, that their answers will assist in identifying learning system problems and in improving instruction, and that their answers will not affect their grades. The questionnaire should be answered anonymously.

After the questionnaire has been completed, students should be invited to participate in an informal discussion of their answers. Participation should be on a voluntary basis. The discussion should permit exploration of all aspects of the learning system. If the students are convinced that the teacher is genuinely interested in improving his instruction and are encouraged to express their opinions openly, many valuable and practical suggestions will usually be received.

An instructor was preparing a student questionnaire. His first draft for the topic, "Interpersonal Relations in the Classroom," included the following items. Which should be eliminated?

1. The instructor often "puts students down." _____

2. Pairing students for mutual tutoring helped me learn. _____

3. The instructor helped me to understand the subject matter. _____

4. The instructor encouraged me to ask questions. _____

INSTRUCTIONAL EFFICIENCY

Suppose an instructor believes that some of his students failed to achieve an objective because they did not have enough practice. To spend more time lecturing might be an inefficient use of class time since not all students need the extra practice. A more efficient procedure might be to design an independent study unit for those students who need it. When considering alternative instructional methods, a teacher should choose those methods that make the most productive use of both the instructor and student time.

Efficiency refers to the resources expended to achieve a particular instructional outcome. In evaluating instructional efficiency, two of the most important resources to be considered are student time and instructor time. If an instructor is considering modifying his instructional procedures, he should take into account the objectives that will be achieved by using the new procedures as well as the amount of time required to implement them.

EVALUATING TWO DIFFERENT LEARNING SYSTEMS

We have thus far been concerned with procedures and criteria used in evaluating a single learning system. The same procedures and criteria are used in comparing two different learning systems. Let us state them.

In evaluating two learning systems:

1. The learning objectives should be the same for both. In this way, the same criteria will be used for comparing the effectiveness of the two systems.

2. The average entry skill level of the students in both systems should be equivalent. This can be achieved by giving the terminal test to all students before instruction begins. Students with equivalent scores should then be paired and different members of each pair as-

---

FEEDBACK:

4.16 3, because the answer indicates no *action* to be taken.

signed to each of the systems.

3. At the end of instruction the systems should be compared with regard to all of the following: student achievement, efficient utilization of student and instructor time, cost of designing and operating each system, and student attitudes.

TABLE 4.5   SOME TOPICS FOR INCLUSION IN A STUDENT OPINION QUESTIONNAIRE AND ILLUSTRATIVE QUESTIONS

A. Instructor Involvement
1. The instructor was enthusiastic when presenting course material.
2. The instructor seemed interested in teaching.
3. The instructor used examples or personal experiences which helped to get points across in class.
4. The instructor seemed to be concerned with whether the students learned the material.
5. The instructor was friendly and relaxed in front of the class.

B. Student Interest
1. I felt this course challenged me intellectually.
2. I was generally attentive in class.
3. I intend to take more courses in this subject.

C. Student-Instructor Interaction
1. The instructor encouraged students to express opinions.
2. I had ample opportunity to ask questions.
3. The instructor appeared receptive to new ideas.

D. Course Demands
1. The instructor attempted to cover too much material.
2. The instructor lectured above my level of comprehension.

E. Course Organization
1. I could see how the concepts in this course were interrelated.
2. The class lectures made for easy note-taking.
3. I knew where the course was heading most of the time.

F. Grading and Examinations
1. The grading system was adequately explained.
2. The answers to exam questions were adequately explained after the exam was given.
3. Course objectives were reflected in the exams.

G. Relevance of the Course
1. I could see how the course material could be applied to my personal problems.
2. I could see how the course material is pertinent to my major field of interest.
3. The instructor made me aware of current problems in the field.

Let us illustrate these procedures with a hypothetical example. In a course in art history, the usual method of preparing students for class was to assign textbook readings. However, most students did not come to class adequately prepared. Therefore, a slide-tape independent study unit was designed for each of the textbook assignments, and a study was conducted to compare the effectiveness of this method with the one previously used.

STUDENT ACHIEVEMENT

A test of achievement of terminal objectives was devised and given to the students at the beginning of the term. The students were then assigned to one or the other of the methods on the basis of their scores on the test so that the average score of each group was equivalent. At the end of the term, students in both groups were given an alternate form of the same terminal test.

The effectiveness of the two systems was determined by the percentage of students who achieved the terminal objectives in each system. The results are summarized in Table 4.6.

TABLE 4.6   PERCENTAGE OF STUDENTS ACHIEVING OBJECTIVES IN ART HISTORY COURSE (HYPOTHETICAL)

Objectives	Slide-Tape Units	Textbook Assignment
O-1	93	70
O-2	98	80
O-3	90	68
O-4	65	92
O-5	87	65

The table shows that for all objectives except objective 4, the slide-tape system was the more effective. The unit for objective four was subsequently modified.

EFFICIENCY

The efficiency of the two systems was compared in two ways: the cost of producing the slide-tape units compared to the cost of textbooks and the student time required. The original cost of producing the slide-tape system was much higher than the cost of the textbooks; however, since the slide-tape units were used for several years before revision was needed, the cost per term was more nearly comparable to the cost of textbooks. Moreover, the more effective learning produced by the slide-tape unit made its increased cost worthwhile.

Students were asked to keep track of the time they spent reading the textbook assignment, and this was compared to the time required to go through the slide-tape units. It was found that there was very little difference in the average time required.

STUDENT QUESTIONNAIRE

A questionnaire was prepared to determine which method the students preferred. The questions were phrased in such a way that they could be answered by students who learned by either method. For example, students were asked to agree or disagree with the statement, "The visual materials helped me to learn the material in this course." This could be asked of both groups and comparisions drawn. A statement such as, "I liked the slides" would be of no use since it applies only to the slide-tape group and would permit no comparisons. The results showed that the students were overwhelmingly in favor of the slide-tape units.

As a result of this evaluation, the slide-tape units were adopted as a permanent component of the learning system.

EVALUATION FOR RECYCLING

In this chapter, we have repeatedly stressed that the purpose of evaluation is to gather information that can be used to improve instruction. Merely gathering and interpreting information is insufficient. The information must be used to modify instructional procedures when a change is indicated.

Before modifying a learning system, the designer should recheck the relevancy of the objectives. This can be done by continually comparing the objectives to the referent situation in which the students will use what they have learned. The referent situation should be examined to see if either the performance requirements or the conditions have changed sufficiently to require a modification in learning objectives.

One method of determining whether or not objectives should be modified is to collect information about how well students who have taken the course succeed in the referent system. An analysis of the difficulties they encounter, the extent their success is related to their achievement in the course, and the kinds of knowledge and skills that are required to learn on the job, will provide some indication of the direction in which the objectives of the learning system should be changed.

SUMMARY

Evaluation is a continuous process of collecting and interpreting information in order to assess decisions made in designing a learning system. A comprehensive evaluation plan should provide information about three topics: (1) the achievement level of students entering the learning system;

(2) the achievement level of students leaving the system; and (3) the effectiveness and efficiency of instructional procedures employed in the learning system.

The usefulness of evaluation information depends upon the properties of the testing instrument used to obtain the information. A good testing instrument has the following properties:

1. Validity   It requires the learner to perform the same behavior under the same conditions specified in a learning objective.

2. Reliability   It provides a consistent measure of a learner's ability to demonstrate achievement of an objective. The reliability of a test may be augmented by increasing the number of opportunities a learner gets to demonstrate achievement, or by reducing extraneous factors that may influence his performance.

3. Objectivity   Two or more competent observers can independently agree whether or not a learner's test performance meets the criteria stated in a learning objective.

4. Differentiality   It includes tasks that only learners who have achieved the objective(s) can perform.

Entry skills are the objectives a student should have achieved before beginning a unit of instruction. There are two reasons for measuring student entry skills: (1) to aid an instructor in verifying (or refuting) his assumptions about whether students are adequately prepared; and (2) to provide a baseline for evaluating instruction. Entry skills information is employed in the following ways: (1) for determining which instructional materials and procedures require modification; (2) to assess the need for remedial instruction; (3) to provide feedback to students; and (4) for comparing the effectiveness of two different learning systems.

Continuous evaluation refers to procedures for collecting information about a learning system while it is in progress. Such information is useful to both learners and instructors. Learners use evaluation information to gauge their own learning progress. Consequently, the information should be made available while students are learning, in a medium that is appropriate to the knowledge or skill being learned.

Instructors use continuous evaluation information for two purposes: as feedback regarding their classroom behavior and as feedback regarding a new learning system in the process of development. A questionnaire which provides information about students' opinions, is an excellent source of feedback for both purposes.

Instructional outcomes are evaluated by assessing: (1) student achievement of objectives; and (2) instructional effectiveness.

Student achievement is measured by a test which includes terminal objectives for the whole course and for each of its subunits. The test should include a sufficient number of items to obtain a stable measure of student achievement of each objective. Each objective should be weighted in proportion to its contribution to successful performance in the referent situation.

Test scores may be translated into grades by any of four methods:
(1) numerical scaling; (2) pass-no pass; (3) number of objectives achieved; and (4) level of objectives achieved.

Instructional effectiveness is measured (1) by the proportion of students achieving each terminal objective for the course as a whole as well as for each subunit of the course; and (2) by the information gathered from student opinions about the course. Taking all of this into account, we can determine why a student may not be achieving an objective. Three possible reasons are: (1) inadequate organization of the subject matter; (2) ineffective instructional procedures; and (3) inadequate student preparation.

Two learning systems may be compared by making equivalent the average student entry skill level and assessing student achievement of the same objectives for both systems.

SUGGESTED READINGS

Block, James H. (ed.): *Mastery Learning*, (New York: Holt, Rinehart and Winston, 1971).

Bloom, Benjamin S., Hastings, J. T., and Madaus, G. F.: *Handbook on Formative and Summative Evaluation of Student Learning*, (New York: McGraw-Hill, 1971). (Especially Section 3: "Evaluation Techniques for Cognitive and Affective Objectives").

Davis, R. H. and Behan, R. A.: "Evaluating System Performance in Simulated Environments," in R. M. Gagné, (Ed.): *Psychological Principles in System Development,* (New York: Holt, Rinehart. and Winston, 1962).

Ebel, R. L.: *Measuring Educational Achievement*, (Englewood Cliffs, N.J.: Prentice Hall, 1965).

Gagné, R. M.: "Learning Hierarchies," *Educational Psychologist,* Vol. 6, No. 1 (1968), pp. 1-9.

Glaser, Robert: "Instructional Technology and the Measurement of Learning Outcomes: Some Questions," *American Psychologist,* Vol. 18 (1963), pp. 519-21.

Glaser, R. and Klaus. D.: "Proficiency Measurement: Assessing Human Performance," in R. M. Gagné: *Psychological Principles in System Development*, (New York: Holt, Rinehart and Winston, 1962), pp. 419-474.

Lumsdaine, A. A.: "Assessing the Effectiveness of Instructional Programs," in Robert

Glaser (ed.): *Teaching Machines and Programed Learning II,* (Washington, D.C.: National Education Association, 1965), pp. 267-320.

Merrill, M.D.: "Necessary Psychological Conditions for Defining Instructional Outcomes," in M. D. Merrill (ed.): *Instructional Design: Readings,* (Englewood Cliffs, N.J.: Prentice Hall, 1971), pp. 173-184.

Scriven, M.: "The Methodology of Evaluation," in R. Tyler (ed.): *AERA Monograph Series on Curriculum Evaluation*, No. 1, (Chicago: Rand McNally, 1967), pp. 39-83.

Tyler, Ralph W.: "Changing Concepts of Educational Evaluation," in R. Tyler (ed.): *AERA Monograph Series on Curriculum Evaluation*, No. 1, (Chicago: Rand McNally, 1967), pp. 13-18.

Wilhelms, Fred T.: *Evaluation as Feedback and Guide*, (Washington, D.C.: Association for Supervision and Curriculum Development, National Education Association, 1967).

Wood, Dorothy A.: *Test Construction*, (Columbus, Ohio: Charles E. Merrill Books, Inc., 1960).

EVALUATION DECISION AID

This decision aid was designed to help you evaluate a learning system. It is divided into three parts.

Part I is a chart to be used for developing an evaluation plan. It will help you to decide on the kind of evaluation information you should collect and how to collect it.

Part II consists of two checklists for designing evaluation instruments. The first is a checklist for designing tests of student achievement. It helps you to specify and check test conditions, characteristics, and instructions. The second checklist is for designing student opinion questionnaires. It will aid you in selecting topics, items, and the type of response students should give. It also helps you plan how to administer the questionnaire.

Part III consists of checklists for interpreting three kinds of evaluation information: student prerequisites, student terminal achievement, and the relevancy of your course objectives. Each checklist helps you decide on an appropriate action to improve the design of your learning system.

Read the entire aid before beginning to plan your evaluation program. The checklists for designing an evaluation instrument will tell you what information you should plan to collect.

PART I: PLANNING FOR EVALUATION

INSTRUCTIONS   The following chart is to help you develop an evaluation plan. The first column lists six kinds of information for evaluating a learning system. For each kind of information, fill in the blanks in the second and third columns. For example, to assess student understanding of course objectives at the beginning of the course, the instructor could ask students to write a sample final exam item that would test achievement of each objective. If no more than 80 percent of the students are able to write correct items, the instructor could distribute correct examples and/or present the course objectives in simpler form. Look at the checklists for designing evaluation instruments before filling in the third column. The checklists will help you plan your evaluation program.

Information Required	What Instrument Do You Plan to Use?*	How and When Will You Collect and Use this Information?
1. Do you wish to assess student understanding of objectives?		
2. Do you wish to assess student prerequisite skills?		
3. Do you wish to assess student achievement during course?		
4. Do you wish to assess student opinions during course?		
5. Do you wish to assess student terminal achievement?		
6. Do you wish to assess student terminal opinions?		

PART II: DESIGNING EVALUATION INSTRUMENTS

INSTRUCTIONS This part of the aid includes two checklists: the first is for designing a test of student achievement; the second is for designing a student opinion questionnaire. For each kind of test you plan to use, as indicated in Part I of this aid, follow the steps in the checklist. After completing each checklist, you should have a test and a plan for administering and scoring it. It may be necessary to write more than one draft of your test and test plan.

*In Part II of this aid are checklists for designing evaluation instruments. Look at these checklists before filling in this column. They will help you to plan your evaluation program.

Test of Student Prerequisites or Achievement (can be used for course as a whole or subunits of a course)

1. Specify testing conditions.

    a. List topics to be covered.
    b. For each topic, list and rank objectives according to importance in referent situation.

2. Design a test.

    a. Write and check the test for each objective.
       1) Are conditions, behavior, and standards the same as in objectives (validity)?
       2) Are there a sufficient number of items to demonstrate achievement (reliability)?
       3) If the test is short-answer, can competent observers agree on correct answer (objectivity)?
       4) Can competent observers agree whether a student has achieved standards (objectivity)?
       5) Can only students who have achieved objectives answer correctly (differentiality)?
          The procedures for answering this question are:
          a) Test students at the beginning of the course.
          b) Test advanced students.
       6) Will students be given feedback so that they can identify correct test performance and errors made (feedback)?
    b. Write and check test instructions.
       1) Ar˜ there jargon words not previously explained to students?
       2) Can independent observers agree on what instructions require?

3. Select one of the following scoring procedures and specify method of assigning grades.

    a. Number of questions answered correctly.
    b. Number of objectives achieved.
    c. Level of objectives achieved.
    d. Pass-no pass.

Student Opinion Questionnaire (can be used during and at end of course)

1. Select topics to be included. Examples are:

    a. Instructor's personal characteristics.
    b. Student interest.
    c. Student-instructor interaction.
    d. Course demands.
    e. Course organization.
    f. Testing and grading practices.
    g. Course relevance.
    h. Open-ended questions (What did you like? What did you dislike? What changes in course procedures would you suggest?

2. Select the type of response to be made by student.

a. Categorical (true-false; yes-no; check-if-agree).
   Example:
   The slide-tape units helped me prepare for exams.   T   F
b. Scale.
   Example:
   The slide-tape units helped me prepare for exams. SA   A   N   D   SD*
        *(strongly agree; agree; neutral; disagree; strongly disagree)
c. Short-answer.
   Example:
   What changes in the slide-tape units would you suggest?

3. Write the questions and then check for the following:

   a. Did you ask for achievement information? (This information can be obtained better by an achievement test.)
   b. Can students answer items from their own experience?
   c. Did you ask a question that will enable you to take some action?

4. Plan administration of questionnaire.

   a. Explain its purpose to students.
   b. Explain that answers are not related to grades.
   c. Students should be instructed to answer the questionnaire anonymously.
   d. State how you will collate and distribute answers to students.
   e. Plan to implement suggestions or explain to students why you cannot.

PART III: INTERPRETING EVALUATION INFORMATION

INSTRUCTIONS This part of the aid includes three checklists for interpreting information obtained from evaluation instruments. In every case, interpretation should be followed by specific plans for future action, that is, the specific things that will be done to improve your learning system. The following checklists will help you formulate these plans. After completing each checklist, you should make a tentative list of actions you intend to take. A final plan for reviewing your learning system should be written after reviewing and integrating your tentative list.

Student Prerequisites

1. What proportion of students achieved each prerequisite on entry skills test?

2. If students do not meet prerequisites, select from following actions:

   a. Prepare review.
   b. Develop special remedial instruction.
   c. Reduce number or level of terminal objectives.
   d. Limit students entering course.
   e. Give feedback to students.

Student Terminal Achievement (for course as a whole or course subunits)

1. What proportion of students achieved each objective on terminal test?

2. If students fail to achieve objectives, select from the following actions:

   a. Review organization of subject matter.

1) Were all enabling objectives identified?
2) Were enabling objectives sequenced correctly?
3) Check student opinion questionnaire.

  b. Review instructional procedures (see Chapters 8 - 9).
    1) Were objectives understood?
    2) Were background and implications of topics presented?
    3) Were examples given?
    4) Was required terminal behavior demonstrated or modeled?
    5) Was sufficient practice provided?
    6) Did students receive feedback?
    7) Check student opinion questionnaire.

  c. Determine whether students are adequately prepared for instruction. Check student achievement of prerequisites.

3. To help you complete items 2a, 2b, and 2c, review student answers to opinion questionnaires.

Check Relevancy of Course Objectives and Content

1. Do students who achieve terminal objectives succeed in referent sitaution?

2. Have conditions, behavior, or standards of referent situation changed?

3. Select from the following actions:

  a. Modify conditions, behavior, or standards of current objectives.
  b. Add additional objectives.
  c. Add or modify course content.

POSTTEST

1. An instructor is designing a learning system. After writing learning objectives, he begins to design an achievement test in order to:

  a. Check whether the objectives stated are in behavioral terms.
  b. Sequence enabling objectives.
  c. Identify prerequisite entry skills.

                                                   _____

2. One of the objectives for a course in art appreciation is: "Given several pictorial examples of the French Impressionist school of art, the student will identify the painter." Which of the following is a valid test of this objective?

  a. Name five painters of the French Impressionist school and give the title of a work of each.
  b. Name five French painters of the French Impressionist school.
  c. Match the following list of painters of the French Impressionist school with a list of paintings.
  d. Name the artist who painted each of the following paintings from the Impressionist school.
  e. All of the above.

3. How can the reliability of a test be increased?

   a. Increase the number of opportunities to demonstrate achievement.
   b. Control temperature and humidity in the testing room.
   c. Use nonjargon words and clear instructions.
   d. a, b, and c are all correct.
   e. None of the above.   _____

4. An instructor wishes to increase the objectivity of his achievement tests. He should begin by:

   a. Measuring terminal achievement.
   b. Writing objectives in behavioral terms.
   c. Designing a multiple-choice test with at least five alternative answers.
   d. Obtaining student opinions.   _____

5. In order to determine whether a final exam has the property of differentiality, you should:

   a. Make sure your objectives are stated in behavioral terms.
   b. Give it to your students on the first day of the course.
   c. Give it to advanced students.
   d. Both b and c.   _____

6. A postclass opinionnaire can provide the following information:

   a. Achievement of terminal objectives.
   b. Achievement of enabling objectives.
   c. Whether examples presented in class are clearly understood.
   d. Both a and b are correct.   _____

7. An instructor is developing a new learning system. He selects a unit of the system for prototype testing. Which of the following methods of collecting evaluative information should he use:

   a. Achievement test of the unit's terminal objectives.
   b. Entry skills test.
   c. Opinion questionnaire.
   d. Informal discussion with the students.
   e. All of the above.   _____

8. In evaluating learning systems, the method of grading on the curve has the following disadvantage(s).

   a. A grade does not reflect achievement of objectives.
   b. Grades provide no information for evaluating instructional procedures.
   c. Grades cannot be used as an indicator of student preparation for future courses.
   d. All of the above.   _____

9. When analyzing student performance on the final exam, an instructor found that many of his students failed to achieve the objectives of one of his instructional units. He checked the entry skills test for the unit and found that all students had passed. What should he do now?

    a. Check to see whether any enabling objectives were omitted.
    b. Check the examples he used to explain the subject matter.
    c. Check whether students were given sufficient practice.
    d. All of the above. _____

10. For which of the following evaluation questions is a student opinion questionnaire NOT appropriate?

    a. Did the teacher seem interested in teaching?
    b. Did students have ample opportunity to ask questions?
    c. Did students perceive the relevance of the objectives?
    d. Did the students have prerequisites? _____

11. If a teacher compares two learning systems, he should:

    a. Use the same learning objectives for both systems.
    b. Keep the average entry skill level of students in both groups about the same.
    c. Give the terminal test to all students before instruction.
    d. Measure student attitudes.
    e. All of the above. _____

Answers to this posttest can be found on page 335.

OVERVIEW OF LEARNING SYSTEM DESIGN • REC OGNIZING WELL-FORMULATED OBJECTIVES • DERIVING AND WRITING LEARNING OBJECTIVES • EVALUATING LEARNING SYSTEMS • **TASK DE SCRIPTIONS**•TYPES OF LEARNING • ANALYZING TASKS, OBJECTIVES, AND LEARNER CHARAC TERISTICS • GENERAL PRINCIPLES OF LEARNING AND MOTIVATION • THE LEARNING AND TEACH ING OF CONCEPTS AND PRINCIPLES •THE LEARN ING AND TEACHING OF PROBLEM SOLVING • PERCEPTUAL-MOTOR SKILLS • THE SYSTEM APPROACH TO INSTRUCTION • OVERVIEW OF LEARNING SYSTEM DESIGN • RECOGNIZING WELL-FORMULATED OBJECTIVES • DERIVING AND WRITING LEARNING OBJECTIVES • EVALUAT ING LEARNING SYSTEMS • **TASK DESCRIPTIONS** • TYPES OF LEARNING   ANALYZING TASKS, OBJEC TIVES, AND LEARNER CHARACTERISTICS • GEN ERAL PRINCIPLES OF LEARNING AND MOTIVA TION • THE LEARNING AND TEACHING OF CON CEPTS AND PRINCIPLES • THE LEARNING AND TEACHING OF PROBLEM SOLVING • PERCEPTUAL- MOTOR SKILLS • THE SYSTEM APPROACH TO INSTRUCTION • OVERVIEW OF LEARNING SYS TEM DESIGN•RECOGNIZING WELL-FORMULATED OBJECTIVES•DERIVING AND WRITING LEARNING OBJECTIVES • EVALUATING LEARNING SYSTEMS • **TASK DESCRIPTIONS**•TYPES OF LEARNING • ANALYZING TASKS, OBJECTIVES, AND LEARNER

5

CHAPTER OBJECTIVES

- Given a series of hypothetical situations, select the most appropriate method of task description, i.e., narrative, flow diagram, or outline.
- Given a set of flow diagram symbols and a list of functions, match the symbol to the function.
- List the types of information normally included in an action task description.
- Given a series of statements dealing with the distinction between fixed and variable sequence tasks, determine whether they are true or false.
- Given a simple fixed sequence action task, draw a flow diagram describing the task. Include all relevant steps.

INTRODUCTION

The learning system designer begins with a large body of material he must teach to someone else. From this body of knowledge, he selects those concepts, principles, and skills to be learned by the student. In general, the designer begins the selection process by deriving and writing a terminal objective which will allow him to concentrate on the most relevant and critical aspects to be learned. He then breaks down the terminal objective into enabling objectives.

How does he establish the enabling objectives? Some enabling objectives may be obvious to the designer. But how can he be sure that he has not overlooked some critical enabling objectives which are not so obvious? And, equally important, how will he decide the sequence in which the objectives must be taught?

The **task description** is a useful tool for breaking terminal objectives down into enabling objectives. It is, as the name implies, a way of describing how a task is performed. Whenever a learning system designer must teach a student tasks, some form of clear-cut task description is useful and valuable. The task description also serves another important function by helping to specify, in precise and operational terms, what the referent system is. In a sense, it is a detailed statement about how a task is performed in the referent system. The following example may help to clarify this point.

Terminal Objective:	Given a standard American-built automobile with power steering, power brakes, and automatic transmission, the learner will be able to drive, unaided, for 1000 miles over different types of terrain and through one or more cities of over 100,000 population, without violating traffic laws or having an accident.

Some of the enabling objectives to meet this terminal objective may be obvious to you immediately. For example, if the student must drive a 1000 miles without breaking any laws, then he will have to know what the laws are. The other enabling objectives may not be so apparent. While we might say that the first step in this task is to plan the trip, the steps in planning a trip can be quite complicated. If he is to plan the entire trip, the student will have to know how to read a map (a new enabling objective) and perhaps how to gather information before departing about motels en route (another new enabling objective) and so on. Notice that these two new enabling objectives were derived from an examination of the first step in the task. If we were to develop a more complete task description, including all the steps in the terminal objective, many new enabling objectives would become apparent to us. In addition to planning the trip, component tasks might have included servicing the car, negotiating through traffic, freeway driving, etc.

A task description is used as a basic planning document in the design process. As you study this lesson, you will discover that a careful task description provides the basis for the design of a great deal of instruction. Students must learn many different tasks, and if we are to teach them these tasks, the knowledge to be taught must be systematically organized so that salient points are identified and so that critical bits and pieces of information are not omitted. The purpose of this chapter is to teach you what a task description is and how to write one. In the next chapter, we will turn to the use of the task description and learning objectives for design purposes.

As you read this chapter, notice how complex seemingly simple tasks actually are. Many teachers perform tasks so automatically that they overlook critical steps and underestimate the difficulty a novice experiences as he tries to learn how to do it. Take a simple task like setting an alarm clock. Most adults perform this task readily and without difficulty. For a child, on the other hand, the task involves many concepts, principles, and perceptual-motor skills he may not have mastered. One need only recall how difficult it is to learn to tell time (a prerequisite skill for setting an alarm clock) to realize how complex such a "simple" task really is. In teaching tasks, therefore, it becomes necessary to explicate all of the steps involved so that nothing will be overlooked.

In the discussion which follows, we will distinguish between two major classes of tasks: action tasks and cognitive tasks. Action tasks are observable and involve an interaction between a person and an object or between one person and another person. There are two types of action tasks: fixed sequence action tasks and variable sequence action tasks. Cognitive tasks may have some observable aspects, but they are largely done mentally or "in one's head."

See if you can recall the types of tasks to be discussed in this chapter.

1. A _ _ _ _ _ tasks.
   a. Fixed _____
   b. Variable _____
2. C _ _ _ _ _ _ _ _ tasks.

ACTION TASKS

The term action task implies that someone is doing something to another person or object; however, it is almost impossible to do anything to other persons or objects without their doing something back. If we turn on the radio, it responds almost immediately with a click, a hum, the voice of an announcer, or music. Similarly, when we smile at a friend, he smiles back, nods, or strikes up a conversation. When we engage in any action task, therefore, the action is never one way; there is always an interaction between a person and an object or a person and another person. One of the major characteristics of any action task is this interaction.

If you will think for a minute about the kinds of activities in which people engage when they perform an action task, you will realize that some objective is always implied. To undertake a task is to do something toward accomplishing a goal; and that means a person must engage in some form of action. Consider the kinds of action implied by the following tasks:

adjust a microscope
tune a television
dial a telephone
teach a child

You will notice that the terms adjust, tune, dial, and teach not only involve action, they also imply that someone or something is modified by the action. It is the microscope that is adjusted, the television that is tuned, the child who is taught, and so on.

DEFINITION:
THE CONCEPT OF AN ACTION TASK, INCLUDES THREE CRITICAL ATTRIBUTES: (1) AN INTER-ACTION BETWEEN A PERSON WITH ANOTHER PERSON OR OBJECT (2) WITH A VIEW TO CHANGING HIM (OR IT) AND (3) IN ORDER TO MEET SOME GOAL.

FEEDBACK:
5.1   1   Action   2   Cognitive
         a   sequence
         b   sequence

Action tasks may be very complex, or quite simple. Some examples of complex action tasks are these: overhaul an automobile engine, repair a radar, interpret an intelligence test. Complex action tasks break down into simpler subtasks. Examples of simple action tasks within the radar repair task are these: replace a tube, adjust a dial, read a radarscope, and so on.

On the first page of most telephone directories there is the following announcement:

FOR INFORMATION ON NUMBERS NOT LISTED IN THIS DIRECTORY, CALL: DIRECTORY ASSISTANCE

• • • • • *Long Distance (for numbers in other places)*

      For numbers inside your Area 517 (for example) Dial 1 + 555-1212

      For numbers outside your Area 517 (for example) Dial 1 + Area Code + 555-1212

1. A user decides to call a friend outside of his area whose telephone number he does not know. The user of the telephone has an objective. What is it?

2. To achieve his objective he must interact with whom or what?

3. Who or what will be changed as a result of the interaction?

F R A M E

5.2

ACTION TASK DESCRIPTIONS

DEFINITION:
THE TASK DESCRIPTION IS A SYSTEMATIC MEANS OF IDENTIFYING AND SEQUENCING SALIENT FEATURES OF A TASK.

Every description of an action task has four critical elements. First, there are signs or cues signaling actions. Generally these cues originate in the external world. The signal may be a flashing light or special sound; it may be a meter reading or written instructions. Actions in tasks are frequently preceded by cues that signal their beginning.

Second, there must be action verbs to describe the behavior of the per-

---

FEEDBACK:

5.2   1   To obtain the telephone number of someone outside his area.

      2   The telephone and an operator in the area he intends to dial—possibly his telephone directory as well.

      3   The user. The objective is to change him from someone who doesn't know the number to someone who does.

former at each step in the task. We have already noted some examples of these action verbs: to adjust a microscope, to dial a telephone, and so on. It is important to note, however, that any one of these tasks would, if described more fully, break down into a number of component steps, each of which would have an action verb associated with it. Take, for example, the task of adjusting the microscope. This task might also involve: selecting a slide, turning on a light, focusing an eyepiece, etc.

Third, there are indications of the persons or objects acted upon. Tasks, as we have observed, involve an interaction of the performer with the world. A task description states with whom or with what he is interacting. The student in the above example of adjusting a microscope is interacting with slides, eyepieces, and another student if he must work in a pair.

Finally, actions are accompanied by feedback that result from the interaction process. At each step along the way, the man performing a task receives some knowledge about his performance. Signals of various kinds come back to him as a direct result of his behavior, providing him with valuable information about his progress.

FRAME 5.3

Every description of an action task contains four critical elements. They are:

1. _____ or _____ to initiate the action.

2. _____ verbs.

3. _____ or _____ acted upon.

4. _____ from the action.

One way to help you appreciate the importance of a task description is to consider a very simple task and the problems involved in teaching it to someone else. Sharpening a pencil will again serve as a good example of this.

Today, one can buy electric pencil sharpeners. These sharpeners are relatively new to the consumer and may require learning how to operate them. Naturally, the designer has made the operation of these sharpeners as simple as possible. They have a hole into which one places the pencil which automatically starts the machine and there is a small light that goes on when the pencil is sharp to signal that it should be withdrawn. Now, consider for a moment this sequence of events which actually occurred in one of our offices.

FEEDBACK:

5.3   1 Signs . . . cues   3 Persons . . . objects
       2 Action   4 Feedback

A woman entered the office in search of a pencil sharpener. We told her there was one on the desk. She looked puzzled.

"It's electric."

"Oh! How does it work?"

"Put your pencil in the hole. When the light goes on, it's sharp. That's all there is to it."

The woman followed directions and sharpened several pencils. Then she said, "I believe it's broken."

"Why?"

"Because the light doesn't go on."

After a brief inspection, we discovered that she was sharpening a red pencil.

"The light won't work with red pencils."

"Why?"

"Perhaps because pencil lead is a conductor of electricity and red pencils do not conduct electricity."

"Oh!" She replied.

She might have asked for more information, but fortunately didn't.

Clearly, the task of sharpening a pencil seems on first consideration to be a remarkably simple one but it does, in fact, involve a number of steps. If we examine the sequence of actions just described, we would discover that the pencil sharpening task has many components. A few of these are:

(1)   Deciding that pencils need to be sharpened

(2)   Finding a pencil sharpener

(3)   Placing a pencil in the sharpener (point first)

(4)   Withdrawing the pencil—on light cue

(5)   Examining the point

The task was further complicated by the discovery that the light did not always work. This led to the learning of a new principle which might have been expanded almost indefinitely had the woman chosen to explore such concepts as the electrical properties of graphite.

The woman in this illustration entered the situation with considerable knowledge. She knew, for example, which end of the pencil to sharpen. She had mastered such simple concepts as what the light meant and the on-off apparatus. She had the perceptual-motor skill to control the pencil and exert appropriate pressure on it. All of these things she had learned in other settings.

FOUR TYPES OF INFORMATION INCLUDED IN ACTION TASK DESCRIPTIONS

As we have already observed, every description of an action task includes information about four different aspects of the task. Let's review these four types of information and relate them to the example of the pencil sharpener. First, the task description contains information about the different actions being taken to reach a goal. In our example of the pencil sharpener, the woman had to take the actions listed above, indicated by such action verbs as decide, find, place, withdraw, and examine. Second, actions are preceded by cues that signal whether or not it is appropriate to take other actions. Before deciding to sharpen the pencil, the woman had undoubtedly noticed that the pencil point was dull an... this cued her subsequent behavior. The cue to withdraw the pencil occurred when the light went on. And so on. Third, every action is followed by some form of feedback. When the woman asked us where she could find a pencil sharpener, she received feedback ("on the desk"); when she looked at the desk, she saw the sharpener (another form of feedback). Generally, feedback from one action, cues the next. Consider for a moment the way the light acts as both a cue to one action and feedback for another. The light is a cue to withdraw the pencil, but it is also feedback to the action of inserting the pencil and applying pressure to it. Every description of an action task contains information about the actions to be taken, the cues that initiate those actions, and the kinds of feedback that follow the actions. Finally, descriptions of action tasks include information about the people or objects acted upon. The woman made a decision about the pencils based on visual cues. She inserted the pencil into the sharpener and waited for the light to glow.

Unfortunately, there is no clear-cut taxonomy for describing tasks, since the method used depends on the type of task. Furthermore, there are many learning activities which are not suited to a task description. Normally, a subtask is broken down until you come to the point at which it cannot be broken down further. No description is necessary or even possible if a subtask cannot be divided. Task descriptions are least useful, therefore, for simple cognitive exercises such as defining, listing, or stating verbal materials. They are very useful when the task involves a **fixed sequence** of steps, or a **variable sequence** of events.

TWO KINDS OF ACTION TASKS

A number of methods have been developed for describing action tasks. We will concentrate on methods which can be applied to fixed sequence and variable sequence action tasks.

FIXED SEQUENCE ACTION TASKS There are many action tasks that require a fixed, predictable sequence of actions. One way to think about such tasks is that they are **algorithmic**. Webster defines an algorithm as a rule or procedure for solving a recurrent mathematical problem. In other words, if we follow a predefined sequence of actions, we will be able to solve a particular type of problem whenever we encounter it. In general, the pencil sharpening task is of this type and involves a fixed, algorithmic sequence.

Check the point ⟶ Decide whether to sharpen ⟶
Walk to pencil sharpener ⟶ Insert pencil ⟶
Watch light ⟶ Withdraw pencil ⟶ Check point

Fixed sequence action tasks often branch and return to the mainstream of action. The feedback after inserting the pencil in the sharpener, for example, is actually the sound of the motor. But suppose the motor does not operate. The absence of this feedback is a cue for an entirely different sequence of actions which presumably would rectify the problem. For example, silence following the insertion of the pencil may signal the user to inspect the plug to see if it is in the socket.

Now inspect this simple schematic of a fixed sequence task with no branches:

Action → A	Feedback A	─Action ─→ B	Feedback B	─Action─→ C	Feedback C
	Cue B		Cue C		Cue D

In some cases, such as the example above in which the motor doesn't operate, the task has branches and an action may be followed by two or more cues signaling different intervening activities. The schematic for a branching action task might look like this.

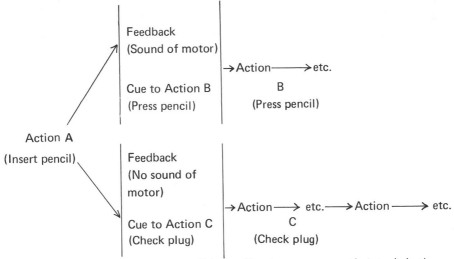

One of the best ways of describing a fixed sequence action task is the use of a flow diagram. Later in this chapter we will explain how a flow diagram is used in describing an action task.

VARIABLE SEQUENCE ACTION TASKS   Many action tasks are not algorithmic and cannot be described in terms of a fixed sequence of actions. Such action tasks generally do not involve a series of discrete actions elicited by particular cues. Instead, the cues are constantly changing. We may, for example, apply the brakes on our automobile, or turn to the right, or depress the accelerator for any of hundreds of different reasons and in response to a variety of cues. Brakes may be applied because of signs, because of bumps, a ball, or glass in the road, or because children are playing alongside the road. There is simply no way of neatly diagraming the flow of events in such action tasks because they are unpredictable, nor would it be adaptive to try to teach such tasks as if they were fixed sequence tasks. Most complex skills like driving a car, playing basketball or football, and flying an airplane, fall into this category. These complex variable sequence action tasks can still be described, but the description is done by dividing the task into subtasks and using outlines, narrative descriptions, and (for fixed sequence subtasks) the flow diagram.

Complex variable sequence action tasks generally involve one or more fixed sequence subtasks. The procedure for starting an automobile is a fixed sequence task which sometimes has branches, but the algorithm is generally highly standardized. Thus, the task of starting the car might be treated as fixed sequence. The same applies to shifting gears in an automobile. Determining which subtasks are fixed sequence can be useful because the fixed sequence subtasks can often be learned more efficiently in isolation rather than in the context of the overall task. A student can be taught to shift gears, for example, while the car is standing still. Learning each subtask individually helps the student towards the larger goal of learning the task. For example, the student who has practiced the fixed sequence action task of shifting gears in a parking lot or driveway until it is automatic will find it easier to maneuver through city traffic.

Decide whether the following are fixed sequence or variable sequence tasks. Avoid looking up the answers until after you have made you response.

	How to:	Fixed Sequence	Variable Sequence
F	1. Thread a movie projector	( )	( )
R	2. Fly an airplane	( )	( )
A	3. Play football	( )	( )
M	4. Polish shoes	( )	( )
E	5. Change a flat tire	( )	( )
5.4	6. Mail a letter	( )	( )

(continued on next page)

7. Solve a long division   ( )   ( )
   problem

DESCRIBING COGNITIVE TASKS

Not all tasks have an overt action component. Many tasks are done at the cognitive level, or in a more popular jargon, "in the head." A number of verbs are used to describe such cognitive tasks. Some of these are: decide, discriminate, or solve. When a manager decides to hire a particular applicant for a job, to invest more money in advertising, or to stop manufacturing a certain item, he is engaging in a cognitive task. When a teacher evaluates her pupils, decides to seek a new job, or selects a husband, she is doing a cognitive task.

Although we do not often know enough about how people actually do such cognitive tasks, it is still helpful to try to identify the component parts or subtasks and list them. In the case of a decision-making task, we sometimes list the criteria for making the decision. These criteria can then be converted into a form of task description.

It is possible to actually describe cognitive tasks: (1) if there are experts who can tell us how to perform the cognitive task; or (2) if there is a generally agreed upon procedure for performing the cognitive task in question. Two examples may help to clarify these points.

In many parts of the United States today, people are learning Zazen, which means "sitting Zen." Students of Zen sit motionless and concentrate on their own breathing in order to suspend the flow of ordinary thought without falling asleep. Obviously, the real experts in Zazen are the Zen Buddhists. If you were to ask a Zen Buddhist how he meditates, however, he would simply laugh and perhaps he would tell you a puzzling and paradoxical **mondo** (a question and answer) to help you discover for yourself how to meditate. Abraham Kaplan, in the New World of Philosophy, reports the following mondo: A monk asked the master to play him a tune on a stringless harp. The master was silent for a few minutes and then said, "There, you hear it, don't you?" The monk replied, "Alas, no, master." The master reproached him with, "Why didn't you ask me louder?" Clearly, Zen masters have very little patience with those who must depend upon others for their entertainment or their instruction. Those who have tried to learn a task such as archery or flower arranging, by the Zen method, describe, in excruciating detail, the years required to discover the Zen ap-

---

FEEDBACK:

5.4	1	Fixed	4	Fixed	7	Fixed
	2	Variable	5	Fixed		
	3	Variable	6	Fixed		

proach to such seemingly simple tasks. A Zen master would never do a task description of how to meditate or arrange flowers or shoot an arrow. Fortunately for the impatient Westerner, however, the task of Zen meditation has been described by men who at least claim to be experts. Here is a task description [Lesh, 1971] of how to meditate:

> Keep your back straight and erect; your hands in your lap, the left hand palm facing inward on the right palm, with the tips of the thumbs touching. Your head too is erect, the ears on the plane of the shoulders, and the nose in line with the navel. You may keep your eyes closed or open as your prefer. If you have them open fix them, unfocused, on the floor at a point about two or three feet in front of you. Now raise your whole body slowly and quietly, move it repeatedly to the left and to the right, forward and around, until you feel the best position.

> Breathe through your nose, inhaling as much as you need, letting the air come in by distending the diaphragm. Don't draw it in, rather let it come to you. Exhale slowly and completely, getting all the air out of your lungs. As you exhale slowly, count "one." Now inhale again, then exhale to the count of "two." And so on up to ten. Then start over again with "one" and repeat up to ten again, etc.

> You will find the counting difficult as your mind will wander. Keep at it though, keep bringing your mind back to the process of counting your breath. As you become able to do the counting with reasonable success, start playing the following game with the counting. As you count "one" and are slowly exhaling, pretend that the "one" is going down, down, down, into your stomach. Then think of its being down there as you inhale, and begin to count "two." As you exhale, bring the "two" down and place it in your stomach beside the "one." Eventually you will find that your mind itself, so to speak, will descend into your stomach. Gradually it will become possible for you to concentrate with more and more success on the numbers. Your mind will wander, and you will find yourself carried away on trains of thought, but it will become easier and easier to bring your mind back to the counting of your breath. Don't try to keep the "alien" thoughts out. Instead just try to concentrate on the counting. You may take note of the thoughts as they come in, if necessary, and then return to the counting. Get rid of the thoughts not by pushing them out of your mind, but by concentrating on the counting.

> You may find that you become anxious or uncomfortable. This is because sitting still and concentrating like this restricts the usual ways we have of avoiding discomfort. If you feel uncomfortable, just accept it. If you feel pleasant, accept that with the same indifference. Eventually you will be able to be quiet in both body and mind.

This example nicely illustrates how a task can be described in a straight narrative form. After considerable practice, the student of Zen can presumably achieve a "primordial state" which has been described as "spiritual." There are no observable criteria provided with this task description to help the student know when he has achieved this state. However, the state is known to be associated with certain changes in brain wave patterns which can be measured and fed back to the student.

A second, more prosaic example, comes from the area of art history. How does a student learn to discriminate a van Gogh from a Rembrandt? Can a learning system designer describe such a purely cognitive task? Not in great detail, but he may be able to list some subtasks or criteria the connoisseur uses to make the discrimination. For example, the connoisseur may:

1. Study the brush strokes for certain characteristic features, e.g.:
   a. Broad, flat, smooth, and bold (van Gogh)
   b. Direction
   c. Length
   d. Texture
2. Note the use of color:
   a. Earth tones (Rembrandt)
   b. Bright, pastel tones (van Gogh)
   c. Attempt to capture the effects of sunlight (van Gogh)
3. Observe the subject matter:
   a. Different historical period and costumes
   b. South France (van Gogh)
   c. Holland (Rembrandt)
      (van Gogh painted in Holland in his early period also)
4. Study the composition:
   a. Bold, striking
   b. Detailed

In point of fact, the connoisseur does not actually go through these various subtasks in a step-by-step fashion. The connoisseur has learned to make the discrimination so well that he, in effect, short-circuits these steps and appears to go directly to the answer. Most amateur art critics can readily distinguish between a van Gogh and a Rembrandt and a child can probably be trained to make the discrimination in very few trials. However, as discriminations become more difficult to teach (for example, the difference between a van Gogh and a Bonnard), a cognitive task description becomes more valuable and useful. Note how the task description in the above case is nothing more than an outline of subtasks. The subtasks are obviously, also, criteria or standards for making a judgment about whether or not a painting is by van Gogh or Rembrandt. Thus, if the strokes are broad, flat and smooth, it is probably a painting by van Gogh.

Creative tasks present a special set of problems. By creative tasks, we mean those tasks which include the production of an original output as their primary goal. When creative tasks are carefully studied, they can generally be broken down into subtasks. Some of the subtasks are describable and some are not. Those subtasks which involve an element of personal taste, preference, or value generally cannot be described. Painting a picture, for example, is clearly a creative task. An expert might describe the tasks as follows:

1. Select a subject.
2. Decide what media will be used.
3. If oil on canvas, stretch canvas.
4. Prepare canvas.
5. Select colors.

Some of these subtasks can be described and some cannot. Stretching a canvas is actually a fixed sequence task, so it can be described using a flow diagram. Deciding what media to use is not. Whenever a task involves an element of personal taste, value, or preference, it is very difficult, if not impossible, to describe it. The selection of a subject, the decision to use a particular medium, the choice of colors, and so on, all involve personal taste, and artists differ greatly in these regards. A man may be laughed at by one generation for departing from accepted form and proclaimed a genius by the next.

Evaluation tasks often have a value, taste, or preference component. Some evaluation subtasks may be described, but those which involve taste or preference generally defy description. Judges of beauty contests and figure skating may use some objective criteria to evaluate the contestants, but their personal tastes and preferences also play a significant role in their choices.

One final fact complicates this analysis of cognitive tasks. Sometimes cognitive tasks are fixed sequence and can be described with a flow diagram. A large number of these fixed sequence tasks are in the area of mathematics, or involve the use of mathematical formulae. Although we may do a mathematical task in our head, it nevertheless often is done using a fixed sequence of steps with decision points, cues for the next step, and feedback for previous steps. Sometimes these fixed sequence cognitive tasks are converted to action tasks by notational systems so that we actually write down and keep a record of the stages as we pass through them. These fixed sequence cognitive tasks can be described using a flow diagram.

COLLECTING INFORMATION ABOUT THE TASK

In order to write a task description, the learning system designer will need to collect information about how the task is performed. The designer may or may not be an expert. If he does not know how the task is performed, then he will have to learn. If the designer does know how the task is performed, he should still collect information about it from others because he may know it so well that he cannot communicate it effectively. This is often due to the fact that the expert performs the task more or less automatically and overlooks important steps in the task.

There are several techniques that can be used to gather the needed information to describe the task. In one way or another, the three methods we will outline involve consulting expert sources.

INDIVIDUAL AND GROUP INTERVIEWS

One of the best ways to find out how a task is performed is to talk to people who know how to do it. This can be done in either a group or individual setting. Whichever method is used, it is important to have a large enough sample to insure that critical actions, cues, subtasks, or types of feedback are not overlooked. How large this sample must be will depend on the task. The more complex the task, the larger the sample should be. One of the best ways to determine the size of the sample is empirically. When the same points are repeated over and over again, you can assume that you have collected all of the relevant information.

Group interviews are expensive and difficult to organize, and so they are generally not recommended. However, they have one or two important advantages which should not be overlooked. For one thing, people in groups tend to remind one another of important points which they might overlook in individual interviews. Also, when people are interviewed in groups, they are able to correct errors and clarify misconceptions. Group interviews are particularly important when the tasks being performed are team tasks and one individual must depend on another in order to do his job effectively.

DIRECT OBSERVATION

Another approach to gathering information for the task description is by direct observation. Actually, one seldom observes a task being performed without also interviewing the person performing it. While watching the individual or group perform, it is important to take detailed and careful notes. Photographic records and other types of data can be helpful. The critical thing is to record every response and to note the cues that signal each response as well as the types of feedback that follow each response.

TECHNICAL MANUALS

Sometimes technical manuals are available to provide valuable information about how a task is performed. They are not always entirely satisfactory as a source of information, however. For one thing, technical manuals are frequently written from an engineering point of view. As a result, they may contain a great deal of superfluous information not readily understood by a layman using them. Another problem is that the information in technical manuals is not always organized in the most useful manner. In addition, critical actions may have been overlooked, because the information for inclusion in the manual is collected at the factory, rather than on a sample of actual users in the field.

FRAME 5.5

List three ways to go about collecting information on the way a task is performed.

1. _____ or _____ interviews.

2. _____ observation.

3. Technical _____.

THE NEED FOR A TASK DESCRIPTION

Task descriptions help the learning system designer identify the enabling objectives needed to meet a terminal objective. In this sense, task descriptions help the learning system designer decide what to teach and how to teach it. It is important to write a task description for four reasons. Two of these reasons concern the content of instruction, or what is to be learned. The other two deal with the methods to be used, or how one goes about teaching a task.

With respect to content, the task description helps to insure that all essential material will be taught, and at the same time, that no unnecessary information will be included in the course. Both of these reasons for performing a task description are based on the assumption of efficiency. Good instruction, as we have already observed, should include all that the learning system designer believes to be important and exclude content which does not contribute to the objectives of the course.

FRAME 5.6

Task descriptions help the designer decide what to leave _____ of the lesson and what to _____ in it.

FEEDBACK:

5.5	1	Individual . . . group	5.6	1 out
	2	Direct		2 keep, include, etc.
	3	manuals		

With respect to methods of instruction, the task description helps the designer to identify the types of learning involved and the order in which to teach subtasks and concepts. There are several different types of learning, including concept learning or perceptual-motor skills learning. As you will discover, one of the most important factors in deciding how to teach something to a student is the type of learning involved. Different types of learning require different approaches to teaching. Furthermore, within any given task, there may be several different types of learning. The task description will help you to identify these types so that they may be taught in the most effective way.

The task description also helps the designer plan the sequence of instruction. The order in which concepts and subtasks are taught will depend upon their hierarchical relationship to one another. All this means is that before we can learn some tasks (or concepts) we must have acquired others. The hierarchical relationship can often be established by writing a task description.

Task descriptions help the designer decide how to teach by enabling him to identify the _____ of learning involved in the task and helping him to _____ the subject matter.

FRAME 5.7

FLOW DIAGRAMING FIXED SEQUENCE TASKS

Flow diagrams are a means of representing fixed sequence tasks in schematic or diagramatic form. Computer programers first used flow diagrams as a means of describing a computer application; a means which was midway between a broad outline and detailed machine coding. Flow diagrams are an aid to visualizing the structure of a task. They provide a convenient method for describing and clarifying relationships between actions, cues, and feedback which might otherwise be obscure and possibly overlooked by the learning system designer.

STRUCTURE OF A FLOW DIAGRAM

In flow diagraming, the steps in a task are represented by a set of symbols. The shape of the symbol used depends on the function being performed. The use of flow diagrams for describing fixed sequence tasks is relatively

---

FEEDBACK:
5.7   1   types
      2   organize, structure, sequence, etc.

new and symbols have not been standardized; however, it is possible to use the symbols commonly employed in computer programing, which are shown in Table 5.1.

TABLE 5.1   SYMBOLS USED IN FLOW DIAGRAMING

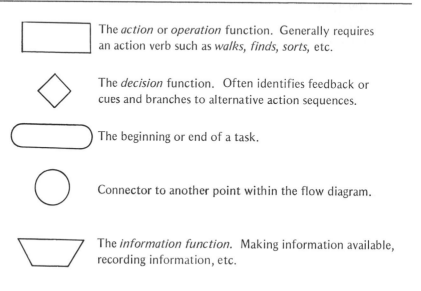

The *action* or *operation* function. Generally requires an action verb such as *walks, finds, sorts,* etc.

The *decision* function. Often identifies feedback or cues and branches to alternative action sequences.

The beginning or end of a task.

Connector to another point within the flow diagram.

The *information function.* Making information available, recording information, etc.

In order to clarify how flow diagrams of fixed sequence tasks are written and used, it will be helpful to recall, once again, the example of the pencil sharpener. An oversimplified view of how this task is performed might look like this:

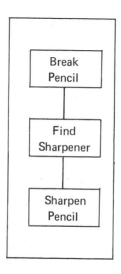

Actually, even such a simple task as sharpening a pencil has far more steps than the above description suggests. It can be a valuable exercise to trace an elementary task of this kind from beginning to end.

Match the number and symbol

Symbol   Number

1. Connector within a program
2. The decision function
3. The action or operation function
4. Information function
5. Beginning or end of the task

Now study the following flow diagram (Table 5.2) of the pencil-sharpening task carefully. Note particularly how the various symbols are used. Try to imagine that you are a completely naive learner—perhaps a man from Mars or a very young child. Are there new concepts you might have to learn in order to do the task? How about coordinated muscular skills such as putting in a plug, or simultaneously pushing on the pencil while turning the crank. Is the flow diagram complete? Remember the episode of the red pencil? Have we taken account of pencils which do not turn the light on even when they are sharp?

FEEDBACK:

5.8   3   5   2   1   4

Theodore Lownik Library
Illinois Benedictine College
Lisle, Illinois 60532

TABLE 5.2   FLOW DIAGRAM OF PENCIL SHARPENING TASK

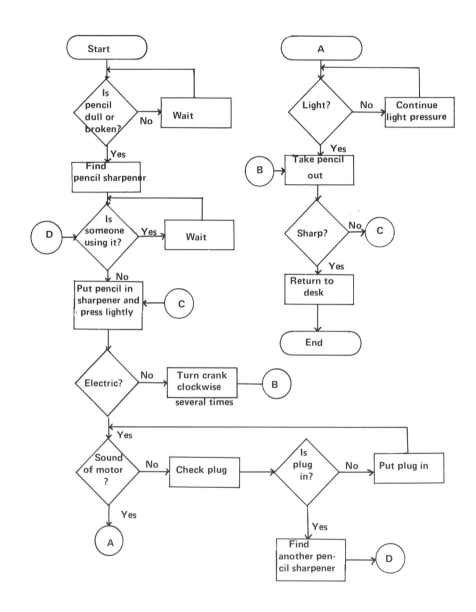

SHAPING BEHAVIOR

There is a training procedure with which all learning system designers should be familiar. It is called shaping and involves a method of successive approximations to teach humans and animals a new skill. It would be inappropriate to attempt to give a detailed account of shaping in a chapter devoted to task descriptions. However, by describing the task of shaping we can help you become familiar with the technique. Remember, however, our principle objective is to illustrate how a flow diagram could help you design a learning system to teach someone else how to shape behavior.

Have you ever watched animals perform very complex skills and wondered how they learned to do them? Pigeons can be taught to play an elementary game of ping pong, for example, or they can be trained to press a colored disc to get food. It is easy to see how a pigeon would go on pressing such a disc once it has learned the connection between the disc and food, but how do you get him to press the disc in the first place? Pigeons are commonly taught to press a disc to get food in order to demonstrate shaping to beginning psychology students, so let's use the procedure to illustrate how shaping is described.

The procedure for training pigeons is described by a well-known psychologist, B. F. Skinner, in his book, **Science and Human Behavior:**

> To get the pigeon to peck the spot as quickly as possible we proceed as follows: We first give the bird food when it turns slightly in the direction of the spot from any part of the cage. This increases the frequency of such behavior. We then withhold reinforcement until a slight movement is made toward the spot. This again alters the general distribution of behavior without producing a new unit. We continue by reinforcing positions successively closer to the spot, then by reinforcing only when the head is moved slightly forward, and finally only when the beak actually makes contact with the spot. We may reach this final response in a remarkably short time. A hungry bird, well adapted to the situation and to the food tray, can usually be brought to respond in this way in two or three minutes.

In a sense, this quotation from Skinner constitutes a task description and the reader should study it carefully. The fact of the matter is no one can be trained to shape a pigeon's behavior using this narrative description alone. Several critical steps have not been included in the process and one would have to look elsewhere in the book in order to determine how a reinforcer is operationally defined. Indeed, the intent of the author was not to teach someone how to shape behavior but to explain what shaping is. If he had wanted to actually teach a student to shape behavior, he might have developed a flow chart something like Table 5.3.

This task description illustrates how difficult it is to learn a simple task

TABLE 5.3   FLOW DIAGRAM OF "SHAPING"

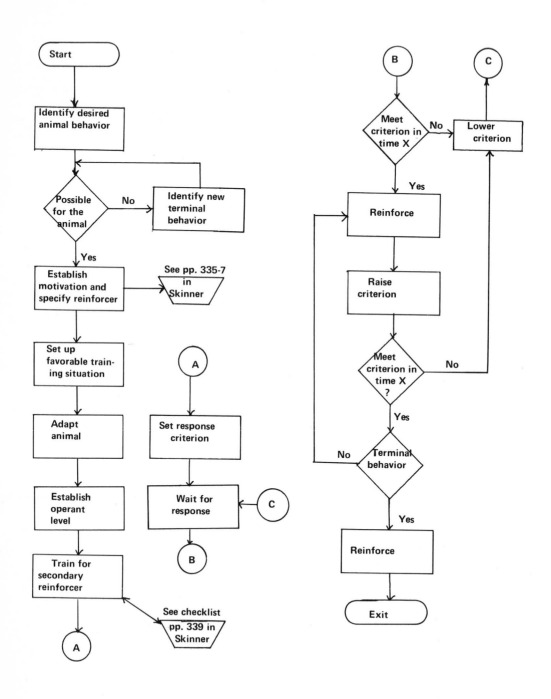

with which we are unfamiliar. The fact of the matter is that shaping is a very simple process. Once you know how, it is only a little more difficult than sharpening a pencil. However, as you can see from an inspection of the flow chart, there are a number of concepts and component skills which should be mastered before one actually attempts to shape behavior. Some of the concepts are: terminal behavior, repertoire, primary reinforcer, favorable training situation, criterion, operant level, etc. An important principle is also embedded in the flow chart: when shaping, you gradually raise the criterion of satisfactory performance so that the learner successively approximates the desired terminal behavior. The flow diagram is drawn to help insure that none of the steps are omitted and that all the concepts, skills, and principles to be taught have been clearly identified.

Notice how the information box is utilized to direct the student to some source of information such as a passage in the textbook or a checklist to help him complete the step in question. This device is frequently used in flow diagrams and can be used to significantly reduce the number of steps included in the diagram. It says to the student, "If you would like to or need to know more about this step or how to perform it, refer to the following source."

There are many times when shaping can be used in the training of humans as well as animals. Most skills, for example, can be shaped. Early in the training of a child, we should reinforce (with praise, for example) any movement in the direction of a desired terminal behavior (catching a ball, for example) and gradually raise the standard of performance needed to earn additional reinforcements.

Match the number to the symbol

Symbol   Number

F
R
A
M
E

5.9

_____

_____

_____

1. Light on?
2. Connect A.
3. Turn switch clockwise.
4. Begin.
5. See telephone directory.

RELATIONSHIP OF OBJECTIVES TO THE TASK DESCRIPTION

As we indicated in the last chapter, behavioral objectives specify what a student will be able to do when he completes a course of instruction, the conditions under which the behavior will be performed, and standards against which the performance will be evaluated. The task description specifies the steps involved in performing a task. Both are useful for designing a learning system. Task descriptions and objectives interact with one another so that subtasks are frequently the result of writing behavioral objectives, and new objectives often emerge when tasks are described in detail.

Many students find it difficult to understand which comes first, the task description or the objectives. It is, indeed, a chicken and egg problem, which brings us back to a point made in Chapter 1. Learning system design is not a fixed sequence task. In practice, the designer employs the most appropriate tools as they are needed. As a general rule, it seems to us that the process resembles a problem-solving activity. The designer of a learning system begins with some sort of problem. He tries to define as carefully as he can what that problem is and, in the process, gathers as much information as possible about it. Slowly he hammers out a terminal objective which, on inspection, reveals specific tasks. He then sets out to describe these tasks. From the task descriptions, new enabling objectives emerge which may, in turn, suggest new tasks. Furthermore, in the process of doing these various things, the designer may have rewritten the original terminal objective and described the initial task several times. In other words, the process is iterative, by which we mean the designer goes back

FEEDBACK:
5.9   3   2
        4   5
        1

over his work and recreates the steps as new dimensions and aspects emerge.

CRITERIA FOR EVALUATING TASK DESCRIPTIONS

When writing a task description, it is important to keep three things in mind. First, the description must be complete. Every step in the task must be included. Second, avoid using words or phrases that can be interpreted in different ways. Try to use action verbs that describe observable behavior. Say exactly what you mean in the simplest and most direct terms. Third, be certain the task is internally consistent, that it doesn't require a man to do two incompatible things at the same time. A man cannot, for example, perform two operations at opposite ends of a room at the same exact time.

SOME PROBLEMS WITH TASK DESCRIPTIONS

A task description is a detailed specification of human behavior. Although psychologists are presumably interested in basic data about human behavior, they have not developed a generally accepted scientific scheme for classifying behavior. Clinical and industrial psychologists have had an interest in this problem for a number of years, but, so far, a useful taxonomy or classification scheme for behavior—particularly normal behavior—has not been developed. Preliminary research suggests that typical task descriptions include four factors: (1) a cognitive factor (a person decides, judges, analyzes, computes); (2) a social factor (a person talks, asks, listens); (3) a procedural factor (a person operates, uses equipment, handles); and (4) a physical factor (a person carries, walks, writes). Obviously, if a more universal scheme for describing human behavior existed, it would be much easier to write task descriptions. It might also help us begin to develop information about how to train people for different types of activities within tasks.

A second problem with the task description is that there is no generally agreed upon way of breaking tasks down into their component subtasks. In effect, we are not really sure whether a task is the appropriate word for a described activity. We speak of the task of flying an airplane and we also refer to the task of sharpening a pencil. Obviously the differences between these two activities are so great that they are not merely quantitative, but qualitative as well. It does not seem reasonable to classify both flying an airplane and sharpening a pencil in the same category. Sometimes the distinction is made between a job and a task, in which case the job is broken down into numerous tasks and the task may be broken down still further into subtasks.

A third and final problem stems from the fact that some behavior is private to the individual and simply cannot be described. Some human behavior can be observed and the steps recorded, but other activities are purely personal and perhaps unique to the individual. The fact is that we simply do not know some of the steps a musician goes through to write a symphony or a poet to write a sonnet. As we have already noted, subtasks which cannot be described involve an element of personal taste, preference, or value.

For all of these reasons, we have tried not to prescribe a rigid approach to the task description. Sometimes, a flow diagram is possible and desirable; sometimes it is not. Try different approaches, particularly if the task is a large one and is a variable sequence task. Use a narrative description or outline if the flow diagram is impractical. The only rule of thumb we advise is that you should not, under any circumstances, attempt to write a task description if it is a creative task which even experts in the subject area can't describe, especially if it involves personal preference or taste.

SUMMARY

A task is some activity (often assigned) in which people engage. There are two major classes of tasks: action tasks and cognitive tasks. Normally the words action task imply that someone is doing something to another person or object. Action tasks may be either fixed sequence (algorithmic) or variable sequence. Cognitive tasks are not performed overtly, but covertly, as mental activities. They are generally described best in outline or narrative form. Some cognitive tasks are fixed sequence and may be described using a flow diagram; such cognitive tasks generally involve mathematical or logical formulae. Task descriptions are a systematic way of identifying and sequencing the salient features of a task. If a task is fixed sequence, it can generally be described with a flow diagram. If it is not fixed sequence, an outline or narrative description may be necessary. Learning objectives and task descriptions interact and tend to evolve together. Information for the task description may be collected by individual or group interviews, direct observations, or technical manuals. Task descriptions help the designer decide what to teach and how to teach it.

SUGGESTED READINGS

Bennett, Corwin A.: "Toward Empirical, Practicable, Comprehensive Task Taxonomy," *Human Factors,* 1971, *13*:3, 229-236.

Fleishman, E. A.: "Performance Assessment Based on an Empirically Derived Task Taxonomy," *Human Factors,* 1967, *9*:4, 349-366.

Herrigel, H.: *Zen in the Art of Archery*, (New York: Vintage Books, 1971).

Kaplan, A.: *The New World of Philosophy*, (New York: Vintage Books, 1961).

Lesh, T. V.: "Zen Meditation and the Development of Empathy in Counselors," in

Barber, T., et.al., *Biofeedback and Self-Control 1970*, (Chicago: Aldine-Atherton, 1971).

Miller, R. B.: "Task Taxonomy: Science or Technology?" *Ergonomics*, 1967, *10:*2, 167-176.

See also the Readings for Chapter 7, Analyzing Tasks, Objectives, and Learner Characteristics.

TASK DESCRIPTION CHECKLIST

Steps in Describing a Task

1. If you are an expert in performing the task, go directly to no. 2. If you are not an expert, learn how the task is performed.

2. Break the task down into subtasks using action verbs such as operate, decide, ask, lift, etc.

3. Identify those subtasks which are fixed sequence (pp. 136 - 137), and describe them using flow diagrams (pp. 145 - 147).

4. Do not attempt to describe subtasks which
    a.   Involve preference, taste, or values.
    b.   Cannot be broken down into more discrete steps.

5. Describe all remaining subtasks using either a narrative form or an outline.

An Example of How One Teacher Used the Task Description Checklist

Task: Painting a Picture

1. Are you an expert?
    Yes.

2. Break the task down into subtasks:
    a.   *Select* a subject.
    b.   *Select* media: oil on canvas.
    c.   *Mount* canvas.
    d.   *Prepare* studio.
    e.   *Sketch* subject on paper.
    f.   *Select* sketch to be painted.
    g.   *Compose.*
    h.   *Sketch* on canvas.
    i.   *Prepare* canvas.
    j.   *Prepare* pallet.
    k.   *Mix* paints.
    l.   *Decide* on treatment and paint.
    m.   *Build* up painting by layers.
    n.   *Allow* painting to dry.
    o.   *Varnish* canvas.
    p.   *Frame.*

3.   Identify fixed sequence subtasks and organize them into a flow diagram.
>   Mount canvas.
>   Varnish canvas.
>   Frame.

4.   Do not attempt to describe tasks which
>   a.   Involve preference or taste or values:
>>   Select subject.
>>   Select media.
>>   Select sketch to be painted.
>>   Decide on treatment and paint initial sketch.
>   b.   Cannot be broken down into more discrete steps:
>>   Allow painting to dry.

5.   Describe all remaining subtasks using narrative form or an outline.
>   Outline all of the following:
>>   Prepare studio.
>>   Sketch subject on paper.
>>   Select sketch to be painted.
>>   Compose.
>>   Sketch on canvas.
>>   Prepare pallet.
>>   Build up painting by layers.

POSTTEST

	T	F
1. If the learning system desginer has written carefully developed behavioral objectives, a task description is unnecessary.	____	____
2. Variable sequence tasks are generally more complex than fixed sequence tasks.	____	____
3. Fixed sequence tasks may be thought of as being algorithmic.	____	____
4. If a designer already knows how a task is performed, he need not do a task description.	____	____
5. Technical manuals are probably the best single source of information for the task description.	____	____
6. The task description helps the learning system designer insure that unnecessary information will not be included in the final product.	____	____
7. Task descriptions are of little help when it comes to the question of types of learning involved in a task.	____	____
8. Shaping the behavior of a pigeon in a Skinner box is probably too complex a task to be described with a standard flow diagram.	____	____
9. Many seemingly simple tasks are quite difficult to describe in detail.	____	____

10. There are no very adequate criteria for evaluating a task
    description once written.   ____   ____

List the four types of information normally included in a description of an
action task:

11. _____

12. _____

13. _____

14. _____

How are the following four symbols used in a task description?

15. _____

16. _____

17. _____

18. _____

    a. Action or operation
    b. Decision
    c. Connector
    d. Beginning or end

You have been asked to design a series of training programs for a nationally known
manufacturer of children's furniture, Playrooms, Inc. The programs are described on
the left. Decide whether or not a task description would probably be helpful and
which type you believe would be preferable and check your answer.

	Flow Diagram	Narrative or Outline	No Task Description
19. Develop a program to help salesmen convince retailers to stock more furniture made by Playrooms, Inc.			
20. Develop a program to train apprentice lathe operators to turn table legs.			
21. Develop a program to train foremen to decide how to minimize machine down time and maximize use of manpower and production.			
22. Develop a new advertising theme and slogans.			

Answers to this posttest can be found on page 335.

OVERVIEW OF LEARNING SYSTEM DESIGN • REC
OGNIZING WELL-FORMULATED OBJECTIVES •
DERIVING AND WRITING LEARNING OBJECTIVES
• EVALUATING LEARNING SYSTEMS • TASK DE
SCRIPTIONS•**TYPES OF LEARNING** • ANALYZING
TASKS, OBJECTIVES, AND LEARNER CHARAC
TERISTICS • GENERAL PRINCIPLES OF LEARNING
AND MOTIVATION • THE LEARNING AND TEACH
ING OF CONCEPTS AND PRINCIPLES •THE LEARN
ING AND TEACHING OF PROBLEM SOLVING •
PERCEPTUAL-MOTOR SKILLS • THE SYSTEM
APPROACH TO INSTRUCTION • OVERVIEW OF
LEARNING SYSTEM DESIGN • RECOGNIZING
WELL-FORMULATED OBJECTIVES • DERIVING
AND WRITING LEARNING OBJECTIVES • EVALUAT
ING LEARNING SYSTEMS •TASK DESCRIPTIONS •
TYPES OF LEARNING ANALYZING TASKS, OBJEC
TIVES, AND LEARNER CHARACTERISTICS • GEN
ERAL PRINCIPLES OF LEARNING AND MOTIVA
TION • THE LEARNING AND TEACHING OF CON
CEPTS AND PRINCIPLES • THE LEARNING AND
TEACHING OF PROBLEM SOLVING • PERCEPTUAL-
MOTOR SKILLS • THE SYSTEM APPROACH TO
INSTRUCTION • OVERVIEW OF LEARNING SYS
TEM DESIGN•RECOGNIZING WELL-FORMULATED
OBJECTIVES•DERIVING AND WRITING LEARNING
OBJECTIVES • EVALUATING LEARNING SYSTEMS
• TASK DESCRIPTIONS•**TYPES OF LEARNING** •
ANALYZING TASKS, OBJECTIVES, AND LEARNER

6

CHAPTER OBJECTIVES

- Given a list of six types of learning, select the four types to be discussed in greater detail in subsequent chapters.

- Given descriptions of six types of learning, match the description with the type name.

- Given a series of statements about types of learning, discriminate those that are true from those that are false.

- Given a series of statements, recognize which statements apply to classical conditioning and which apply to operant conditioning.

INTRODUCTION

One of the most obvious things about learning something new is that it changes our behavior. It is therefore convenient to talk about learning in these terms. We have referred to this in previous chapters as terminal behavior. Consider the following list of different behavioral outcomes of learning:

To spell the word *compensate*
To define the word *compensate*
To sew a zipper in a dress
To write a theme
To drive an automobile
To calculate a square root
To hate Shakespeare
To love Shakespeare
To name the characters in *Hamlet*
To be less aggressive
To be more thoughtful
To play the piano
To swim across the pool
To get along with others

As you review these different outcomes of learning, ask yourself whether or not the indicated behaviors seem to reflect a common underlying process. When a child learns to swim, is that the same process as learning to get along with other children, or are essentially different processes involved? In other words, is there only one kind of learning, or are there different types?

Another way of looking at this problem is through an analogy. Consider a concept like temperature, which is essentially unitary. No matter how we go about measuring temperature, the measures will be highly correlated, because one underlying process in involved. We can measure temperature in several different ways but all yield basically the same results. Now, is this true of learning?

The answer is no. We can, and do, measure learning in different ways, but the measures are not all highly correlated. Indeed, some measures of learning are very poorly correlated with one another. The reason for this may be that the measures of learning are just not very good, or that when we measure learning we are not always measuring the same thing since there are, in fact, different kinds of learning.

Think for a minute about the typical classroom learning situation. What kinds of measures can a teacher take to estimate the amount his students have learned?

FRAME 6.1

There is another piece of evidence to suggest that learning is not of a single type. Ways to improve learning seem to be different depending on the desired outcome. A good golf coach uses some principles that are not necessarily very relevant to a psychologist trying to help a child learn to be less aggressive. Both are trying to help another person learn something, but the methods are different. There are some psychologists who would claim that underlying learning processes (and even the principles) are essentially the same. Our position is that learning is not unitary, and that there are several different types of learning. This is a lesson about some of the types of learning.

WHAT IS LEARNING?

The word learning commonly evokes memories of teachers, classrooms, and schools. For most of us, this is the setting in which learning occurs. In reality, any view which restricts learning to such formal settings as these is far too narrow. Learning begins at birth and ends at death; it is one of the most pervasive phenomena to be observed on earth. Indeed, the capacity to learn is perhaps one of the most distinguishing characteristics of animal life. From amoeba to man, animals learn. When they cease to learn, animals are, for all intents and purposes, either dead or vegetating.

FEEDBACK:

6.1   Time it takes to learn; number of errors on tests; items correct on tests; retention of items learned over a given period of time. (The reader may be able to think of other appropriate examples.)

People learn under a wide range of conditions and circumstances. We learn more or less continuously: at home, on the street, at the office or factory, and in the classroom. This learning often takes place under the most casual and unplanned conditions; at other times, it occurs in environments especially structured to bring learning about.

In normal, daily experience, the consequences of our behavior are unintentional, but teach us things. If we fail to hold the nail properly, we smash a finger. If we watch the milk on the stove closely and test it occasionally, we will not scald it. If the baby places his finger across the light socket, he receives a shock. The contingencies between a response and its consequences under such circumstances as these are fortuitous. No one has purposely arranged the environment so as to elicit the desired behaviors and then to reward or punish them. Under such circumstances as these, "nature" is often the teacher in the sense that it punishes or rewards everyday behavior and thereby determines what is learned.

When we speak of designing a learning system, we mean that the contingencies are not accidental. Someone—in the parlance of this book, a learning system designer— has structured the conditions to elicit desired behaviors along with what is being learned. In the design of a learning system, we are concerned with the structure and organization of the environment to bring about learning in an optimal way.

If we are to structure efficient learning systems, it is obvious that we must know what learning is and how to bring it about. Despite the fact that learning, as we have already noted, makes a tremendous contribution to our everyday life, the conditions under which we learn best are not readily apparent. In our daily life, we exercise almost no control over the learning process whatever. We rely on common sense to direct the process, and while it often works, there are times when our common sense fails us.

More often than not, relying on common sense has drawbacks. The teacher scores his examinations, returns them days or weeks after the test, and assumes the system works because his students appear to learn. Why they have learned is not absolutely clear, but at some level, he judges that they have learned something and he therefore accepts the system. Because he has not tested in a controlled way the consequences of immediate versus delayed knowledge of examination results for the students, he cannot know that delayed knowledge of results are far less effective. The same can be said of a whole host of variables having to do with the conditions of practice, the arrangement or sequencing of learning, the rewards or punishment which follow behavior, and so on. We seldom exert the necessary controls in everyday life needed to establish the most efficient methods of bringing learning about.

You are a learning system designer. One day, while walking along the street with your son and his dog, the dog runs across the street to investigate a street lamp. Your son calls to the dog but it refuses to come to him. He calls again— now somewhat angry—and the dog looks at him. After a number of angry, insistent calls from your son, the dog slowly slinks across the street and very reluctantly approaches the boy. When the boy gets hold of his collar, he spanks the dog. What might you say to your son **about the effects of reward and punishment on learning?**

One of the problems in this regard is that we can never observe learning directly. Learning is an intervening variable, i.e., it intervenes between something that happens in the world and the subsequent behavior of the learner. We must infer learning by observing a learner's behavior. Unfortunately, it is not always easy to tell whether or not learning has occurred, and it is even more difficult to know how much learning has taken place. Since this is the case, we are often wrong in our common sense assumptions about how learning occurs. If we could actually see the learning rise and fall like water in a glass, we might rapidly master the variables controlling it. But since that is impossible, we must adopt a different strategy. The strategy involves the careful control and observation of behavior and the conducting of experiments to test hypotheses about it. The results of such studies as these have a great deal to say about how one should design a learning system.

Since learning is not something directly seen or felt or heard, we can only know it has taken place by observing behavior. This implies that after learning, some change in behavior will have occurred. But this situation is complicated by the fact that not all changes in behavior are the result of learning. Behavior changes for reasons other than learning. Our behavior is different when we are sleepy or fatigued; we become less alert, "all thumbs" as the saying goes. Drugs frequently cause a marked change in behavior. Drivers are warned not to take barbiturates or tranquilizers. A great deal of change in behavior is directly attributable to growth or maturation. Children seem not to have to learn to creep, for example; it just happens naturally as a consequence of the growing process.

This being the case, how are we to know when a change in behavior is attributable to learning? There are several theories about this but it can

FEEDBACK:
6.2 "Son," you might say, "You are not using your common sense. You are punishing your dog for obeying you! Give him a big hug and lots of praise instead."
(Your answer may be somewhat different from this one.)

generally be said that learned changes in behavior are brought about through practice or experience. Furthermore, it is often observed that these changes are relatively permanent. Learning systems have as their major, overall objective the modification of student behavior through practice and experience.

DEFINITION:
THE COMPLETE DEFINITION OF LEARNING EM-
PHASIZES THE NOTION OF A RELATIVELY PERM-
ANENT CHANGE IN BEHAVIOR AS A FUNCTION
OF PRACTICE OR EXPERIENCE.

F
R
A
M
E

6.3

We know a man has learned something because his behavior _____.

But all _____ in behavior is *not* due to learning.

IN WHAT WAYS DOES BEHAVIOR CHANGE WITH LEARNING?

This definition of learning emphasizes a change of behavior. But we might well ask, what is the nature of that change? There are, in fact, a number of ways in which behavior changes as learning proceeds. Let us consider some of these.

First of all, as we learn, stimuli frequently acquire new meanings. In other words, as learning proceeds, we become more sensitive to stimuli which in the early stages of learning have little, if any, meaning for us. The many sounds of an automobile engine provide important clues to the experienced driver which are often overlooked by the beginner. In effect, our perceptions are enriched as stimuli acquire new and different meanings. At the outset, milk is just something to drink, but gradually, the stimulus of milk comes to have a set of related connotations: cows, cheese, dairies, Pasteur, homogenized. As this process of enrichment continues, we come to respond to milk in some subtle and complex ways. We prefer cream rather than just plain milk in our coffee and write checks to dairies.

A second kind of behavioral modification that occurs as learning progresses is that extraneous (and often interfering) factors are eliminated.

FEEDBACK:
6.3   1   changes
       2   change

We are sometimes tense and embarrassed when we begin to learn, but these interfering responses gradually fall by the wayside. In skills training, useless motions are gradually eliminated.

Another way in which extraneous factors are eliminated is through **stimulus redintegration.** This occurs when a smaller part of the total stimulus is needed for us to make a response. Have you ever noticed, for example, how difficult it is to recognize a new acquaintance, if he is not wearing his glasses, or if he has grown a beard or if he is dressed differently? Yet, when you know a person well (that is, as your learning about him proceeds) you can recognize him from a good distance—even though he is walking away from you. This points up the fact that a response (like recalling a person's correct name) requires only a part of the total original stimulus once the connection is well learned.

Behavior also changes with learning when certain stimuli become substitutes for others. At first, it may be necessary to explain to a child in detail what is desired of him, but later, a simple look can communicate the entire message.

When behavior becomes better integrated and more autonomous, change is again indicated. In the learning of a complex skill, the skill is eventually executed more smoothly—the independent bits of behavior are tied together in a more closely integrated fashion. It becomes autonomous in the sense that we can often carry on other activities simultaneously. The new driver, for example, must concentrate all of his attention and energy on the task at hand; the skilled driver can carry on a conversation, and even fasten his seat belt while driving, although it is not recommended, of course.

The student should not be under the impression that these different ways behavior changes are necessarily independent of one another. They are all interrelated. One of the reasons behavior becomes better integrated with learning, for example, is that useless false bits of behavior are gradually eliminated.

Place the correct letter in the blanks after the phrases below:

F
R
A
M
E

6.4

    a.   Stimuli acquire new meanings.

    b.   Extraneous and interfering factors are eliminated.

    c.   Some stimuli come to substitute for others.

    d   Behavior is better integrated.

1. The beginner at poker concentrates on the cards; but he gradually   ( )
learns to watch both the cards and the behavior (facial expressions)
of his adversaries.

2. A teacher habitually closes her books before dismissing class and   ( )
students learn to leave the room as she closes the book.

(continued on next page)

3. A student in public speaking stops stammering and looking at his feet.   ( )

4. The worker on an assembly line puts together a complex piece of electronic equipment all the time thinking about his problems with his mother-in-law.   ( )

FOUR TYPES OF LEARNING

A number of different psychologists and educators have tried to classify types of learning. In this section, we will discuss some of these classifications.

Several years ago in a book called, **The Conditions of Learning**, Robert M. Gagné proposed a hierarchical set which included eight different types of learning. Gagné considered the types hierarchical in the sense that they were arranged in a series and all of the lower types contributed to and were included within the higher types. His list included the following eight types arranged in order of their complexity:

1. Signal learning (classical conditioning)
2. Stimulus-Response learning (operant conditioning)
3. Chaining (stimulus-response chains)
4. Verbal association (also rote learning)
5. Multiple discrimination
6. Concept learning
7. Principle learning
8. Problem solving

If we ignore for a moment the hierarchical aspect of this system, most of what commonly goes on in the classroom falls under the last three types, namely, concept learning, principle learning, and problem solving. In addition, the learning system designer must often deal with a type of learning which Gagné does not include as a separate type in his hierarchy, namely, perceptual-motor skills, such as those involved in athletics, vocational, and military training. In our discussion, we will focus on these four types: concept learning, principle learning, problem solving, and learning of perceptual-motor skills. An additional section on classical and operant conditioning will be included in this chapter only. Before turning to a discussion of these two types of learning, let's briefly look at the four types that will be taken up in greater detail in Chapters 9 - 11.

FEEDBACK:
6.4   a   b
       c   d

Place the correct letter (a or b) in the table head:

1. ( )

Classical conditioning
Operant conditioning

2. ( )

Concept learning
Principle learning
Problem solving
Perceptual-Motor skills

a. Sufficiently complex to require separate chapters
b. Lower in the hierarchy of types and of more theoretical interest

CONCEPTS

The word **concept** is a part of our everyday vocabulary. The dictionary defines the term as "an abstract idea generalized from particular instances." Although some psychologists might be loathe to accept this more or less popular definition, the fact of the matter is, it is a relatively good first approximation. Some psychologists treat concepts as if they existed "out there" as stimuli; some treat concepts as "ideas" inside of the student. One psychologist, for example, says a concept is "a class of stimuli which have common characteristics." Another psychologist of a more cognitive bent has defined concepts as "properties of organismic experience—more particularly they are abstracted and often cognitively structured classes of 'mental experiences' learned by organisms in their life histories." In either case, concepts are abstractions from our experience of the world. They do not refer to particular events, but to some abstract property which cuts across diverse events. If it were not for the fact that men and animals form concepts, it would be extremely difficult to deal with the complexity of stimuli which we encounter in everyday life. Concepts help us organize and classify experience.

Here are some examples of concepts:

Round	Lake
Red	Tort
Up	Beside
Love	Dog
Building	Concept
Aggression	Deductive
Democracy	Tourist
Atom	Many
Few	Average

FEEDBACK:
6.5   1   b
       2   a

Obviously, a large part of what we learn in school consists of concepts. When we have learned a concept, we are able to respond to the abstract properties of a series of objects or events, and not merely to their unique characteristics. Red is red, whether we are talking about sweaters, automobiles, houses, or toy trains. Once we have learned the concept of a building, we are able to correctly classify a wide range of structures from the Empire State Building to a local two-story bank building.

Lower animals can and do learn concepts, but they cannot name them. Thus, although an animal may be able to respond consistently to the concept of red, it cannot name it. Once humans have learned a concept, they can often name it as well. Our capacity to verbalize also enables us to talk about a concept, to describe its attributes and properties. Another way in which we demonstrate that we have learned a concept is by using other concepts to describe it. Finally, once we have learned a concept, we can correctly identify instances of it. Even lower animals are able to do this, although they must indicate that they can select correct instances of the concept nonverbally, for example, by the choices they make between alleys in a maze or doors in a puzzle box.

One of the types of learning we shall have more to say about in Chapter 9 is concept learning. At that time, we will develop some general principles for learning and teaching concepts.

FRAME 6.6

Check the items below which are concepts:

The Queen Mary	_____
Automobile	_____
Columbus	_____
Few	_____

PRINCIPLES

Concepts help us to classify diverse phenomena; principles enable us to predict, explain, and control phenomena. There are different kinds of principles: some are empirically rooted in scientific discovery; others are matters of common agreement or definition. Regardless of their origin, principles state relationships between two or more concepts. In general, principles can be converted into "if-then" statements.

FEEDBACK:
6.6 Automobile
Few
(The Queen Mary and Columbus are a specific object and person, not a class.)

Let's take a simple example of a principle and try to show how it may be used to predict, explain, and control phenomena. Take the following principle: My neighbor's dog barks when strangers are nearby. This statement obviously contains a number of concepts: neighbor, dog, bark, strangers, nearby. These concepts have been organized together in a particular relationship which, as we have already observed, can be converted into an "if-then" statement: If strangers are nearby, my neighbor's dog barks. The concepts might have been organized differently as indicated in the following principle: The stranger's dog barks at my nearby neighbors. Now, compare the two sentences we have just analyzed and note how the syntax changes their meaning.

- The stranger's dog barks at my nearby neighbors.
- My neighbor's dog barks at nearby strangers.

Principles organize concepts in particular ways and the meaning of the principle is partially determined by the grammatical structure of the sentence.

Rearrange the concepts contained in the following principle to form a new principle:

Defective airplanes are dangerous for pilots

F
R
A
M
E

6.7

The statement, my neighbor's dog barks when strangers are nearby, enables you to both predict and explain. If you are staying at your neighbor's house and you hear his dog bark, you can explain the fact by invoking the principle: the dog is barking because a stranger is nearby. On the other hand, you can predict that if a stranger is approaching, the dog will bark. Knowing these facts, you can exercise some control over the situation by keeping strangers away, for example, or putting the dog in the basement when strangers are nearby. Thus, prediction, explanation, and control are all interrelated.

Many of the principles which students learn are developed as a consequence of scientific observation and research. Psychologists have observed that the strength of behavior increases if it is positively reinforced (or in more popular jargon, rewarded). This observation became known

---

FEEDBACK:

6.7 Defective pilots are dangerous for airplanes. (Note how the arrangement of the concepts has changed the meaning.)

as the **principle of reinforcement.** Physicists have developed the principle: force equals mass times acceleration. Many principles are not empirical, but are simply a matter of definition. For example, there is nothing in nature to demand that every state must be represented by two senators or that a two-thirds vote is required to override a presidential veto; these principles are true only by definition, i.e., because people have decided they are true.

When a student has learned a principle, he can generally do more than simply state the principle. Indeed, the fact that he can state the principle is not very good evidence that he really knows the principle; he may only have memorized it by rote. If a student has really learned a principle, he should be able to make some predictions from it and explain appropriate events using the principle. This topic will be treated in greater detail in Chapter 9.

PROBLEM SOLVING

Frequently, we encounter situations in life for which no appropriate response is immediately available to us. These are called **problem situations.** Here are some examples of problem situations:

- A man sells two radios at $100 each. On one he makes a profit of 25 percent; on the other he loses 25 percent on cost. Did he gain or lose on the whole transaction?

- An engineer wishes to redesign a spaceship so that it will not require a thick permanent heat shield to protect astronauts.

- A performer asks his audience for a three-digit number and then correctly predicts the sum of this number and four other three-digit numbers yet to be supplied (two by the audience and two by the performer). How does he do it?

- A graduate student tries to decide whether to buy or rent a house in the university community in which he will be living for two years.

- A Russian spy wonders if there isn't some better way to collect information from the CIA than by visiting it personally.

In each of these cases, someone is trying to discover a solution to a problem. In order to solve the problem, he will have to invoke concepts and principles learned in other contexts. Furthermore, after solving the problem he will, in all probability, have learned something about how to approach and solve similiar, but not necessarily identical, problems. When a student learns to solve problems he integrates previously learned knowledge together into new and higher order principles. For this reason, it should be treated as a type of learning which goes beyond the learning of principles, per se.

Problem solving is the most advanced type of learning. Frequently, it is treated as discovery learning because there is a major element of discovery involved in it. In problem solving, the student develops the higher order principle(s) himself and is not guided directly to the solution as is frequently the case in principle learning. The process of discovery is more or less orderly and has been extensively studied. Although various psychologists have used somewhat different terms to describe problem-solving stages, generally they agree that the student begins by preparing for the problem (organizing and understanding it); he then analyzes and carries out a plan and afterwards goes on to test and verify the appropriateness of the action.

PERCEPTUAL-MOTOR SKILLS

In Chapter 11, we define perceptual-motor skills as coordinated muscular movements employed to successfully complete a desired act or task. The word **perceptual** refers to a complex process. Basically, we depend on our senses for knowledge about the world. The senses transmit what might be thought of as unprocessed data to the central nervous system. We call this raw data a **stimulus** or **stimuli** (plural). As a result of learning, our raw impressions (the unprocessed data) of the world are constantly being modified. For instance, as skilled drivers, we perceive a parking place differently from the way we did as children, although it might be considered the same set of stimuli to both the adult and the child. We are able to judge its size and the appropriateness of using a space better than a child. Perceptions provide the information necessary to coordinate. motor movements, giving rise to the concept of **perceptual-motor skills.** Of course, we aren't necessarily aware of all of the information being used by our bodies when we perform a perceptual-motor skill. The high diver and the pole-vaulter are processing perceptual information without necessarily being conscious of this fact.

One of the characteristics of the industrial revolution, which began several hundred years ago, is a rapid increase in technological development. Technology is not confined to the factory, however, and all around us we are daily confronted with a bewildering array of machines. Some of these machines are designed to make our lives easier by doing work for us.

Walk around your house or apartment and take a look at some of the gadgets there: power mowers, dishwashers, electric coffee pots, frying pans, toasters, vacuum cleaners, radios, tape recorders, washing machines, and clothes dryers. Technology has also resulted in a host of mechanical things to make life more pleasurable or efficient outside of the home: automobiles, snowmobiles, bicycles, camping equipment, skis, tennis rackets, scuba diving outfits, private airplanes, equipment for arts and crafts, and so on.

It would be literally impossible to list even a small fraction of the gadgets, from typewriters to computers, which are to be found in offices, factories, scientific laboratories, schools, and colleges across the country. Although the designers of all these mechanical things are beginning to pay more and more attention to making these as foolproof and easy to operate as possible, the fact of the matter is people still must develop the perceptual-motor skills necessary to use these gadgets.

Paralleling the rise of technology, there has been a steadily increasing pressure on the society to provide the trained people to run the machines. Rather than replacing man, machines seem to displace them to tasks demanding higher and higher degrees of skill. Many vocational skills are primarily perceptual-motor.

In recent years there has also been an increase in leisure time, and that time is frequently used to improve perceptual-motor skills involved in such activities as golf, sailing, painting, and so on.

TWO ADDITIONAL TYPES OF LEARNING

The four types of learning just discussed will all be developed in greater detail. But now, let's consider two additional types of learning which will not be covered beyond this chapter.

CLASSICAL CONDITIONING

As we have already said, there are two different kinds of conditioning: **classical** and **operant**. Classical conditioning is most closely identified with the great Russian physiologist, Ivan Pavlov. Pavlov was particularly interested in the digestive processes, and he developed a number of techniques for measuring gastric secretion. Food was used since it stimulates such secretion naturally. When a stimulus (food) invariably elicits a particular response (salivation) without any prior training, it is called a reflex. Pavlov was studying this reflex and he observed that when a neutral stimulus, such as a bell or metronome or the sound of the experimenter coming into a room, was closely and consistently paired with the presentation of food, dogs learned to salivate. Thus, the neutral stimulus came to substitute for the originally effective stimulus. Today, we show this paradigm in the following way. The **neutral stimulus** or bell is called the **conditioned stimulus**. The **effective stimulus**, or food in this case, is called an **unconditioned stimulus**. Once the response of salivation is learned to the sound of the bell, it is called a **conditioned response**.

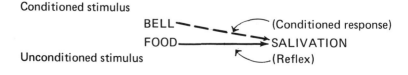

Conditioned stimulus

BELL — — — (Conditioned response)
FOOD————→SALIVATION

Unconditioned stimulus (Reflex)

Here is a second example of classical conditioning. A bright light in the eye causes the pupil to close. Pair a bright light with a neutral stimulus, such as a buzzer. In the following paradigm, the terms have been left blank. Fill in the terms using the example of the light and the pupil.

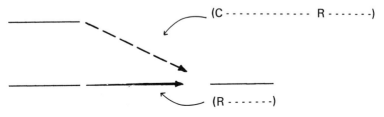

Pavlov actually discovered conditioning about the turn of the century and spent the next several decades of his life studying the process. We don't have time to consider all of the ways in which he manipulated this basic situation. It is enough to observe that he studied the conditioned reflex exhaustively and that psychologists owe him an enormous debt for his insight and methodological sophistication. Today we call this type of conditioning, classical or sometimes respondent conditioning.

OPERANT CONDITIONING

At about the same time that Pavlov discovered the conditioned reflex, an American psychologist by the name of Edward Lee Thorndike was studying a different kind of conditioning which we now call operant conditioning. Basically, operant conditioning involves strengthening a particular response by reinforcing it. Thorndike studied cats in a puzzle box. To escape from the puzzle box, a cat had to learn to pull a string. When the cat pulled the string and escaped, he was reinforced by getting a piece of fish. Some people might say rewarded with fish, rather than reinforced, but today psychologists prefer to use the word reinforcement (although it has a rather technical definition which need not concern us here). The significant point is that this model of conditioning is different from the one identified with Pavlov. Let's take a look at the paradigm for operant conditioning.

FEEDBACK:

6.8   Buzzer   (Conditioned response)

       Light   Pupil
       (Reflex)

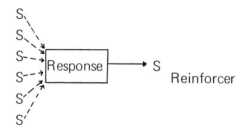

In operant conditioning, the response is emitted. No particular stimulus necessarily elicits it; it occurs. Sometimes, teachers go to great pains to get the response to occur by providing guidance or modeling the desired behavior. Sometimes the response is shaped using the process we described in Chapter 5 on Task Descriptions. Once the response occurs, it is followed by some reinforcer such as the word, "good," or objects such as food or money. Once reinforced, the response is strengthened and its probability of occurrence in that particular stimulus complex increases.

F
R
A
M
E

6.9

Try drawing an operant paradigm for the following situation.

> Everytime a boy's dog walks into the kitchen at
> suppertime, the boy gives him some of his meat.

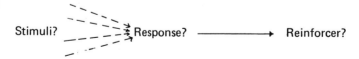

Stimuli?   Response? ⟶ Reinforcer?

Now it will pay to consider some of the ways in which these two kinds of conditioning are different from one another.

First of all, the two paradigms are different. In classical conditioning a particular stimulus elicits the response. Food elicits the response of salivation, just as the conditioned stimulus comes to elicit salivation. In operant conditioning there is no eliciting stimulus. The response in operant conditioning is said to be emitted. Look at the diagram. Notice that the arrows in classical conditioning go from specific stimuli,

---

FEEDBACK:

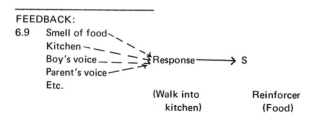

6.9   Smell of food
Kitchen
Boy's voice   Response ⟶ S
Parent's voice
Etc.

(Walk into   Reinforcer
kitchen)   (Food)

called the unconditioned stimulus and conditioned stimulus, directly to a particular response. In operant conditioning, there is no such direct connection. In fact, we may not know what stimulus or stimuli led the cat to pull the string and escape from the box.

Second, in classical conditioning, one stimulus comes to substitute for another. The conditioned stimulus (a bell) replaces the unconditioned stimulus (the food). In operant conditioning, there is no stimulus substitution of this kind. Indeed, we may not know what stimulus is controlling the behavior of the cat.

Third, using operant conditioning, the cat's behavior is strengthened by reinforcement. We can identify this reinforcer and know that it always follows the response it strengthens. In the case of the cat, the reinforcer is fish. Escape may also be a reinforcer. They both follow the response of pulling the string. In our example of classical conditioning, food might be considered a reinforcer, but it doesn't follow the learned response. It precedes it. Furthermore, unconditioned stimuli, in general, do not strengthen responses—they elicit them. Another example of an unconditioned stimulus is a bright light in the eye which elicits the response of closing the pupil. Does a bright light in this case act in the same way as fish for the cat? Probably not.

Fourth and last, many psychologists believe that classical and operant conditioning affect entirely different parts of the nervous system. While we do not wish to spend too much time on this question, it is important to at least recognize this fact because both types of conditioning may be going on in the typical classroom. Most of us are familiar with the somatic nervous system which controls so-called voluntary activity and thinking. There is a second system which is concerned primarily with the glands of our body; it controls most of our reflexes and is involved when we are afraid, anxious, or otherwise emotionally disturbed. There are a number of psychologists who say that operant conditioning is basic to what we would call classroom learning and skills learning; in fact, most of the kinds of learning normally taught to a child. But classical conditioning is the way we learn emotional things—such as being afraid of the dark or to hate school. Whatever the case, these two kinds of conditioning are sometimes thought of as separate types of learning, basic to all others.

SOME CONCLUDING REMARKS

Before concluding this overview of the types of learning, let's examine again the two reasons for breaking learning down into separate types.

First, it does not appear to be a genuinely unitary concept. As we have already stated, the amount of learning can be measured in a wide variety of ways—many of which are not highly correlated. For example, it is possible to measure classical conditioning by the magnitude of a reflex or its latency, but these measures are not necessarily highly correlated. Equally important is the fact that a measure like rate of responding may be very useful for one type of learning, i.e., operant conditioning, but less useful for another type such as classical conditioning. Thus, for different types of learning, different measures are often appropriate. To take a more ordinary example, consider a skill like golf and the learning of a concept. In golf, one measure of learning to drive might be the distance a ball travels in a specific direction, but in concept learning, we might wish to determine whether learning has occurred by asking the student to correctly identify instances that illustrate a concept or to define a concept. For each type of learning the measures often differ, and where it is possible to take two or more measures, they are frequently not highly correlated.

The second reason for talking about different types of learning is that the principles involved in teaching them often vary. By principles, we mean the rules or conditions that promote learning.

Consider the difference between the two types of conditioning which we have just been studying as a way of illustrating this point. One principle to promote or encourage operant conditioning is this: the reinforcer should follow the learned response as closely in time as possible. When the cat pulls the string and escapes from the box, fish should be available immediately. A principle of classical conditioning is this: the conditioned stimulus should precede the unconditioned stimulus by a very short interval of time. The bell should sound just before the dog receives the food powder. Since the reinforcer does not follow the learned response, the principle which is essential to operant conditioning is not applicable in classical conditioning. Two different principles are involved for the two types of learning.

In this unit, we have discussed the fact that there are different types of learning and some of the principles important to them. In subsequent units, we will consider still other types of learning and the principles that promote them. We will also further discuss concept learning, principle learning, perceptual-motor skills learning, and problem solving in much greater detail and develop their governing principles.

See if you can associate the correct term with the paradigm shown by placing the appropriate letter in the boxes below.

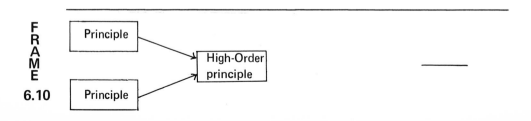

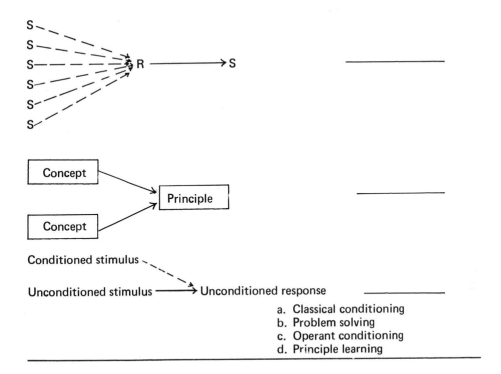

a. Classical conditioning
b. Problem solving
c. Operant conditioning
d. Principle learning

SUMMARY

Learning is defined as a change of behavior resulting from practice or experience. Some ways in which learning changes behavior are: stimuli acquire new meanings; new responses are learned to stimuli; nonessentials are eliminated; and behavior becomes better integrated and more autonomous. There are different types of learning, but no general agreement among psychologists and educators as to the categories. Six types are described: classical and operant conditioning, concept learning, the learning of principles, problem solving, and perceptual-motor skills. Although there is some disagreement over the classification of learning, distinguishing among the various types is important for learning system design because different principles seem to be involved in teaching them.

SUGGESTED READINGS

DeCecco, J.P.: *The Psychology of Learning and Instruction: Educational Psychology,* (New Jersey: Prentice-Hall, Inc., 1968).

FEEDBACK:
6.10   b   d
          c   a

Desse, J. & Hulse, S.: *The Psychology of Learning,* (New York: McGraw-Hill Book Co., 1967).

Gagné R. M.: *The Conditions of Learning,* (2nd ed.), (New York: Holt, Rinehart & Winston, 1970).

Kimble, A.: *Hilgard and Marquis' Conditioning and Learning,* (Rev. ed.), (New York: Appleton-Century-Crofts, Inc., 1961).

Melton, A.W.: *Categories of Human Learning,* (New York: Academic Press, 1964).

Skinner, B. F.: *Science and Human Behavior,* (New York: The Free Press, 1965).

POSTTEST

	T	F
1. Whenever behavior changes, it is evidence that learning has occurred.	___	___
2. There is little disagreement regarding the different types of learning.	___	___
3. Learning is essentially a unitary concept—i.e., no matter how it is measured, the outcomes are highly correlated.	___	___
4. One reason for asserting there is more than one type of learning is that the principles for teaching students different kinds of behaviors are not the same.	___	___

Decide which of the following characteristics apply to operant conditioning and which apply to classical conditioning. Put a check in the correct column.

	Operant conditioning	Classical conditioning
5. The reinforcer follows the learned response.	_____	_____
6. One stimulus comes to substitute for another.	_____	_____
7. The response is emitted.	_____	_____
8. Involved in the learning of "emotional" responses.	_____	_____
9. As learning proceeds, stimuli often tend to acquire new meaning.	_____	_____

10. From the following list of types of learning, check the ones that will be discussed in subsequent chapters.

Concept learning _____

Principle learning _____

Problem solving _____

Operant conditioning _____

Classical conditioning _____

Perceptual-Motor skills _____

The major type of learning involved in each of the following examples is:

11. A student must learn to recognize an oak leaf. _____   a. Principle learning

12. A dog learns to salivate to the sound of a bell. _____   b. Perceptual-Motor skill

13. A child has difficulty with her multiplication _____   c. Problem solving
    tables, particularly her 9s. She is told "to
    subtract 1 from the number she is multiplying   d. Operant conditioning
    by nine to get the first digit in the answer and
    then to add enough to the first digit to equal   e. Concept learning
    nine to get the second digit." After a few ex-
    amples and some practice, she is able to do her   f. Classical conditioning
    9s without error.

14. A pigeon learns to peck a disc to obtain food. _____

15. A child learns to ride a bicycle. _____

16. Troubled by a clogged tube from his gas tank _____
    to his carburetor, the owner of an automobile
    discovers that he can blow the dirt out of it
    by using a tire pump.

Answers to this posttest can be found on page 336.

OVERVIEW OF LEARNING SYSTEM DESIGN • REC
OGNIZING WELL-FORMULATED OBJECTIVES •
DERIVING AND WRITING LEARNING OBJECTIVES
• EVALUATING LEARNING SYSTEMS • TASK DE
SCRIPTIONS•TYPES OF LEARNING • **ANALYZING
TASKS, OBJECTIVES, AND LEARNER CHARAC
TERISTICS** • GENERAL PRINCIPLES OF LEARNING
AND MOTIVATION • THE LEARNING AND TEACH
ING OF CONCEPTS AND PRINCIPLES •THE LEARN
ING AND TEACHING OF PROBLEM SOLVING •
PERCEPTUAL-MOTOR SKILLS • THE SYSTEM
APPROACH TO INSTRUCTION • OVERVIEW OF
LEARNING SYSTEM DESIGN • RECOGNIZING
WELL-FORMULATED OBJECTIVES • DERIVING
AND WRITING LEARNING OBJECTIVES • EVALUAT
ING LEARNING SYSTEMS •TASK DESCRIPTIONS •
TYPES OF LEARNING • **ANALYZING TASKS, OBJEC
TIVES, AND LEARNER CHARACTERISTICS** • GEN
ERAL PRINCIPLES OF LEARNING AND MOTIVA
TION • THE LEARNING AND TEACHING OF CON
CEPTS AND PRINCIPLES • THE LEARNING AND
TEACHING OF PROBLEM SOLVING • PERCEPTUAL-
MOTOR SKILLS • THE SYSTEM APPROACH TO
INSTRUCTION • OVERVIEW OF LEARNING SYS
TEM DESIGN•RECOGNIZING WELL-FORMULATED
OBJECTIVES•DERIVING AND WRITING LEARNING
OBJECTIVES • EVALUATING LEARNING SYSTEMS
• TASK DESCRIPTIONS•TYPES OF LEARNING •
ANALYZING TASKS, OBJECTIVES, AND LEARNER

7

CHAPTER OBJECTIVES

- Given a series of examples, the student will be able to correctly label those that are task analyses and those that are task descriptions.
- Given a series of possible attributes of a task analysis, the student will be able to select the three key attributes that should be included.
- Given a series of true-false statements about the use of task analyses and individual differences among learners, the student will be able to select those that are true.

INTRODUCTION

Early in the learning system design process, the teacher specifies a set of terminal objectives or writes a task description, or does both of these. Once the terminal objectives have been defined and broken down into tasks and enabling objectives, the next step in the process is to analyze the tasks and the objectives. For convenience, we call this process task analysis, even though at times it only involves an analysis of objectives and not of a task. The task analysis involves a careful examination of the enabling objectives or task descriptions in an effort to identify those factors which will influence the final design of the learning system.

Three kinds of factors should be considered: (1) the characteristics of the learner or learners; (2) the types of learning; and (3) special conditions or constraints influencing the learning process. Unless these three factors are specified, the designer will be unable to decide how best to proceed with the presentation and organization of the material to be learned.

A task description and behaviorally stated objectives contain important clues to help the learning system designer identify task-related concepts, principles, and perceptual-motor skills which must be mastered by the learner in order for him to do the task. By helping the designer identify prerequisite concepts and principles, the analysis of the task and the objectives becomes an aid for curriculum planning. Using the objectives and the task description to perform a task analysis, the learning system designer is better able to specify the content and sequence of course materials. In addition, he will be able to identify the types of learning involved which, as we learned in the last chapter, can be used to help specify how the content of the course should be taught.

In a sense, a task description is like a road map. If we are preparing to take a trip—and want to do the job efficiently—the road map serves as a rough guide. But there are many aspects of the trip which the road map cannot and does not deal with, and we will need to analyze the trip more carefully. We may want to stop for the night in certain cities, for example, and to wire ahead for reservations. The road map cannot specify for us which cities are the best ones for us to stop in. There are too many variables involved in making such a complex decision. By using special aids, such as guide books to hotels, motels, and restaurants, the decision may be made somewhat easier. But, there is still much to be considered. Whether we plan to drive 200 or 600 miles a day will depend not only on the roads, but on the weather and our fatigue or our willingness to risk driving after dark. If there are deserts or mountains to be crossed, special preparations may be necessary. Obviously, total trip-planning must also take into account whether we are traveling in a large air-conditioned car, a Volkswagen, or whether we are on a motorcycle, a bicycle, or even on foot.

If the task description is analogous to a road map, the task analysis is more like a trip plan. The task description provides a schematic outline of how a task is performed, but it does not specify all the special constraints and conditions that will influence how the task will actually be carried out in real life, nor can the task description develop all of the concepts and principles one will have to know in order to perform the task. The task description tells how a task is performed. The task analysis deals with the question of how it shall be taught, to whom, when, and where. Once the task description or the objectives are written, a task analysis is conducted in order to answer such questions as these:

- What types of learning are involved in the objectives and/or the task?

- What entry skills do the learners already possess?

- Under what conditions will the task have to be performed or the learning demonstrated?

- What are the characteristics of the learners? Age? Sex?

This is a chapter about the task analysis and how it is performed. Just as there are vast skills differences among drivers intending to take a long distance trip, there are always differences among people in any group about to learn how to perform a new task. One of the most critical aspects of any task analysis is the evaluation of these differences among learners; therefore, we call this chapter, Analyzing Tasks, Objectives, and Learner Characteristics.

F
R
A
M
E

7.1

In a previous chapter, we dealt with task descriptions. This chapter focuses
on the task (1) _____ . Normally the task (2) _____
follows (is done after) the task (3) _____ .

THE TASK ANALYSIS

We have observed that the task description is like a schematic drawing or
map; it is a rough outline of how a task is performed. The task description does not delve into details about the learner, the types of learning
involved, or special conditions or constraints. It says nothing, for
example, about the intelligence of the learner, his age, level of maturity,
or his special abilities. The task description only hints at the kinds of
skills the learner will have to possess in order to perform the task; it does
not exhaustively analyze these and identify the kinds of learning which
are involved. Finally, the task description does not tell us whether the
task will have to be performed with or without special aids, in the tropics
or the Arctic, while wearing a full field pack or perhaps gloves, or even
underwater. Obviously, such factors as these will all bear on the kind of
learning system which ultimately gets designed. As part of the design
process, it is important to conduct a careful analysis of the task with such
factors as these in mind.

F
R
A
M
E

7.2

The task analysis is an examination of the task descriptions or a set of objectives in an effort to identify: (1) assumptions about the _____'s characteristics; (2) the _____ of learning involved; and (3) special _____
or _____ on the performance of the task.

Let us examine these three factors in greater detail.

LEARNER CHARACTERISTICS

The fact that men differ from one another along a number of dimensions
has probably never been seriously questioned. Differences in physical
prowess, age, sex, and maturity are easily discriminated and apparent to
the most casual observer. Even psychological differences in talent or

---

FEEDBACK:

7.1	1	analysis	7.2	1	learner
	2	analysis		2	types
	3	description		3	conditions . . . constraints

basic abilities are readily apparent, an observation noted by novelists, philosophers, and poets long before the emergence of scientific psychology. Some of the differences among men are hereditary; others result from their unique learning histories. Whatever the source of the differences, they have a substantial impact on the way in which learning systems are designed. Most learning system design questions can only be resolved if the characteristics of the learners are known. How a learning system is designed will always depend upon who the learners are.

ENTRY BEHAVIORS One of the ways learners differ is in their entry behaviors. Entry behaviors are the skills and learning sets which students bring with them to the learning situation. By **learning sets**, we mean prior learning available to a student for use in the new situation. If, for example, a student is to learn to solve problems in long division and he is able to recite the multiplication tables, then we refer to this capacity to recite the multiplication tables as a learning set.

It is possible to think of entry behaviors in two quite different ways. As we have just suggested, entry behaviors can be defined in terms of the skills and learning sets possessed by a student when he begins to learn a task or skill. But, it would also be possible to define entry behaviors in terms of the initial skills needed to successfully learn a new task or skill. There is often a discrepancy between the entry behaviors possessed by a student and those needed to successfully learn a new task. Therefore, two critical questions arise in connection with the learner's entry behavior. First, what does he need to know in order to enter the learning system (or what assumptions has the designer made about his prior learning)? And second, which of the assumed learning sets does the student actually possess?

The first of these questions can only be answered by carefully reviewing the things you plan to teach the learner and identifying the prerequisite knowledge he requires to successfully complete a sequence of instruction. The second question can be answered in one or two ways. It is possible to actually assess each student's level of knowledge and prscribe a course of instruction guaranteed to provide him with the necessary entry skills. This alternative is illustrated in Fig. 7.1. Once the objectives have been identified and the task described, tests are administered to establish the skills possessed by the learner (actual entry behaviors). These are compared with the entry behaviors needed for the learning system and remediation is prescribed if necessary.

An alternative is to design the system so that it is matched to the measured characteristics of a particular population. If a designer knows, for example, that most high school graduates possess the entry skills required for the learning system he is creating, he may simply establish

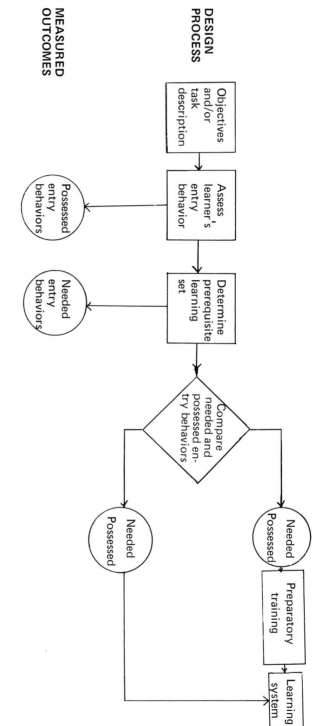

Figure 7.1 One important function of the task analysis is to help the learning system designer develop a training strategy, taking into account differences in skills possessed by a learner and those needed to successfully enter the system and negotiate it.

high school graduation as a selection criterion and attempt to solve the entry behavior problem in this way.

To the extent that the designer can control the entry behaviors and characteristics of the group to be trained, the learning system design task will be made easier. The task analysis may reveal that the task can only be learned in the time available by trainees of above average intelligence or mechanical ability. Likewise, the analysis might suggest the need for normal eyesight. Such control over the population to be trained is, of course, not always possible. But when it is, the design process is generally more straightforward. A simpler linear learning sequence can be devised; no special provisions need to be made for branching deviant learners; and fewer training aids will be needed.

List some of the entry behaviors a child ought to possess if he is to learn to read a map and "navigate" for his father on a cross-country trip.

FRAME 7.3

PHYSIOLOGICAL MATURATION The word maturation implies changes in an individual's behavior which are a function of natural growth or development as opposed to formal learning. Commonly, such changes are normative. That is, it is possible to prescribe norms for different species depending on their chronological age or stage of development. Thus, we expect children to walk and talk and gain control over given muscles at approximately the same chronological age.

Obviously, children cannot be taught skills which demand a degree of muscular control they do not yet possess. Learning systems designed for children, must be accommodated to their level of physiological maturation. The learning environment must be organized taking into account the fact that children are smaller, weaker and less coordinated than adults. Frequently, when this is done, one discovers that children are able to learn many skills which may, at first, seem beyond their capacities.

An interesting example of this is in the area of reading and writing. For many years, it was assumed that most preschoolers simply could not be taught to read or write. Handwriting, in particular, involves complex perceptual-motor coordination beyond the capacity of most children under five years of age. But writing does not necessarily have to be done in the traditional way. Using a device called the Edison Responsive Environment

FEEDBACK:

7.3 Can read place names, road signs, etc.; can discriminate left from right; understands concept of distance, miles, etc.; recognizes numbers; can add.

or "talking typewriter" children as young as three years of age have been taught successfully. The Edison Responsive Environment consists of a jam-proof electric typewriter, a slide projector, and a tape recorder attached to a computer. The teacher's voice is recorded on tape and when a child pushes a key, he hears the name of the letter spoken by his teacher. After the child loses interest in playing with the typewriter operated in this mode, a letter is displayed on the screen, the voice names it, and all keys, except the one for the letter displayed, are locked. The child explores to discover the unlocked key. When the child has learned several letters in this way, letters are formed into words.

In this example, the task is to teach students to read. The designer of the Edison Responsive Environment recognized in analyzing the task that special consideration would have to be given to the physical maturational level of the learners.

COGNITIVE MATURATION Just as a child passes through certain preestablished stages in his physical development as he grows older, he also goes through a relatively fixed sequence in his mental or cognitive development. It is easy to observe the changes that occur as a child matures physically, and on this basis, no one would question the difference between children and adults. Cognitive changes, on the other hand, cannot be observed; they must be inferred. As a result, there is a tendency to conclude that a child's cognitive world is essentially the same as an adult's, or that the child is a miniature adult in terms of his cognitive abilities. This is actually a distorted and erroneous impression. The quality of a child's thought is significantly different from an adult's. A child's unique approach to reality and his or her view of the world have important implications for the design of learning systems.

The great Swiss psychologist, Jean Piaget, has devoted a large part of his professional life to the study of the stages in a child's cognitive development. It would be inappropriate to attempt to review Piaget's ideas in a chapter on task analyses, but some appreciation for the educational implications of the theory will help the reader understand why it is important to take cognitive maturation into account in the design of learning systems.

Piaget distinguishes three broad periods of cognitive maturation: the Sensorimotor Period (0 - 2 years); the Concrete Operations Period (2 - 11 years); and the Formal Operations Period (11 - 15 years). As children pass through these three periods, they become better able to deal with certain complex concepts. According to Piaget, all children must pass through these stages in their growth process.

One of the points which Piaget makes is that very young children tend to understand reality best in terms of concrete operations. They must interact with physical objects in the real world in order to grasp complex concepts. Detailed verbal explanations are of only marginal value to them.

Piaget also notes that there are some concepts young children cannot understand no matter how concretely they are presented. For example, children under seven years of age who see water poured from a short fat container into another tall skinny container, actually believe the quantity of water changes in the process. They are unable to recognize that the two amounts are equal regardless of the shape of the container, i.e., that quantity is conserved. In another example, a child is given two clay balls which he agrees are of equal size. One is rolled into the shape of a sausage; the other is left unchanged. Again, the child under seven tends to say they are no longer equal. Because children tend to make errors of this kind, there are some concepts which cannot be taught until they have reached the appropriate stage of cognitive development.

Although one might cite many similar principles from Piaget's work, these two should be sufficient to highlight the importance of cognitive maturation for the design of learning systems. The important thing to remember is this: if you are designing a learning system for younger children, it is essential to take into account their stage of cognitive development in the task analysis. You would therefore be well advised to study the works of Jean Piaget and other experts in this area.

Both (1) _____ and (2) _____ maturation are a function of age. The older a child the more mature he is apt to be along both of these dimensions.

F R A M E

7.4

PSYCHOLOGICAL ABILITIES AND APTITUDES   If you were to observe a large number of people learning a specific task, differences in performance would be readily apparent to you. Some people learn the task faster than others; some people retain the material learned longer; some make fewer errors; and so on. Such differences in performance may be due to the factors already listed, such as variation in past learning or maturational level. But variation in performance may also be caused by differences among individuals in basic abilities and aptitudes. Some learners are more intelligent than others or may possess special aptitudes for music or mathematics. Such special abilities provide these learners with the capacity to acquire certain skills more readily than others. One important implica-

FEEDBACK:
7.4   1   physiological
      2   cognitive

tion of this fact is that learning environments should be designed to take into account ability and aptitude differences. As long as the subject matter is appropriately organized and presented, even so-called retarded learners may be taught relatively complex skills.

Having observed that one should take individual differences in basic ability and aptitude into account when designing learning systems, the question of how to do this naturally arises; we are now faced with the fact that we know very little about how to do it. For many years, educational research workers focused their attention on a somewhat different class of questions, largely ignoring the issue of individual differences. It may help if we briefly review the history of this problem and develop a general design principle.

A very large number of studies have compared different methods of instruction in terms of their effects on final examination scores. Discussion groups have been compared with lectures; closed circuit television with live instruction; and so on. In general, consistent results favoring one method of instruction over another are seldom, if ever, observed. More often than not, no differences are obtained. If differences are observed, they are almost never consistently observed in one direction. Thus, if "live" teaching proves superior to television teaching in one study, it is very likely that additional studies will demonstrate that television is sometimes better than live instruction.

Since most studies comparing alternative methods of teaching use averaged data, it has been hypothesized that the effects of individual differences are canceled out. In other words, if we looked at the effects of educational treatments on individuals, rather than groups, significant differences would be obtained.

One implication of this analysis is that educational treatments should be prescribed for learners based on individual differences among them. The problem with this formulation is that we know very little about the relationship of instructional methods to individual differences, and a great deal of research remains to be done before we can prescribe educational treatments for different learners with any confidence. One tentative generalization, however, is possible at this time. Low ability subjects appear to require more systematically structured learning materials than high ability subjects. Another way of saying this is that very bright students will probably be able to learn material no matter how poorly it is organized, and sometimes even when it is presented in a random order. Such students seem to have the capacity to reorganize and restructure even the most inept presentations.

This may seem like a slender thread on which to hang so critical a set of decisions but it is about all we have. We are slowly amassing data relating instructional treatments to various measures of individual differences, such as reading ability, introversion-extroversion and anxiety level, but the results are not at all conclusive. The best the system designer can do at this time is to recognize that individuals differ and empirically develop materials that take this fact into account.

Psychologists and educators have studied the way different students respond to programed instruction. In programed instruction, the material is broken down into small steps or frames, carefully sequenced and presented to students who respond to each frame and receive immediate reinforcement. Suppose the frames were put on 3 x 5 cards and shuffled like a deck of cards so that they were randomized. Which of the following would you predict:

F
R
A
M
E

7.5

1. More intelligent students will do better than less intelligent students.
2. More intelligent and less intelligent students will do about equally well.
3. Less intelligent students will do better than more intelligent students.

TYPES OF LEARNING

Chapter 6 pointed out that there are different types of learning and that the designer must tailor this teaching approach to these different types of learning. A major objective of the task analysis is the isolation and identification of the different elements in the tasks to be learned so that the designer can decide what types of learning are involved and how to go about teaching the various concepts, principles and perceptual-motor skills embedded in a task. This point can probably be understood best by using a specific example, so let's look again at the pencil-sharpening task described in Chapter 5 and consider the concepts, principles, and perceptual-motor skills a student will need to know in order to actually perform the task.

Concepts: Dull, broken, sharp, electric, motor, light etc.

Principle: If a black (graphite) pencil is placed in the electric sharpener and pressed gently, a light will glow when it is sharp.

Perceptual-Motor Skill: Press pencil gently.

Now let's pursue this trivial example of a task analysis in somewhat greater detail. The designer might now begin to ask himself some of the following kinds of questions:

FEEDBACK:

7.5　1

- Which of the prerequisite concepts will the person learning this skill already know?

- How old are the learners?

- Where should they be taught the prerequisite concepts? How should these concepts be taught?

- At what level should the concepts be taught? Does the student need to know the electrical and chemical properties of graphite, for example? How much does the student need to know about electrical motors?

- Is the objective, as developed in the task description, merely to have the student be able to sharpen a pencil, or are there other objectives? Do we want the student to know how to empty the sharpener, for example?

To analyze such an insignificant task in such depth may seem to the reader unnecessary, and it probably is. But it makes the point that a task analysis involves a careful examination of the task and/or objectives in an effort to determine such things as how the task will be taught, to whom, when, and where.

In the chapter on Task Descriptions (Chapter 5), we described another task which was a good deal more complex, i.e., how to shape the behavior of an animal. It would pay to reexamine the flow diagram of that task and inspect it for concepts, principles, and perceptual-motor skills. As we examine this task, we are immediately aware of the fact that there are many concepts which even the beginning student of psychology would have to learn: motivation, reinforcer, operant level, criterion, and so on. One basic principle involved in shaping is to wait until an approximation of the desired terminal behavior occurs and then to reinforce it—but keep in mind the other factors needed to set up a favorable training environment. Finally, perceptual-motor skills have a part in watching the animal and reinforcing just the right approximation to the final desired terminal behavior. Once again, we might ask how and where and by whom these things are going to be taught. Here, the entry behavior, age, cognitive maturation, and abilities of the student become critical.

In Chapters 8 - 11, we will attempt to develop some general design principles for teaching these different types of learning. But even a preliminary analysis can be helpful. For one thing, it breaks the task down into meaningful elements so that the designer can begin to raise critical questions about these elements. In what order should the task elements be taught? Where and under what conditions should each task element be taught? On the job? In a classroom? How extensively should concepts and principles be developed? Operant level, in the above example, may be measured in different ways. How deeply are these things to be explored? And, finally, what sorts of training aids might be created to help the student master some of these concepts, principles, and skills more easily?

SPECIAL CONDITIONS AND CONSTRAINTS

There is a third and final set of factors which must be taken into account when analyzing a task. These are the special conditions or constraints that may surround the performance of a task. It is one thing to drive an automobile on a hard, dry road, and quite another to control the same car on an icy surface. Very different training procedures are implied by the two conditions although the task description might reveal little, if any, difference.

Three kinds of special conditions should be considered. First, there are environmental conditions, such as level of ambient illumination, temperature, mechanical restraints, and so on. Second, there are operator conditions. Is the man to perform the task when fatigued, hungry, ill, weak, or under the influence of drugs? Third, there are social conditions that may significantly affect the performance of a task. Will the trainee perform the task with other individuals? How will they share the load? Are there apt to be personality differences? Sex differences?

The practical implications for learning system design which emerge from these observations are generally classified under the topic of **transfer of training**. A basic assumption underlying all training is that it will transfer from one situation (generally the original learning environment) to some other situation which we call the **referent system**. More often than not, the original learning situation does not look exactly like the one in which the task will ultimately be performed. Indeed, there are often great differences among them. Frequently, a task (such as driving an automobile) must be performed under a wide variety of conditions which only more or less approximate the original learning condition. One general principle seems to emerge from the work on transfer of training which the reader should be aware of: try to include as many elements from the real-life situation in the training conditions as possible. At the start, the designer will want to abstract away a good deal of the complexity so that the learner does not have to cope with too many variables at once, but gradually he will have to prepare the learner to deal with the task outside of the classroom where it will often be extremely complex. This means that sooner or later the practice situation must resemble as nearly as possible the conditions under which terminal behaviors are to be performed. The wise director of a play will hold a dress rehearsal which forces the learner to respond in a situation which resembles the opening night as nearly as possible. It is the same with other kinds of learning situations.

SUMMARY

The task description is a simple straightforward account of how a task is performed. But the task description does not: (1) consider characteristics of the learner performing the task; (2) specify the types of learning involved; (3) identify special conditions or constraints on the performance of the task. A task analysis is an examination of the task description in an effort to identify: (1) assumptions about the learner's entry behavior; (2) the types of learning involved; and (3) the effects of unusual conditions or constraints on the performance of the task, and hence the conditions of learning. Entry behaviors are those skills and learning sets which a learner brings with him to the learning situation. Special constraints include unusual environmental, social, or operator conditions that will influence the way a task should be taught.

SUGGESTED READINGS

Annett, J., & Duncan, K. D.: *Task Analysis and Training Design* (Mimeo), ERIC 019566, 1967.

Miller, R. B.: *A Method for Man-Machine Task Analysis,* WADC TR 53-137. Dayton, Ohio: Wright Air Development Center, 1953.

Miller, R. B.: "Analysis and Specification of Behavior for Training" in Glaser, R. (Ed.) *Training Research and Education,* (New York: Wiley, 1962).

Miller, R. B.: "Task Description and Analysis" in Gagné, R.M.: *Psychological Principles in System Development,* (New York: Holt, Rinehart and Winston, 1962).

Phillips, J. L.: *The Origins of Intellect: Piaget's Theory,* (San Francisco: W. H. Freeman and Co., 1969).

Smith, R. G.: *The Development of Training Objectives,* (Washington, D. C.: The George Washington Univ. (HumRRO), 1964).

Whelder, B., & Piaget, J.: *The Growth of Logical Thinking from Childhood to Adolescence,* (New York: Basic Books, 1958).

POSTTEST

	T	F
1. The task analysis is normally performed before the task description.	____	____
2. Types of learning are a critical part of the task analysis.	____	____
3. Physiological maturation is an important consideration in the design of learning systems for children.	____	____
4. Cognitive maturation is more important in the design of learning systems for children than older adults.	____	____

5. Entry behaviors can refer to either the behaviors possessed by a learner or the behaviors needed by a learner.   _____   _____

6. To determine prerequisite learning sets, one need not analyze a task.   _____   _____

7. Differences among children in speed or amount of learning are generally a function of both past learning and special abilities.   _____   _____

8. We know very little about how to design learning systems taking into account individual differences.   _____   _____

9. Studies comparing methods of instruction generally show no differences consistently favoring one method over another.   _____   _____

10. Low ability students appear to require more systematically structured learning materials than high ability students.   _____   _____

Decide which of the following are task descriptions and which are task analyses.

Task Description   A
Task Analysis   B

                                                              A or B

11. An outline of the roles and responsibilities of defensive backs in football when employing the zone defense.   _____

12. A list of the assumed entry skills, the concepts, and principles to be learned for a unit of a course in driver education.   _____

13. A list of objectives with an indication for each objective of the particular perceptual-motor skills involved in the objective along with some notations as to the assumed entry skills.   _____

14. A flow diagram showing how to dismantle a machine gun.   _____

Which of the following are outputs of a task analysis? Check three.

15. An evaluation plan.   _____

16. Assumptions about entry skills.   _____

17. The system operating description.   _____

18. Types of learning involved.   _____

19. Special constraints.   _____

20. An objective examination.   _____

Answers to this posttest can be found on page 336.

OVERVIEW OF LEARNING SYSTEM DESIGN • REC OGNIZING WELL-FORMULATED OBJECTIVES • DERIVING AND WRITING LEARNING OBJECTIVES • EVALUATING LEARNING SYSTEMS • TASK DE SCRIPTIONS•TYPES OF LEARNING • ANALYZING TASKS, OBJECTIVES, AND LEARNER CHARAC TERISTICS • **GENERAL PRINCIPLES OF LEARNING AND MOTIVATION** • THE LEARNING AND TEACH ING OF CONCEPTS AND PRINCIPLES •THE LEARN ING AND TEACHING OF PROBLEM SOLVING • PERCEPTUAL-MOTOR SKILLS • THE SYSTEM APPROACH TO INSTRUCTION • OVERVIEW OF LEARNING SYSTEM DESIGN • RECOGNIZING WELL-FORMULATED OBJECTIVES • DERIVING AND WRITING LEARNING OBJECTIVES • EVALUAT ING LEARNING SYSTEMS • TASK DESCRIPTIONS • TYPES OF LEARNING • ANALYZING TASKS, OBJEC TIVES, AND LEARNER CHARACTERISTICS • **GEN ERAL PRINCIPLES OF LEARNING AND MOTIVA TION** • THE LEARNING AND TEACHING OF CON CEPTS AND PRINCIPLES • THE LEARNING AND TEACHING OF PROBLEM SOLVING • PERCEPTUAL- MOTOR SKILLS • THE SYSTEM APPROACH TO INSTRUCTION • OVERVIEW OF LEARNING SYS TEM DESIGN•RECOGNIZING WELL-FORMULATED OBJECTIVES•DERIVING AND WRITING LEARNING OBJECTIVES • EVALUATING LEARNING SYSTEMS • TASK DESCRIPTIONS•TYPES OF LEARNING • ANALYZING TASKS, OBJECTIVES, AND LEARNER

8

CHAPTER OBJECTIVES

After reading this chapter, you should be able to:

- Select evidence that indicates a violation of a given principle.
- Select changes to remedy an instructional problem based on one of the nine principles in the chapter.

INTRODUCTION

This chapter describes nine basic principles of student learning and motivation. These principles were derived from psychological experimentation and data. They can be applied in any learning system regardless of the age of the learner, the subject matter, or the type of learning. The principles will help provide solutions for typical problems such as these:

- How can student interest be maintained?
- How does teacher behavior influence student learning?
- Is it a good practice to tell students exactly what they are expected to learn?
- Should a teacher's presentations make learning easy for a student?
- Is punishment the best way to change student behavior?
- How can a teacher keep student attention?
- How should practice be arranged for students?

GENERAL PRINCIPLES OF LEARNING AND MOTIVATION

PRINCIPLE 1—MEANINGFULNESS:
A STUDENT IS LIKELY TO BE MOTIVATED TO LEARN THINGS THAT ARE MEANINGFUL TO HIM.

Meangfulness is a personal thing. Something that is meaningful to you is apt to be important to you personally. Therefore it is not likely that everything taught in a given class will be meaningful to every student. Each student is motivated by what he can relate to his experience, his future, and his interests and values. Yet, on the other hand, everything taught in a class is likely to be relevant and meaningful to someone at some time. With these limits in mind, a course of instruction may be considered meaningful to the extent that each student is able to relate the course objectives and methods to his own past experiences, his future goals, and his interests and values.

RELATING INSTRUCTION TO STUDENTS' EXPERIENCES

To make a course meaningful, try to explain to students how the subject relates to their experience. For example, they may be shown how many times each day they apply a simple principle from physics. Ask questions which will help them to make these connections: Have you ever heard the term velocity? Have you ever seen a quarterback throw into the wind? Did you ever throw a football into the wind? If by some chance, students have not had the experiences you refer to, arrange to provide them. For example, "Let's go outside and throw. . ."

Instruction which is frequently unrelated to the experiences of students—as when children are taught the Pledge of Allegiance—is often learned incorrectly and with little enthusiasm. When little effort is made to relate the Pledge to their backgrounds, children tend to learn it by rote and frequently create their own versions of it in order to try to give it some meaning. Listen some day to young children repeating the Pledge of Allegiance. You may hear some of these bizarre recitations: "I purge a regents to. . ."; "One naked individual. . ."; "And to the republic where Richard stands. . ." Try to prevent meaningless instruction by relating student experience to student learning.

RELATING INSTRUCTION TO STUDENTS' INTERESTS AND VALUES

Participative management is an organizational scheme that allows the people affected by a particular decision to have a voice in making that decision. The use of this type of management is widespread in industry. Industrial psychologists have reported that people work harder when they have helped plan the work. The notion of participative managment can be used to make a course more meaningful by allowing students as much voice as possible in many of the decisions that affect them and their learning. If possible, you might permit students to choose what they will learn from a variety of objectives. Allow capable students to make decisions on both course objectives and procedures. In a course where students might not have the opportunity to choose the objectives, they may be allowed to choose from among objectives; they may suggest changes in some objectives; and they may have a say in the way they reach the objectives. Allow students to choose their own learning rate and practice time. Sometimes, let things happen simply because students want them to happen.

Setting up a very specific curriculum is likely to restrict student choice. Whenever possible, consider students' advice before instituting a new course. However, students should clearly understand that it is sometimes in their best long-range interest to learn some things which may not have an immediate payoff for them and may not be particularly meaningful at the moment. When a student finishes school, he may find that if he has learned a complete set of skills from a well organized curriculum, his choices are increased in the long run. A student who has had a comprehensive curriculum can choose from among his many skills to solve a particular problem, and he may also have a greater number of possible career paths which he can follow.

RELATING INSTRUCTION TO THE STUDENTS' FUTURE

Teachers should have some idea of situations that the students will encounter in the future, including skills they may need in everyday life or in the job market. One way to relate learning to the students' future is to develop a statement that provides an overview of the subject to be learned and relate it to future activities outside of school. One teacher, while fascinated by his subject, atomic chemistry, was sensitive enough to realize that his students might not share his fascination for the subject. Although he was afraid he might be wasting class time, he spent three class periods explaining how the information in the course was organized and what students would be able to do with it in the future. As a result, students became quite interested in the subject and asked only a few elementary questions about the usefulness of learning chemistry.

In summary, making learning meaningful consists of three techniques. First, relate students' past experience to the learning. Second, relate the students' interests and values to the learning by using participative management techniques. Third, relate students' goals to the learning by providing an overview of the subject while describing its possible future applications.

F R A M E

8.1

You are observing Mr. Rhebus, a teacher. Mr. Rhebus says, "Write your weekly report on 'Uses of Mathematics During the Neolithic Era'." A student asks, "Couldn't we report on something like 'Uses of Math in the Space Program'?" Another student asks, "How will doing this paper help me outside of school?" Mr. Rhebus responds, "You cannot report on math in the space program. You can only do what I assign. If I am to be fair, I cannot allow any exceptions. If you cannot see the obvious importance of writing this report, I have doubts about your success in the course. Hopefully, by doing the paper you will infer its use for you."

> Which instructor behavior and instructional conditions show that the principle of meaningfulness is being **violated?**

FEEDBACK:

8.1   1   Refuses student's choice of topics
            (or some similar statement).

        2   Refuses to relate assignment to activities outside
            of school (or some similar statement).

PRINCIPLE 2—PREREQUISITES:
A STUDENT IS MORE LIKELY TO LEARN SOMETHING
NEW IF HE HAS ALL THE PREREQUISITES.

A student's past learning is probably the most important factor determining his success or failure in learning. He has a good chance of learning when he knows the information and can perform the skills underlying a new performance. For example, a student who has learned to add, subtract, and multiply whole numbers has all the prerequisites for learning to divide, and is more likely to learn division than a student who has not learned the prerequisite skills.

Always try to identify the prerequisites needed to teach the subject matter for which you are responsible. Prerequisites for a given terminal behavior are often identified as a result of the analysis of a task or the learning objectives.

Many teachers ignore the principle of prerequisites and assume that all students have the same prerequisite skills. As a result, some students are bored while others are frustrated. Those who are bored frequently have enough prerequisite skills to master the skill very rapidly and are forced to move more slowly than they should. Other students are frustrated because they didn't have the prerequisites needed to begin to learn the required skills and therefore, can't learn. Rather than assuming that students have knowledge and skill prerequisites, a teacher should test students for the prerequisites.

If a student has the prerequisites for a set of instructional objectives, he is likely to find the instruction meaningful. He will be capable of perceiving the relationship between the relatively simple knowledge he possesses and the more complex knowledge that he is going to learn.

"Hello, I'm John Skipper. What would you like to know about instruction? How do I begin my course? I whip out the overhead projector and flip up some new problems, and the students and I begin talking about them. Not all the students join in, but I understand that. They're shy with a new teacher. As the course progresses, I usually start a unit with a section of basic material, continue with intermediate material, and finish with advanced material. Another good thing I do is skip around. I skip around by presenting the intermediate or advanced material first. That seems to keep the students on their toes. As with most classes, some of the students do not catch on to that approach."

FRAME

8.2

What would you advise John Skipper to do to be in accord with the principle of prerequisites?

(continued on next page)

1. Begin class with a pretest for prerequisites.
2. Review prerequisites.
3. Take students who are majors only into your class.
4. Go more slowly.
5. Get students of approximately the same age.

PRINCIPLE 3—MODELING:
THE STUDENT IS MORE LIKELY TO ACQUIRE NEW
BEHAVIOR IF HE IS PRESENTED WITH A MODEL
PERFORMANCE TO WATCH AND IMITATE.

Heed what the scholar said, "children have more need of models than critics." Behave in the same fashion that you want students to behave. Rather than just telling students how to do something correctly, show them. Don't tell students **how** to present a logical argument; present a logical argument for them to hear.

Here are five helpful hints for teachers who follow this principle:

1. Teachers should label important aspects of the behavior being modeled as it is being demonstrated. As you show your students how to do something such as clean a carburetor, solve an equation, or analyze a problem, point out each step and each decision you make in a self-conscious manner.

2. Students should witness the model receiving rewards for his behavior.

3. The model should be perceived as a person of high status. Remember, however, your notion about someone with high status may not be the same as your students.

4. If a model's behavior is in conflict with a student's values or beliefs, or if he is punished for his behavior, the student is not very likely to imitate the model. Don't punish the student!

5. Modeling applies when teaching technical or social skills.

Be aware that students are likely to imitate anything you do. Based on what is known about modeling, the cliche, "Those who know, do; those who don't know, teach," should be rephrased. "Those who know, teach by modeling; those who don't know, teach by telling." We could add that students of those who teach by modeling are more likely to learn than the students of those who teach by telling.

FEEDBACK:
8.2   1, 2

Perhaps you have observed events similar to these:

- A teacher scolding a student in front of his peers for being impolite and tactless.
- A teacher lecturing about how to conduct an interview.
- A teacher punishing a child for being aggressive.
- A teacher exhorting students never to make generalizations.

In each of these cases, the students' behavior is not apt to change. Why? Because the students are probably imitating the teacher's behavior. Prevent these unwanted results by modeling the behavior you expect from your students.

There is a conflict in the history class. Mr. Washington is disturbed by his students' alleged dishonesty. He possesses evidence that students have copied old term papers and plagiarized from the literature. He insists that his students must learn the value of honesty and he lectures about it frequently. The students do not admit anything. They complain that Mr. Washington, the respected authority on prerevolutionary America, reads other peoples' lectures in class and reproduces articles for course handouts without obtaining permission of the author.

What instructor behavior and class conditions indicate that the principle of modeling is being violated?

FRAME 8.3

PRINCIPLE 4—OPEN COMMUNICATION:
THE STUDENT IS MORE LIKELY TO LEARN IF THE PRESENTATION IS STRUCTURED SO THAT THE INSTRUCTOR'S MESSAGES ARE OPEN TO THE STUDENTS' INSPECTION.

State all the messages you intend to have the students receive in a way that will insure their reception. There are five useful tips with regard to the principle of open communication:

1. State objectives to your students. Among other things, the objectives tell the students exactly what to attend to.
2. Point out relationships, give cues and prompts to students to be sure they understand what is being said.

FEEDBACK:
8.3 1 Tells students to be honest.
    2 Uses other people's lectures.
    3 Uses articles without permission.

3. Whenever possible, try to avoid talking about something in its absence. For instance, if you are talking about aspects of French culture, show students pictures and films illustrating your point.

4. Whenever possible, stimulate all sensory channels by structuring visual and auditory media so that a student can see and hear all possible features when they are mentioned.

5. Ask students questions to verify communication.

The open communication principle is violated continually in many courses. Course requirements, information, and examples are so unclear at times that students begin to believe they are a secret. These violations make students feel as if they are being taken on a mystery tour. If you have a message for your students, don't play Hide-and-Seek or Twenty Questions; give them the message in the clearest, easiest way possible and then check to see if they got it.

F R A M E

8.4

You are observing Miss Monroe. She introduces her presentation on exponents: "Exponents are very important; pay attention to what I say." Miss Monroe rapidly proceeds to fill the blackboard with equations. When the board is full, she erases the equations and continues to refill the board. As she writes, she continues to talk, at times referring to the equations she has already erased. Some of the students from the math class complained to their advisers. They said that they were confused by the presentations; they never knew what was important, and they never knew what to expect in tests.

What instructor behavior and instructional conditions indicate that the principle of open communication is being violated?

PRINCIPLE 5—NOVELTY:
A STUDENT IS MORE LIKELY TO LEARN IF HIS ATTENTION IS ATTRACTED BY RELATIVELY NOVEL PRESENTATIONS.

Present stimuli that you want students to notice in a fashion that is relatively novel to them. Consider what students usually see and hear. Vary your style and means of presentation from the usual. For instance, if they haven't seen a movie recently, the use of a movie as an instructional aid becomes a novelty.

Novelty does not necessarily imply telling jokes or being a classroom

---

FEEDBACK:
8.4 1 Gives vague directions regarding what to pay attention to.
       2 Erases equations and then talks about them.

ham. It does imply that your voice is modulated, that lectures are alternated with different approaches, that various sorts of assignments are given, that formats used for tests vary, and that different types of examples are included in presentations. For example, in a course on learning systems, we try to use a variety of appropriate yet novel presentations and activities for the student. Lectures, films, role plays, slide-tape presentations, programed texts and discussions are used when appropriate. Students are given assignments to do alone, in pairs, in small groups, in large groups, and as a panel. Sometimes we make the extra effort to convert common titles for topics studied in the class to novel ones. Thus, the title "How to Recognize a Problem" becomes "So, What Seems To Be the Problem?" and the title "Task Analysis" becomes "Who Needs Analysis? You, That's Who."

For three days in a row, class time was used for small group discussion on the same topic: infant care. On the fourth and fifth day, attendance dropped. Those students who came to class discussed everything but infant care in their small group.

FRAME 8.5

What teacher behavior and instructional conditions indicate that the principle of novelty is being violated?

PRINCIPLE 6—ACTIVE APPROPRIATE PRACTICE:
THE STUDENT IS MORE LIKELY TO LEARN IF HE TAKES AN ACTIVE PART IN PRACTICE GEARED TO REACH AN INSTRUCTIONAL OBJECTIVE.

Most teaching includes an active instructional agent and a passive student. Lectures, films, and educational TV require minimal student participation. However, in order to learn, students should respond actively. The practice should not only be active, but should also be as similar as possible to that required in the referent system. Listening to a lecture or taking notes while observing an artist at work is insufficient and inappropriate practice for learning to paint. In contrast, painting is active, appropriate practice for learning to paint.

There are three useful suggestions to aid in adapting teaching to this principle:

FEEDBACK:

8.5   1 Uses the same topic.

      2 Uses the same mode of practice for a week.

1. Require students to answer questions. Ask as many students as possible to respond. Have all students write answers down and have a few state them orally.

2. Ask students to organize or reorganize information found in their reading.

3. Set up laboratories and on-the-job learning situations when the course objectives call for them.

Some teachers are able to stimulate active appropriate practice even when there are a large number of students in class. For example, a teacher may describe different types of research to his students and then ask the question, "Here is a research report. . .what type of research is it?" Students must respond by writing their answers. Afterwards, the teacher would check the results, provide his answer, and discuss alternative answers. Under these conditions, students are more apt to pay close attention to information presented in class and perform well on tests.

Some teachers use games and simulations to stimulate active practice. One business teacher had his students set up a business and conduct an advertising campaign. A geology teacher had his students buy what they felt might be oil-rich land in a simulated environment. A political science teacher had his students make decisions as foreign ministers of mythical countries.

Other teachers use tutorial methods. Pairs of students are assigned to teach each other. In one such case, each student prepared questions to ask his partner, and following the partner's response, told him if his answer was right or wrong.

F R A M E

8.6

Mr. Binary introduced the new section of the course: "Now I will demonstrate and explain how to sign on to the computer and run through a program. I will test each of you individually on November 18. You will have to sign on and run through a program. Now watch carefully as I point out the procedures. We do not have enough time for each of you to sign on and work a program through before the 18th, so please watch very carefully." On the 18th, many students did not perform well. They said that they could tell how to do the task, but they could not actually do it.

What advice would you give Mr. Binary so that his behavior would be in accord with the principle of active appropriate practice?

1. Change objective if resources are scarce.
2. If possible, move test date back and let each student practice procedure.
3. If possible, simulate a situation where student must make the same steps and decisions as he would on the computer.

4. Give a better demonstration and explanation.
5. Let the student watch more closely, perhaps with the aid of a video recorder.

PRINCIPLE 7–DISTRIBUTED PRACTICE:
A STUDENT IS MORE LIKELY TO LEARN IF HIS
PRACTICE IS SCHEDULED IN SHORT PERIODS
DISTRIBUTED OVER TIME.

Space short practice sessions over a period of time. It is better, for example, to have the student practice French or study science for about 1 hour in the morning and in the afternoon each day, than to have him practice for long periods of time with only short breaks between practice sessions. Many teachers may have the students practice French or study science 2 hours in a row and provide a 20-minute break between the 2 hour practice sessions. This sort of practice schedule leads to fatigue, unpleasant associations with the subject matter, and mistakes in practice. Instead, use short practice sessions spaced over time.

Here is part of a brochure describing a workshop. "Participants will practice new laboratory procedures."

F
R
A
M
E

8.7

> Calendar: Aug. 23, 24, 25
> 8 A.M. to 12 P.M. – 1 P.M. to 5 P.M.

A participant reports, "It was a marathon. We were tired from the first day on. By the third day, we wanted to quit. The materials were valuable, but I cannot remember half the procedures. The last day I made a number of errors. At this point, I still avoid using these procedures."

> What instructor behavior and instructional conditions show that
> the principle of distributed practice is being violated?

PRINCIPLE 8–FADING:
A STUDENT IS MORE LIKELY TO LEARN IF INSTRUC-
TIONAL PROMPTS ARE WITHDRAWN GRADUALLY.

At the beginning of instruction, help a student learn by providing prompts and hints. As the student becomes proficient, systematically

FEEDBACK:
8.6	1, 3	8.7	1	Four-hour practice sessions.
			2	One break in an eight-hour span.
			3	Three days in a row of steady practice.

withdraw or fade out the prompts. For instance, to teach blind students Braille, beginners use widely spaced bumps; later, the space is narrowed to standard Braille distance. By using this principle, the students are able to learn to perform by themselves without gaps or errors in their performance.

If fading does not proceed systematically, students may become dependent on the prompts. If fading proceeds too rapidly, students make errors. In one case, an English teacher used an extra line as a prompt to teach foreign students to recognize the difference between the letter d and the letter b. The extra line was put to the left of each letter to accentuate the difference of the shapes of the d and b. The teacher was surprised when students handed in tests where the letters were represented by the letter with an added line to its left.

PRINCIPLE 9—PLEASANT CONDITIONS AND CONSEQUENCES:
A STUDENT IS MORE LIKELY TO CONTINUE LEARNING IF INSTRUCTIONAL CONDITIONS ARE MADE PLEASANT.

To provide pleasant conditions and consequences, you must first eliminate the negative aspects of instruction; then, you must accentuate the positive aspects.

If you want students to feel good about the things they have learned and to use this knowledge after they leave school, you must reduce the possibility of school being boring, frustrating, and unpleasant. To do so, we must recognize those occasions in school that are aversive.

AVOIDING AVERSIVE OR UNPLEASANT CONDITIONS AND CONSEQUENCES

There are four ways that students are often inadvertently exposed to aversive stimuli in class:

1. Students are bored. The lack of challenge and variety, the demand to repeat what they already know, the interminable waiting, and the monotonous tone of the teacher are all conditions that contribute to boredom.

2. Students are subjected to unpleasant physical conditions. Extreme heat or cold of the room, having to remain in one place, the distractions in the environment, and occasional corporal punishment contribute to unpleasant physical conditions in class.

3. Students are **frustrated** by being placed in situations where unattainable, unreasonable demands are made and no escape is allowed. Giving students information for which they have no prerequisites, demanding top flight performance when students are fatigued,

hiding necessary information from students, continually failing students, and demanding that students pay attention when they cannot hear or see, are all contributing factors to frustration.

4. Students are **hurt emotionally.** The avoidance of personal contact by the teacher, harsh public comparisons of students' work, crude jokes with the student as the butt, and threats of failure all contribute to hurt students emotionally.

RESULTS OF AVERSIVE CONDITIONS AND CONSEQUENCES

The use of aversive conditions and consequences results in a temporary cessation of the behavior preceding the aversive stimulation; unpleasant association with other events, objects, or people present at the time; and avoidance of the entire situation in the future. As a result of continual unplesantness, the subject matter itself acquires unpleasant overtones; the teacher becomes unpleasant; and school in general becomes unpleasant. Finally, the student uses whatever means he has to avoid coming to class and learning the subject matter. If punishment is continued, intensive, or combined with frustration, the student may exhibit maladaptive behavior. He or she may show unusual conformity, unwarranted worrying, unspecified fears, shyness, acquiescence, lack of self-confidence, and a lack of productivity.

You are a student. During one of your biology classes, another student asked the teacher to explain the course requirements. "What are the objectives of this course?" The teacher responded, "The requirements of this course are obvious. However, I can see why *you* might ask a question like that when I recall your performance on the last assignment. If I were you, I would start working and stop asking stupid questions. Actually, if I didn't know any better I would have thought you were doing a satire of the last assignment." During the few times the student attended class, he remained silent. At the end of the term, he changed his major from biology to chemistry.

F
R
A
M
E

8.8

What instructor behavior and classroom conditions show that the teacher was not avoiding aversive conditions and consequences?

PROVIDING PLEASANT CONDITIONS

What makes some teachers popular? Although there are distinct differences in teaching style among popular teachers, each in his own way makes learning pleasant for students. Some make their students laugh.

FEEDBACK:
8.8   1   The public embarrassment caused by the teacher's sarcasm.
        2   Tells the student to work hard and stop asking stupid questions.

Others excite their students with their own enthusiasm. Some provoke the students' intellectual curiosity. Some teachers simply treat their students as respectable human beings. To some extent at least, these examples reflect personality differences among teachers.

Obviously, the way a teacher approaches his class depends upon his personality. Personality may be changed, but not by reading a chapter in a book. In addition to the general principles already discussed, we recommend three procedures that most teachers, regardless of basic personality patterns, could use to make learning more pleasant.

1. Set challenging tasks during training. A challenging task is neither too hard nor too easy. A task with a 90 percent probability of success is too easy; one with a 10 percent chance is too hard; neither is a challenge. Chance of success depends on individual ability. A task with approximately a 50 percent chance of success is about right. For most beginners, sinking a 5 foot putt in golf would be a challenge. A 5 foot putt for an expert would be rather easy. On the other hand, a 20 foot putt would be too hard for a beginner and a 1 foot putt might be too easy. If a teacher provides tasks that are too easy, students will be bored. If a teacher provides tasks that are too difficult, the result may be nonadaptive, rigid behaviors characteristic of frustration. Determine the specific task that should be assigned to a particular student on the basis of the assessment of prerequisites as mentioned in Principle 2. One exception might be mentioned. A challenging task based on the students' ability should not be presented to students who have continually failed to learn. Give these students tasks which guarantee success. As these students succeed, increase the task difficulty until it becomes challenging.

2. Give students knowledge of results. A report of this sort should include what students did well, what students did poorly, what made the performance poor, and what to do to improve it. Their correct choices should be confirmed and their errors should be corrected. Knowledge of results serves to improve performance and provide an incentive to work. Don't overlook the fact that unsuccessful students need feedback most.

3. Reward students' efforts. Unfortunately, many desirable student behaviors go unrewarded, and many undesirable student behaviors are rewarded. This may result from certain misconceptions about rewards.

   • Rewards are not just concrete objects such as money, food, or presents. Many rewards are subtle and intangible. Attention from people, opportunity for novel experience, and being able to exert power may also serve as rewards.

- Achievement is not always its own reward. Other rewards may be necessary. Achievement becomes a reward by association with other rewards.

- Rewards should be tailored to the individual. Different people have different tastes. What is rewarding for one person may not be rewarding for another person.

- Rewards are not bribery. Rewarding a student for a job well done is no more bribery than paying for his labor.

- Reward a desirable action as soon as you can after detecting its occurrence. If you want to reward a student for asking a good question, don't wait. The action immediately preceding the reward is the one which will continue. An immediate reward minimizes the possibility of rewarding an undesirable behavior.

- Rewarding a student every time he responds correctly is excellent for initiating behavior, but is not necessary to maintain participation over time. Intermittent rewards given for a number of responses or for an amount of time at work is the best way to maintain a high rate of participation over time. The tenacious performance of gamblers illustrates the power of intermittent payoffs.

In summary, teachers can make practice conditions pleasant in three ways. First, they can set challenging tasks. Second, they can give students feedback. And, third, they can reward students' efforts.

The Eureka school system decided to reward students by giving them money for coming to school during the summer. When a student would come to school and stay the day, he would be given some cash. As a result, everyone and his brother spent his summer in school raising havoc. The teachers paid most attention to the students who were not learning and were causing problems. The few students who were reading or asking questions were ignored by the teachers. When one of the worst troublemakers did read something, the teacher praised him loudly, "Good boy," she said. The student turned abruptly and said, "I'm not your boy."

F
R
A
M
E

8.9

What instructor behavior and instructional conditions indicate that the principle of making learning pleasant is being violated?

FEEDBACK:

8.9   1   The school was giving a cash reward for attendance, not learning.

2   Teachers ignored students who were reading.

3   Teachers were not aware of what was rewarding to certain children.

4   Teachers paid attention to students who were not learning.

SUMMARY

This chapter contains nine general principles of motivation and learning. These principles deal with (1) making the subject matter more meaningful; (2) knowledge of prerequisite concepts and principles; (3) modeling; (4) open communication, (5) novelty; (6) active and (7) distributed practice; (8) fading prompts; and (9) the consequences of instruction. An instructor can use these principles to improve his teaching. In addition, it helps the teacher predict what will happen to student learning and motivation if certain procedures are followed and to infer possible reasons that students fail to learn. These general principles of learning and motivation are the basis for more specific principles related to teaching concepts, principles, problem solving, and skills.

SUGGESTED READINGS

De Cecco, John P.: "Motivation: How to Increase Student Vim & Vigor," *The Psychology of Learning and Instruction: Educational Psychology,* (New Jersey: Prentice-Hall, Inc., 1968).

Gagné, R. M.: "The Design of Instruction," *The Conditions of Learning,* (New York: Holt, Rinehart, & Winston, 1970).

Mager, Robert F.: *Developing Attitude Toward Learning*, (Palo Alto, California: Fearon Publishers, 1968).

Rogers, Carl R.: *Freedom to Learn,* (Columbia, Ohio: Charles E. Merrill Publishing Company, 1969).

Silverman, Robert E.: "Using the S-R Reinforcement Model," *Educational Technology.*

Thiagarian, S.: "Programed Instruction in the Affective Domain," *N.S.P.I. Journal*, Vol. 10, No. 6, July, 1971.

DECISION AID

This decision aid will help you make decisions about teaching based on principles of learning and motivation. The decision aid is divided into two columns—factors and outcomes. The outcomes refer to your desired objectives—increased learning and motivation. The factors are those elements in the classroom that need to be arranged to achieve the desired objectives.

HOW TO USE THE DECISION AID

FOR MAKING PREDICTIONS   Find the classroom factor(s) that will best help you achieve your objective. Then predict the instructional outcome. If, for example, you are making your course more meaningful, student motivation should increase.

FOR INFERRING ANTECEDENT CONDITIONS   Find an instructional outcome present in your course; then note the classroom factors which may contribute to that outcome. If student practice is maintained, i.e., they are working hard, the practice is probably challenging, they are being rewarded, and getting feedback.

FOR EVALUATING INSTRUCTION Use the list of classroom factors as a checklist. You might ask yourself if you are incorporating the classroom factors into your instruction.

Instructional Outcomes	Classroom Factors
1. Positive student *attitude* and student *motivation* to learn increases as . . .	. . . the course of instruction becomes *meaningful* to the student.

2. Learning is more likely to occur if . . .	. . . learning is made meaningful in these ways:
	  a. Relate it to student's experience.
	  b. Relate it to the student's goals.
	  c. Relate it to the student's interests and values.
	. . . the student can demonstrate on entry to the course the number and quality of *prerequisite* abilities required.

3. The student will be more likely to learn from a *presentation* if . . .	. . . the required behavior is *modeled* and labeled. . . . the information is readily *open to inspection* of the student. . . . the presentation is relatively *novel* in some aspect.
4. The probability that a student will *learn from practice* will increase if . . .	. . . students have *active, appropriate* practice. . . . practice is taken in relatively small amounts, and practice *sessions are separated over time (distributed practice).*

5. The probability that student *practice* and *learning* will be maintained is increased when . . .	. . . instructional cues are systematically withdrawn *(fading).*
	. . . the amount of aversive conditions and consequences associated with or resulting from learning is avoided in these forms:
	  a. Boredom.
	  b. Unpleasant physical conditions.
	  c. Frustration.
	  d. Unpleasant emotional states.
	. . . practice is made pleasant for the student in these ways:

a. Practice tasks are challenging (not too hard, not too easy).
b. Students are given feedback to confirm and correct their choices and actions.
c. *Rewards* are given for desirable behavior.

POSTTEST

More than one answer may be correct.

1. You are observing a teacher. He asks his students, "What do you think about the objectives I have listed?" A student answers, "I cannot see what all those objectives have to do with urban affairs." The teacher says, "I hope that by the end of this course that will become clear to you." A second student asks,"I'm very interested in the topic of pollution in urban areas; can we include that topic?" The teacher answered, "No, we won't include that topic. I'm not too interested in it and I'm not much of an expert in the area."

   What would you advise the teacher to do to be *in accord with* the principle of *meaningfulness?*

   a. Include fewer more clearly stated objectives.
   b. State an overview relating the objectives and the "real world."
   c. The teacher should be interested in all related topics.
   d. Assign special interest areas as independent study topics.
   e. Let students conduct the course themselves.

2. The gym teacher began, "Good morning. Today, during our first hour of class, we will start preparing for your intermediate skills tests on the uneven parallel bars. I assume you all have the basic skills. Well, let's begin." Some students were injured in attempting the intermediate skills during the first hour. Some students did not try to perform during the first few weeks. Weeks later the teacher discovered he had to take time to teach several students the basic skills.

   What instructor behavior and classroom conditions indicate that the principle of *prerequisites* is being *violated?*

3. A citizenship teacher wanted his students to learn to solve problems in a democratic fashion. He said to his students, "The class will be run my way. This class will run democratically because that's the way I want it." It is well known that students in this class solve social problems by ordering each other about rather than arriving at a group decision.

What would you advise this teacher to do to be *in accord with* the principle of *modeling*?

a. Change his course objectives.
b. Use democratic procedures to determine how the class will be run.
c. Punish students for ordering each other around.
d. Solve all problems by group decision.
e. Stick to citizenship facts and stop bothering with class procedures.

4. You are evaluating an English course taught to foreign students. You observe. When the teacher begins the hour she says, "Today we will study transportation." She continues, "I know some of you have never seen a train. Here is a picture of a train." She shows a picture of the front view of a steam locomotive in a snowstorm. The students express their confusion, "What are we supposed to learn? What is a train?"

What teacher behavior and classroom conditions indicate that the principle of *open communication* is being *violated*?

5. A colleague is opening his heart to you, "Why don't my students come to class? Why do those who attend class read newspapers and draw instead of participating? I tell them interesting things in class. To be sure the students remember the interesting things, I take special pains to repeat them each day."

What advice would you give to the teacher so that the instructional conditions would be *in accord with* the principle of *novelty?*

a. Tell the students new, interesting things each day.
b. Ban newspapers and drawing equipment from the class.
c. Don't worry about keeping the students interested.
d. Avoid repeating topics in the same fashion.
e. Relate the class topics to newspapers.

6. An advanced medical student states that he is anxious about his internship. He is concerned because at this time, he cannot do what his internship is designed to enable him to do. After his internship he will be required to demonstrate his learning by interviewing and treating real patients. He is now in a special program. He is spending a part of his internship in a general practitioner's office. The M.D. does not trust the student's abilities, so he just allows him to watch his office practice.

What advice would you give the M.D. so that the internship will be *in accord with* the principle of *active appropriate practice?*

a. Let the student watch the M.D. interview and treat real patients.
b. Let the student interview real patients.
c. Let the student interview and treat real patients under supervision.

   d. Let the student treat selected patients according to the M.D.'s prescribed treatments.

   e. Let the student state how he would interview and treat real patients.

7. A student is describing summer school. He says, "I didn't like it. I got tired. Everyone got tired. We had to do the same amount of problems in seven weeks that we would do in fifteen weeks during an ordinary term. When I continued the course sequence in the fall, the teacher had to provide intensive review for those of us who took the course during the summer. I didn't remember much."

   What conditions should summer school include to be *in accord with* the principle of *distributed practice?*

   a. Give easier problems

   b. Eliminate summer school.

   c. Give more problems during summer school.

   d. Give half the problems they work on now.

   e. Lengthen summer session to fifteen weeks so practice sessions are short and spaced.

8. An anonymous teacher is overheard to say, "I can't understand why the students don't work by themselves. They depend on their classmates or me for help. I help them all the time with their work. What can I do? When they need help I give it to them."

   What teacher behavior and instructional conditions show that the *fading principle* is being *violated?*

9. Larry said, "When I heard about the requirements for the five-week course I almost fainted. I wasn't afraid, I simply knew that I could never learn that much that fast. I was a nervous wreck through that course. As the course progressed, I became more convinced that the work was too hard for me. The tests and assignments I did gave no evidence to the contrary. Actually, once I handed something in, I never saw it again."

   What advice would you give to the teacher of the course so that it might be *in accord with* the principle of *making learning pleasant?*

   a. Make work in the course not too hard nor too easy for the students.

   b. Don't give tests and assignments.

   c. Return assignments and tests to students with criticism.

   d. Give out lots of candy during the course.

   e. Tell a lot of good jokes.

10. Most students thought that history class was a circus. It didn't matter how poorly Richard did; when he handed his work in to the teacher, she accepted it. Miss Taylor would say, "He's such a gentleman; how could I refuse?"
Some student reactions to Miss Taylor were:

"For assignments well done, she would give us passes to the educational movies after school. None of us ever went to the movies and our assignments rarely improved."

"At first we would ask many questions about current events. Miss Taylor said that she would answer the question later, but she never did. We stopped asking questions."

What would you tell the teacher to do to be *in accord with* the principle of *making learning pleasant?*

a. Don't accept anything Richard hands in.
b. Don't accept poor work from Richard.
c. Answer students' questions and remember to answer questions put off.
d. Find out what students would like as a reward and give them that.
e. Stop bribing students with movie tickets.

Answers to this posttest can be found on page 336.

OVERVIEW OF LEARNING SYSTEM DESIGN • REC
OGNIZING WELL-FORMULATED OBJECTIVES •
DERIVING AND WRITING LEARNING OBJECTIVES
• EVALUATING LEARNING SYSTEMS • TASK DE
SCRIPTIONS•TYPES OF LEARNING • ANALYZING
TASKS, OBJECTIVES, AND LEARNER CHARAC
TERISTICS • GENERAL PRINCIPLES OF LEARNING
AND MOTIVATION • **THE LEARNING AND TEACH
ING OF CONCEPTS AND PRINCIPLES** • THE LEARN
ING AND TEACHING OF PROBLEM SOLVING •
PERCEPTUAL-MOTOR SKILLS • THE SYSTEM
APPROACH TO INSTRUCTION • OVERVIEW OF
LEARNING SYSTEM DESIGN • RECOGNIZING
WELL-FORMULATED OBJECTIVES • DERIVING
AND WRITING LEARNING OBJECTIVES • EVALUAT
ING LEARNING SYSTEMS • TASK DESCRIPTIONS •
TYPES OF LEARNING • ANALYZING TASKS, OBJEC
TIVES, AND LEARNER CHARACTERISTICS • GEN
ERAL PRINCIPLES OF LEARNING AND MOTIVA
TION • **THE LEARNING AND TEACHING OF CON
CEPTS AND PRINCIPLES** • THE LEARNING AND
TEACHING OF PROBLEM SOLVING • PERCEPTUAL-
MOTOR SKILLS • THE SYSTEM APPROACH TO
INSTRUCTION • OVERVIEW OF LEARNING SYS
TEM DESIGN•RECOGNIZING WELL-FORMULATED
OBJECTIVES•DERIVING AND WRITING LEARNING
OBJECTIVES • EVALUATING LEARNING SYSTEMS
• TASK DESCRIPTIONS•TYPES OF LEARNING •
ANALYZING TASKS, OBJECTIVES, AND LEARNER

9

CHAPTER OBJECTIVES

After reading this chapter, you should be able to:

- Develop a plan for teaching prerequisite concepts, given the results of a pretest.
- Choose a behavioral objective that demonstrates whether a student knows a concept.
- Choose a concept teaching presentation approach.
- Determine if given statements about concept teaching are true or false.
- Select examples of concepts according to their use in concept instruction.
- Choose the type of practice required to teach a given concept.
- Select those statements, in a given list, which are principles.
- Evaluate an objective for a given principle.
- Choose prerequisites for teaching a principle.
- State the steps for presenting and practicing principles in accord with the principles in the chapter.

INTRODUCTION

This chapter provides basic information about how students learn concepts and principles and how they should be taught. The ability to teach concepts and principles is essential to every teacher. Concepts and principles are the basic ideas in a field of study. A student who has truly mastered basic concepts and principles has increased chances for success in advanced study and a greater ability to recognize and solve problems.

CONCEPTS AND PRINCIPLES

At birth, the child's world consists of a collection of completely disorganized stimuli which are only gradually given order and meaning. One important way of organizing perceptions is to classify and label them. When we do this, we form concepts. There are, for example, literally thousands of different **sets of stimuli** which we classify and label using the term, dog. No two of these sets of stimuli are ever exactly alike, and as a matter of fact, some are so different that we may wonder why they should be placed in the same class.

A concept is a class of stimuli which have common attributes. Democracy, honor, horse, building, embarrassment, automobile, ocean, river, and love are all examples of concepts from everyday life. Common classroom examples of concepts include psychotic, mass, society, catalyst, organ, and many more.

As the child grows older, he discovers that he can control objects and people, predict events, and solve problems. In effect, the child is applying principles: If I hold a glass with both hands, it is less likely to spill. If I scream, my mother will surrender. If I drop the plastic cup, it won't break; but if I drop the glass cup, it probably will break. If I want to get the cookie jar on the top shelf, I reach for it with a stick. As you probably realize, principles are sometimes referred to as scientific laws, rules, or generalizations, and are composed of many concepts.

In this chapter, we will show you how to teach concepts and principles. In the first part of the chapter, we will describe concept teaching and show you how to perform the following instructional procedures: test for knowledge of a concept; test for prerequisites; select an approach to teaching concepts; choose appropriate examples for illustrating concepts; provide appropriate practice; and plan a valid posttest.

In the second portion of the chapter we will describe how to teach principles as well as how to carry out the following teaching activities: test for knowledge of a principle; assess prerequisite knowledge; select a strategy for teaching a principle; and provide appropriate student practice.

TESTING FOR KNOWLEDGE OF CONCEPTS

When a student knows a concept, he can do at least four things. First, he can name examples of the concept when he sees them. For example, when he sees a dog or a cow or some other animal belonging to the same class, he can say, "That's a mammal." Second, he can state the properties of the concept such as, "A mammal is an animal with hair and breasts." Third, he can choose examples from nonexamples like: "That kangaroo and that monkey are mammals, but that shark and eagle are not." Fourth, he is probably better able to solve problems which include the concept such as: Could a mammal survive in the Arctic region?

The best way of testing a student's knowledge of a concept is by asking him to indicate which of many examples belong to the category in question. Knowing a concept involves being able to classify objects or events. When a student picks examples from among nonexamples, he is demonstrating his knowledge of the class of objects or events.

The three other methods of demonstrating knowledge of concepts each have weaknesses. From your own experience, you probably realize that stating a concept name, even in the correct context, is not necessarily a demonstration of the attainment of that concept. To illustrate, many people talk as if they were psychologists, referring to Oedipus complexes, anal retentiveness, psychotic behavior, instincts, and learning without knowing the essential properties of the categories or being able to differentiate examples from nonexamples. Furthermore, given enough time, anyone could teach a student to parrot definitions of concepts. Reciting definitions and identifying examples require different levels of knowledge.

Even solving a problem which incorporates some concept is not a sure test of concept attainment. It is feasible that a problem could be solved without knowing one of several concepts involved.

Therefore, when writing a complete behavioral objective for a concept, keep in mind that the best demonstration of knowledge of the concept is the student's ability to differentiate examples from nonexamples. The conditions of the objective should ask for examples and nonexamples of the concept being taught; for instance, "the student will be given examples and nonexamples of the concept herbivores." The terminal behavior should require the student to indicate which examples belong to the concept in question; using the same examples, the student will now point to examples of herbivores. The criterion should require that the student discriminate between examples and nonexamples that are difficult for most people; to do this, he could be asked to choose all examples belonging to the category.

F R A M E 9.1

A nonprofit service organization wants to have local representatives in all sections of the country. They demand that each representative be able to express himself in standard English and in the regional dialect. They realize that none of their present staff members could tell when a person was expressing himself well in a particular regional dialect. They submit that staff members must be taught *how to tell the difference between people who express themselves well and those who do not.* Choose the portions of an objective for the present staff members which will enable them to identify the concept "Northern Appalachian dialect."

Condition   1.   a. Given samples of written statements.
b. Given samples of several American dialects on audiotape.
c. Given a sample of Northern Appalachian dialect on audiotape.

Terminal   2.   a. The student will say when he hears Northern Appalachian
Behavior   dialect.
b. The student will speak the Northern Appalachian dialect.
c. The student will underline examples of the dialect.

Criterion   3.   a. The student's pronunciation must be according to the manual.
b. The student will distinguish between Northern Appalachian dialect and other closely associated dialects according to the manual.
c. The student's underlined portions must fit the definition of the dialect.

FEEDBACK:
9.1   1   b
2   a
3   b

TESTING FOR PREREQUISITES

After specifying the objective for concept teaching, an instructor must assess his students' understanding of the ideas underlying the concept to be taught. These underlying ideas are referred to as **prerequisite knowledge.** The most important factor in teaching a concept is to guarantee that students understand the prerequisite knowledge. Determining what the prerequisites are and whether students know them should be an essential part of planning to teach a concept. Specifically, students should be pretested on the prerequisite knowledge nested in the concept being learned and given review of these prerequisites following the pretest. Consider the following concept definition: "A bird is a warm-blooded vertebrate with wings and feathers." The attributes of a bird that can be listed as prerequisite concepts are: warm-blooded vertebrate, wings, feathers.

For those who teach large groups of students, the nature of the review of prerequisite knowledge depends on the results of the pretest. If all students demonstrate that they know a concept, exclude it from the course. If all or almost all students demonstrate they do not know a concept, include that concept in the course objectives and the instruction. If some students don't know a concept, use one or more of the following four review procedures: (1) if almost everyone missed the concepts, review them with the whole class; (2) students who know the concepts can tutor others as a review measure (This method of review is most appropriate where there are equal numbers of students who know the concepts and who do not know the concepts.); (3) pretest items can be keyed to sources and references which present the concepts, and students can review them independently using these sources (This review method can be used at any time by any number of students.); (4) review concepts with individual students during office hours.

Read the following problem and then indicate your advice to the teacher by putting the appropriate number from the "Procedures" column into the column labeled "Action."

"Look at this will you? These are the results of my pretest. The number next to each sign or concept name is the number of students out of forty that knew the concept. Would you do me a favor and jot down next to each result what I should do next?"

	Concept	Number	Action		Procedure
a.	$\bar{X}$	35	___	1.	Include in course—review with whole class.
b.	Md.	12	___		
c.	s.d.	3	___	2.	Exclude from course.

(continued on next page)

d.	Σ	23	_____	3. Some students tutor others in pairs.
e.	N	21	_____	
f.	Frequency	40	_____	4. Students review independently or individually with me.

SELECTING BASIC APPROACHES TO TEACHING A CONCEPT

There are two basic ways to present information about a concept (Fig. 9.1). The two approaches can be used separately or in combination. The first is deductive. The deductive approach consists of a definiton followed by examples. The definition is given by the teacher, the examples may be given by the teacher or sought by the students. The second approach is inductive. The teacher presents examples which are followed by a definition. The definition is often discovered by the students. Students learn equally well by either approach. The choice of approach is based on considerations of time and desired results.

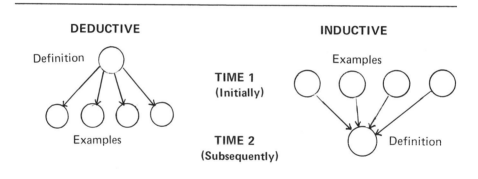

Figure 9.1 Two basic presentation approaches.

The deductive approach is most useful when there is a limited amount of instructional time. Using the deductive approach, students learn concepts more quickly than when using the inductive approach. However, the inductive approach may aid in learning other concepts; i.e., in the inductive approach students learn how to learn. In contrast, the deductive approach may result in longer retention of learning. These factors are summarized in Table 9.1.

FEEDBACK:
9.2 a 4   d 3
     b 1   e 3
     c 4   f 2

TABLE 9.1   CONSIDERATIONS IN CHOOSING INDUCTIVE AND DEDUCTIVE APPROACH

Choice Consideration	Deductive	Inductive
Time	Limited time OK	Need plenty of time
Results	Long retention	Learn how to learn

1. A law professor wants his students to learn the various types of murder charges. The professor realizes that in the future his students will have to find out about concepts of this sort by themselves. In other words, he also wants his students to learn how to learn these kinds of concepts. As a consultant, which approach would you suggest he use? _____.

2. A medical professor wants his students to learn anatomy concepts. He is rather sure that his students know how to learn concepts of this sort. He says that his problem is a limited amount of time for instruction. Which approach would you suggest he use? _____.

F
R
A
M
E
9.3

CONCEPT DEFINITIONS IN THE DEDUCTIVE APPROACH

As we have already stated, the deductive approach consists of a definition followed by examples. When you present examples, relate the example to the properties or attributes in the definition. For instance, if you were using the deductive approach to teach the concept **bird**, you might say, "A bird is a warm-blooded vertebrate with wings and feathers. This is a dodo bird. Notice these wings and these feathers. These attributes make it a bird." In the deductive approach, the accuracy of the definition is of primary importance.

Sometimes, writing a definition that differentiates examples from non-examples is difficult. Consider the problems of the courts in defining a concept such as obscenity, which has never been clearly defined. There are several concepts which present this problem. Adding to the difficulty, concept meanings change over time and even vary from one section of the country to another. Different generations and people from different cultures within the same country often have difficulty communicating. A teacher misunderstood a young student when the student remarked that the teacher's sideburns were "bad." The teacher responded, "They're

FEEDBACK:
9.3   1   Inductive
        2   Deductive

bad. You don't like them?" The student laughed and said, "No, I like them. I mean they're bad, man."

A good definition has all the defining properties of the concept. Defining properties are those properties stated in the definition which serve to place limits on the category. Any given example of a concept may have many properties other than the defining properties, but not all of these need to be mentioned in the definition. Probably all apples have skins; but that property is not normally given as one of its defining properties.

THE DISCOVERY METHOD

When using the inductive approach, the concept definition follows the examples. The teacher might present the definition or the students might have to discover it. When using the discovery method, you should consider these two points. First, be sure that examples and nonexamples are readily available to the student. If examples are not readily available, the student cannot learn. Second, be sure that students do not discover the wrong definition. A young student might make the false discovery that mammals are mother animals if the only examples available are all females. To help a student avoid erroneous discoveries, use a monitoring procedure and check his tentative definitions periodically. If a student has made an erroneous choice of properties to include in the definition, give him labeled examples which would counter the error; in the example above, you could present labeled male mammals.

TWO SPECIAL POINTS ON PRESENTATION STRATEGIES

There is one combination of the two basic presentation sequences worth noting. An excellent sequence to explain a concept is definition-example-definition. In this combination, the teacher explains the definition, relates examples to the definitions as in the deductive approach, and repeats the definition.

In cases where the student has demonstrated that he knows the subordinate concepts nested in the definition, and that he has previously encountered examples of the concept, it may only be necessary to give students a definition.

F R A M E

9.4

1. In using a discovery technique, examples should be easily available to the student.   T   F

2. In a discovery technique, a teacher should check the students' concept definitions periodically.   T   F

3. Presenting definition - example - definition is a good way of explaining concepts.   T   F

4. You can teach a concept by definition alone when a student knows   T   F
     prerequisite concepts and has seen examples previously.

CHOOSING EXAMPLES FOR CONCEPT TEACHING

Examples are used throughout concept instruction. For the purpose of discussion, it will be convenient to consider some differences among the kinds of examples used for the initial presentation and practice, for preview purposes, for advanced practice, and for inclusion in the posttest.

INITIAL PRESENTATION AND PRACTICE

Examples chosen for the initial presentation and practice should be simple and obvious. That means the defining properties of the examples should be easily recognized. The wings of the bird presented should be spread out; a close-up might even reveal separate feathers.

Four of the many ways to accentuate defining properties are:

1. Present pairs of examples and nonexamples simultaneously or in close succession so that students can easily recognize the properties that differentiate examples from nonexamples. For instance, when teaching a student to recognize a van Gogh, present a van Gogh closely followed by other Impressionist painters. In this way, differences among the painters become apparent. When teaching the visual symptoms of scarlet fever, present a picture of a case of scarlet fever next to a picture of a case of rubella and other diseases. Also show photographs comparing the child with and without scarlet fever.

2. Whenever possible, present examples and nonexamples that vary on only one property at a time. Here is an example and a nonexample presented simultaneously which vary in only one property.

TO ILLUSTRATE THE CONCEPT OF THE LOGICAL FALLACY OF ASSERTING THE CONSEQUENT, A POSITIVE AND NEGATIVE EXAMPLE CAN BE PRESENTED TOGETHER

NEGATIVE	POSITIVE
If instructors are trained, then teaching will improve.	If instructors are trained, then teaching will improve.
Instructors are trained; therefore, instruction will improve.	Instruction does improve; therefore, teachers are trained.

FEEDBACK:
9.4   All true

Give several examples for each defining property or attribute and present as many pairs in this fashion as there are properties in the definition. In this way the student will learn to discriminate each defining property.

3. Eliminate those properties not included in the definition from the example. For example, for the concept **ellipse,** it would be better to present a line drawing of an ellipse rather than presenting an ellipse embedded in other figures.

4. Use artificial prompts such as arrows, labels, and pointers to direct attention to the defining properties. When using slides or transparencies, it is possible to highlight or otherwise cause an important attribute to stand out so that it will become obvious to the student. Similarly, critical sounds may be increased in volume in order to help the students discriminate them from background noise. In all such cases, however, it is important to recognize that these artificial prompts are crutches which must gradually be removed or faded so that ultimately the students will learn to use the concept without them.

PREVIEW

Encourage students to preview examples to be used in a presentation. Previews of materials may include manipulating physical machinery or reading written examples, such as reading several short stories which contain examples of the use of symbolism. Students should be given enough time to inspect the examples carefully and to note their properties. In contrast, many teachers present concepts without letting their students study them before the presentation. As a consequence, students often do not know the aspects of the examples to which they should pay attention.

ADVANCED PRACTICE

Once a student can discriminate between examples and nonexamples presented initially, provide him with advanced practice. In advanced practice, the examples are more complex; i.e., their properties are not easily pointed out, they contain many properties not considered defining properties, they differ on more than one defining property, and there are no artificial prompts. In this way, students practice discriminating examples as they are encountered outside the classroom. One early example of the concept **mammal** (defining properties: hair and breast) might be a line drawing of a man and a line drawing of a large fish. In contrast, later practice might include a photograph of a duck-billed platypus in water compared to a photograph of a duck walking on land or a photo of an armadillo on a hillside compared to a photo of a frog on a lily pad.

POSTTESTING CONCEPTS

When students have mastered the discriminations required of advanced practice, they are ready for the posttest. Students should be given completely new examples in the posttest. Even before giving the posttest, be sure that students can discriminate examples that most people find difficult to distinguish. Thorough knowledge of a concept implies that a student can make discriminations that untrained people are incapable of making. When it comes to discriminating one wine from another, the concept of sweet-dry has a far more subtle meaning to the expert than the amateur.

A colleague has called on you for advice. He asks you to choose the best example of three different concepts to be presented to students. The concepts are: square, high, and noun. Take into consideration that the examples chosen are to be used in the initial presentation of the concept. Circle your choice of the best examples.

Concept

1. Square

a. Square   Not a square   b. Square   c. Square   Not a square

2. High

a. Higher   b. Higher   Not higher   c. Higher

3. Nouns

a. Watch   Not a noun   Watch   Noun   b. Watch - Noun   c. Noun   Watch the watch

---

FEEDBACK:
9.5
    2 b
    3 a

FRAME 9.6

A student has tried and mastered discriminations between the difficult examples and nonexamples of the concept *molecular structure of chemical compounds* that you have presented. What kinds of examples would you use on the posttest?

FRAME 9.7

Help a teacher choose an example to be used to teach the concept *noun*. Which of the examples listed below would you use for *later* practice. Choose a or b.

a.   your rose   he rose   b.   The President Hoover rose is in bloom.

He rose early in the morning.

PROVIDING APPROPRIATE PRACTICE TO LEARN CONCEPTS

The most appropriate practice for learning a concept is to discriminate examples from nonexamples. While the student practices doing this, he should be required to state or point out which properties or attributes of the sample make it an example of the concept.

When a student responds correctly or incorrectly in practice he should be given immediate feedback or confirmation. The confirmation a student receives should include praise and information that is relevant. When the student makes an incorrect choice, the properties that he overlooked should be pointed out but he should be given the opportunity to choose again. A student should never be ridiculed or embarrassed for making the wrong choice.

FRAME 9.8

Imagine teaching a course about propaganda. How would you have your students practice to learn the concept *grey propaganda?*

a.   Present labeled examples to review.
b.   Show him many positive examples to review.
c.   Give him pairs of examples and nonexamples to distinguish.
d.   Ask him to define the concept.
e.   Ask him to analyze examples.

FEEDBACK:

9.6   You want to know if the student can identify examples with which he has not practiced to see if he has learned the critical properties and not simply an association between an object or event and a word.

9.7   b. Because the defining properties are subtle, the example differs on more than one property, and many extra properties are included.

9.8   c

The thread which ties all aspects of concept teaching together is **discrimination**. The best test of knowledge of a concept is a student's ability to discriminate between examples and nonexamples. Both the inductive and deductive approaches attempt to familiarize the student with critical properties to use in making the discrimination. During practice, a student is required to differentiate between examples and nonexamples. Once a student is capable of making discriminations, he is ready to use the concept in conjunction with other concepts to form principles.

PRINCIPLE TEACHING

In the structure of knowledge, concepts are combined into principles. Consider the concepts embedded in these simplified examples of principles: round things roll; hot air rises; frustration yields aggression; $E = MC^2$; speed kills; eye color is inherited.

A principle is not simply a number of concepts linked in the same sentence. A principle states a relationship between classes of events which enable us to: (1) predict consequences; (2) explain events; (3) infer causes; (4) control situations; and (5) solve problems. Suppose, for example, that the following principle of human behavior has been validated: "A person's actions depend on the existence of skill and motivation. Both factors must be present and the greater the amount of either skill or motivation, the more likely the action." Knowing this general principle, we can predict that if a person has skill and is motivated, he is apt to perform an activity; we can explain his performing the activity by saying, he has skill and is motivated; we can control his behavior by establishing the conditions that assure his performance of the activity, i.e., by motivating him and teaching him the skill; and we can use this principle, along with other principles, to solve problems.

Principles are different from concepts and facts in their properties and uses. Consider each of the statements below in which the word action is used differently.

- Action is an observable movement of an object or person.
- There was plenty of action yesterday on campus.
- Action depends on the presence of skill and motivation.

The first statement describes the properties of a class of events. Actions, i.e., those events that include observable movement of an object or person, comprise one class of events. Types of statements like the first one above are used to identify or classify. This type of statement is called a concept definition.

The second statement describes an event that occurred which fits the definition of the concept **action**. This sort of statement is used to record events and is called a statement of fact.

The third statement describes a generalized relationship between events and is classed as a principle.

In preparation for teaching, you are reading over the notes relating to the study of ecological systems. Check those which are *principles:*

a. There are two systems under consideration.
b. Ecology is the study of the interaction of systems.
c. Affecting one part of an ecological system affects all other parts.
d. Air pollution is sometimes caused by inversion of air masses.
e. The more phosphates dumped into streams and ponds, the greater the rate of growth of the plant life.
f. The more plant life, the less room for other living things.

SPECIFYING THE OBJECTIVE

When teaching principles, it is important to state an objective that clearly specifies what you want your students to be able to do with the principle. Should the student be able to make predictions? Explain observed phenomena? Solve problems? In Table 9.2, we have developed a model objective for each of five potential applications of a principle. Note that the table is divided into two parts. Study the table carefully and then refer to the example in part B. The objectives are stated in different ways depending on the desired outcome. Five different possible outcomes are developed in Table 9.2: (1) prediction; (2) inference; (3) control; (4) explanation; and (5) problem solving.

Let's consider an example of the use of Table 9.2 to develop a procedure for testing an objective. In this case, the objective is for a student teacher to learn to apply a specific principle. The principle is stated, "Periods of practice separated by periods of rest achieve efficient learning." Now, suppose that we want the student teacher to use the principle to control outcomes. Table 9.2 (part B) can be used to design a situation to test the specific objective. Following the format in the table, a student teacher, for example, might be assigned three hours for practice, an objective to work with, a textbook, and a timer. Within the assigned time, the student teacher might be required to provide practice for his pupils. His performance would be judged by his conformity to the principle and by the resultant learning. In the same fashion, an instructor could use the format given in Table 9.2 for prediction, inference, explanation, and problem solving.

FEEDBACK:
9.9   c, d, e, f
        a is a fact; b is a concept definition.

TABLE 9.2   TYPES OF OBJECTIVES FOR PRINCIPLES

A. GENERAL FORMAT
APPLICATIONS OF PRINCIPLES

Components of Objective	Prediction	Control	Explanation	Inference	Problem Solving
Conditions	Given antecedent conditions	Given sufficient materials to compose antecedent condition	Given a situation including antecedent conditions, consequences, and irrelevant cues	Given a consequence	Given a formulated problem solvable by use of the target principles
Terminal behavior	Student states consequences	Student arranges materials	Student states which antecedent conditions are related to the consequences and how they are related	Student states the antecedent conditions which may have occurred	Student solves the problem by arranging antecedent conditions
Criterion	According to the properties of the principle	So that the consequences approximate consequences of the principle	So that the statements approximate the relationship of the antecedent conditions and consequences of the principle	So that they approximate the antecedent conditions which lead to similar consequences as stated in the principle	According to the properties of the stated principle

B. SPECIFIC EXAMPLE FOR THIS PRINCIPLE: Periods of practice separated by periods of rest achieve efficient learning (as compared to periods of practice with few or no interruptions).

Components of Objective	Prediction	Control	Explanation	Inference	Problem Solving
Conditions	Given a period of time used for practice in a certain way	Given a period of time to be used for practice, practice materials, and a clock	Given a complete practice sequence including the practice times, the learning outcomes, and other information about practice	Given a learning outcome	Given a problem such as: a certain degree of learning is required
Terminal behavior	Student states the amount or quality of learning	Student conducts a practice session	Student states which properties of the practice sequence are related to the learning and how they are related	Student states the practice conditions	Student provides practice conditions
Criterion	According to the properties of the distributed practice principle	So that the learning is efficient as stated in the principle	So that the statements approximate the relationship of the antecedent conditions and consequences of the distributed practice principle	So that they approximate the antecedent conditions which lead to similar consequences as stated in the distributed practice principle	According to the properties of the distributed practice principle

TESTING FOR PREREQUISITE KNOWLEDGE

After writing objectives, an instructor should derive the prerequisite concepts for the principle to be learned and test to determine whether or not the student knows them. To find prerequisites for a given principle, begin by stating the principle fully and identify all of the concepts embedded in the statement. A common error is to choose only the concepts represented by nouns. Don't forget the concepts which include a relationship between events such as: **is a function of, increases as,** and **decreases as.** Include any such parts of speech.

F R A M E

9.10

You are training scouts to survive under adverse conditions. Because you cannot predict the exact conditions they will face, you decide to teach them principles that can apply broadly. Consider this principle:

Combustion depends upon heat, oxygen, and fuel.

What concepts would you include on the pretest?

SELECTING APPROACHES TO PRINCIPLE TEACHING

In general, there are three phases in teaching a principle. During the first time period, the student is motivated to find out the nature of a particular principle. In this phase, as in the others to follow, the conditions for motivation and learning may be arranged by the student or instructor. During the second phase of learning, the principle is composed. In the last instructional period, the student practices applying the principles.

MOTIVATION TO LEARN

A person who is curious about new things he is faced with is more likely to be interested in learning a principle. Curiosity is aroused when a person is puzzled by events which take place and are inconsistent with his knowledge. Because of his lack of knowledge of principles in such puzzling situations, the person cannot explain what is happening, nor can he predict what will happen next, infer what caused the event, or control the situation. A child might ask: "Why is Mrs. Moore's belly sticking out?" "How did the baby get in there?" "How come airplanes can fly and I can't?" An adult might ask: "Why are some people so high strung and some so calm?" "Why is there an epidemic of venereal disease?" "Why doesn't inflation stop?"

FEEDBACK:

9.10 Combustion   heat   fuel
      depends upon   oxygen

When curiosity is exhibited by a student, an instructor should capitalize on it by pursuing the student's question. Unfortunately, most students hold their questions in abeyance and the instructor must arrange conditions to foster curiosity. To promote curiosity, an instructor might set up events which are inconsistent with a student's present beliefs. Here are two suggested procedures:

1. Make provocative statements or ask provocative questions: "A government run by a dictator gets the job done best." "Does air weigh anything?"

2. Demonstrate a relationship or show an event which reveals some new knowledge: support water in an inverted glass by a piece of paper, or show time-lapse photography of a plant's growth with and without moon dust. Before a demonstration, ask the students to predict what will happen. After a demonstration, ask the students if they would actually like to perform the demonstration themselves or use the principle in a practical situation.

COMPOSING THE PRINCIPLE

After prerequisites are assessed and motivation is present, the student should be ready and willing to figure out the relationship of events elaborated in a principle.

Three approaches to composing a principle are:

1. **Ask** the student a series of **questions** which will result in having him **develop the principle**. This approach is used when you can group students who possess the same prerequisite knowledge, when the students are highly motivated, when time is available, and when you desire to teach students the process of discovery.

2. When time is short and students have the same prerequisites, the **instructor may tell** the students how the principle is formed.

3. For objectives including more complex principles, especially for those dealing with control and problem solving, the **instructor may demonstrate** applications of the principle.

Telling and **demonstrating** a principle are both relatively obvious straightforward approaches to teaching it. It is somewhat more difficult to help a student actually develop a principle himself. The dialogue on page 236 illustrates the latter approach. In this dialogue, the teacher leads student to compose the principle from its components by asking questions. Preceding the dialogue, the teacher and student have determined that the student knows the prerequisite concepts, i.e., the student can identify the following concepts—action, skills, and states of motivation—when he sees them, but he cannot predict the action outcome. The teacher has explained to the student that he will be able to predict using the principle: action is a function of skill and motivation.

Teacher:	At this point, you and I are fairly certain that you have the prerequisites for learning the action principle.
Student:	Yes, I did pretty well on the pretest.
Teacher:	From your own experience, describe an action that occurred in some situation.
Student:	Any one?
Teacher:	Yes.
Student:	Last Saturday I read *Stranger in a Strange Land* by Heinlein.
Teacher:	Good book. Why did you do that?
Student:	I read short stories by Heinlein and liked them. I wanted to read a complete novel by him.
Teacher:	What skill and information did you need in order to read the novel?
Student:	I had to be able to read, I had to know certain vocabulary, and I had to be able to look up some words in the dictionary.
Teacher:	Good. In general, what two conditions had to be met before you read the book?
Student:	Wanting to read it and being able to read it. I get it—motivation and skill.
Teacher:	Right. Would you have read the book even if you were able, had you not wanted to?
Student:	No.
Teacher:	Why is it that you did not read it a couple of years ago?
Student:	I couldn't read well enough, and I really didn't want to read it.
Teacher:	Why read it now?
Student:	I had more motivation and greater skill.
Teacher:	Right! That makes up the essence of this principle. How would you state the principle in your own words?
Student:	You have to have some motivation and skill to get some action going. The more of each one; the more likely you are to see some action.

So far, the teacher had led the student to compose the principle from its components. Now he will provide for practice.

When an instructor lectures on the nature of a principle, he describes the events to be related and then draws the relationship. The key to a good explanation is to elaborate on each part of the principle and how it fits into the relationship, as in the above example.

In demonstrating the application of a principle, an instructor should clearly label his own performance as he progresses in his demonstration according to the concepts and relationships implied in the principle. It is a good practice to have the fully stated principle in view to refer to as the demonstration takes place.

PRACTICE AND POSTTEST

Once the principle has been composed, the student should be given the opportunity to apply it as required in the objective. Practice is essential because the use of a principle is reinforcing to the student. Principles are functional: they enable people to do all sorts of things. If a student is given practice exercises, he is more likely to get concrete payoffs for his effort and, in addition, see the relevance of his learning. Thus, students should be allowed to practice mastery to increase their motivation. As practice proceeds, the teacher should provide feedback; at the end of practice, a posttest should be given.

Suppose you were teaching students principles of political science. What steps would you pursue in teaching the students?

1.
2.
3.
4.
5.

F
R
A
M
E

9.11

SUMMARY

Concepts and principles are included in all subjects. Since a large part of the time in a formal classroom setting is devoted to teaching concepts and principles, it is imperative for teachers to understand how they are learned and taught.

   To teach a concept, an instructor formulates an objective which requires a student to differentiate between examples and nonexamples. He derives and tests for the prerequisite concepts embedded in the definition. Depending on the time available and the learning desired, an instructor chooses either an inductive or deductive approach. He provides for practice by asking the student to choose examples of the concept. At first the discriminations are kept simple, but later they are made more difficult. After practice is complete, the posttest follows. New examples are used on the posttest.

   An instructor writes an objective for principle teaching which requires a

---

FEEDBACK:

9.11 1 State the objective—prediction, inference, control, explanation, or problem solving.
      2 Test prerequisite concepts embedded in the principle.
      3 Compose the principle—question, tell, or demonstrate.
      4 Let students practice according to the objective.
      5 Give a posttest.

student to predict, infer, explain, control, or problem solve. Knowledge of concepts embedded in the principle is assessed. The principle is then composed by questioning the student, lecturing on the nature of the principle or by demonstrating its application. The instructor provides for practice according to the requirements of the objective and then he gives a posttest.

SUGGESTED READINGS

Carrol, John B.: "Words, Meaning & Concepts," *Educational Review,* Vol. 34, 178-202, 1964.

DeCecco, John P.: "The Teaching and Learning of Concepts and Principles," *The Psychology of Learning and Instruction: Educational Psychology*, (New Jersey: Prentice-Hall, Inc., 1968).

Gagné, R. M.: "The Learning of Principles, " *Analyses of Concept Learning,* H. J. Klausmeier and C. W. Harris (Eds.), (N.Y. Academic Press, 1966), 81-95.

Gagné, R. M.: "Discrimination: Concrete Concept Learning," *The Conditions of Learning,* (New York: Holt, Rinehart, & Winston, 1970).

Markle, Susan M. & Teimann, Phillip W.: "Conceptual Learning & Instructional Design," *The Journal of Educational Technology*, Vol. 1, No. 1, (London: Councils & Ed. Press, Ltd.), January, 1970.

Mechner, Francis : "The Teaching of Concepts and Chains," *Science Education and Behavioral Technology, In: Teaching Machines and Programed Learning II,* (Washington, D.C.: Robom, NEA, 1965), 461-484.

PLANNING CHECKLIST FOR CONCEPTS

This checklist presents the steps to be followed in teaching a concept. It will help you set up conditions for instruction which conform to the way people learn concepts.

Operations	Decisions
1. PLANNING OBJECTIVES AND PREREQUISITE CONCEPTS	
a. State behavioral objectives for the concepts listed.	Have you stated behavioral instructional objectives which describe a final test in which the learner is required to distinguish examples of the concept from nonexamples?
b. For each concept listed, state its prerequisite concepts.	For each concept listed, have you stated those concepts which are nested in each definition?

Operations	Decisions
2. PLANNING A PRETEST AND REVIEW	
a. Write a pretest.	Have you written a pretest which requires the learner to demonstrate that he knows the prerequisite concepts?
b. State plans for a review.	Have you reviewed the concepts which students did not know on the pretest?
3. PLANNING PRESENTATION OF INFORMATION	
a. Choose a presentation approach.	Deductive: You have limited time and do not wish to teach students how to go about learning similar concepts.
	If you are using a deductive approach, have you stated a definition a student could use to discriminate between examples and nonexamples of the defined concept?
	Inductive: You have ample time and want students to learn how to go about learning similar concepts.
	If you are using the inductive approach, have you: (1) stated examples which emphasize the defining properties and are readily available to the student? (2) planned a monitoring procedure which prevents erroneous discoveries?
b. Plan the examples to be used for initial presentation.	Have you planned examples in which the defining properties are easily pointed out?
c. Plan a review.	Have you planned to let the students preview those examples which will be used in the presentation to illustrate the concept?
4. PLANNING CONDITIONS FOR PRACTICE	
a. Require practice.	Are students required to practice by choosing between examples and non-examples?
	When students identify examples do you ask them to state the distinguishing properties of the examples?
b. Confirm student's choices.	When individual student's choices are correct, are they confirmed immediately?

Operations	Decisions

	When an individual student responds incorrectly, instead of punishing the student, do you:
	    Review the properties the student overlooked?
	    Require the student to try again until the response is correct?

c. Require advanced practice.	When students can discriminate between relatively simple choices of examples and nonexamples, are they then required to choose between examples and nonexamples whose defining properties are not easily pointed out?
	Do you require students to continue practice until they can choose between examples and nonexamples used for advanced practice?
	Does the advanced practice insure that the students can distinguish between the examples that most people find difficult to classify?

5. PLANNING A POSTTEST	
	Does your posttest include examples and nonexamples not encountered previously by the student?

PLANNING CHECKLIST FOR PRINCIPLES

Conditions for Learning Principles

1. The objective

    a. State the principle.

        1) Does the principle include:

            a) A set of antecedent conditions? For example, "If so and so . . . ."

            b) A set of consequences? "Then the following will happen . . . ."

            c) A relationship between the antecedent conditions and consequences which will enable a person to explain, control, predict, and solve problems?

    b. State the objective in one or more of these general formats:

        1) Prediction

            a) Conditions: Given antecedent conditions

       b) Terminal behavior: Student states consequences

       c) Criterion: According to the properties of the principle.

    2) Inference

       a) Conditions: Given a consequence

       b) Terminal behavior: Student states antecedent conditions which may have occurred

       c) Criterion: So that they approximate antecedent conditions which lead to similar consequences as stated in the principle.

    3) Control

       a) Conditions: Given sufficient materials to compose antecedent conditions

       b) Terminal behavior: Student arranges materials

       c) Criterion: So that consequences approximate consequences of the principle.

    4) Explanation

       a) Conditions: Given a situation including antecedent conditions, consequences, and irrelevant cues

       b) Terminal behavior: Student states which antecedent conditions are related to consequences, and how they are related

       c) Criterion: So that the statements approximate the relationship of antecedent conditions and consequences in the principle.

    5) Application to problems (to assess principles only)

       a) Conditions: Given a formulated problem solvable by use of the target principle

       b) Terminal behavior: Student solves the problem by arranging antecedent conditions

       c) Criterion: According to the properties of the stated principle

  c. Communicate the objective to the student.

2. Pretest and review.

  a. Pretest for prerequisite concepts.

  b. Review by asking questions which require the identification of prerequisite concepts.

3. Presentation and practice.

  a. Ask questions or give assignments that require the student to put the components of the principle together. Demonstrate the principle or explain it to the student.

  b. Require the student to demonstrate his knowledge of the principle in the same fashion as the terminal behavior in the objective.

4. Posttest

POSTTEST

To answer the first five questions of this posttest read the following two memos. Then indicate what you would do with the concepts numbered 1-5 in the first memo by assigning each a letter from the procedures listed in the second memo.

Memo

To: You
From: Chris Shendo, Music Teacher

These are the results of my pretest. The column of numbers indicates the number of students who were able to identify that prerequisite concept. I have 30 students.

Test Item No.   1. Sonata   2 _____
                  2. Symphony 15 _____
                  3. Concert   28 _____
                  4. Rhapsody 24 _____
                  5. Baroque   30 _____

What do I do now?

Memo

To: Chris
From: You

Here's what you do now—

I've assigned the letters associated with the suggestions listed to the numbered items above.

   a.   Include in the course, review with whole class.
   b.   Exclude from the course.
   c.   Students tutor each other in pairs.
   d.   Students review independently or individually with instructor.

Answer questions 6-8 on the basis of the following paragraph:

The geology teacher wants his students to know a potentially good oil deposit when they work in a land area. He asks: "How would I know they knew this?" Write an objective which would describe the student's performance indicating his knowledge of the complex concept *a potentially good oil deposit*. Be sure to strive for the closest simulation to the performance required in the referent situation. Choose the portions of an objective that will enable them to identify the concept.

6.   Conditions
   a.   When given a number of defining characteristics.
   b.   When given geological data regarding a section of land and a map.
   c.   When given a map.

7.   Terminal behavior
   a.   The student will choose a tract of land on a map for purposes of exploration.
   b.   The student will write a definition of potentially good oil deposit.
   c.   The student will define potentially good oil deposit as he would in the real world.

8.   Criteria
   a.   According to the concepts in the textbook.
   b.   According to actual oil findings in the area.
   c.   According to the definition given by the teacher.

9.   The supervisor of medical interns wants his students to learn many concepts on their internship. At the same time he wants the interns to become independent learners of concepts as they would in practice. Which approach do you suggest he use? Inductive or Deductive?

10.   A history professor has a list of concepts that he wants his students to learn in a few short weeks. He knows that they all know how to learn concepts already. What presentation approach do you suggest he use? Inductive or Deductive?

11.   Suppose a colleague writes to you and asks you how to present examples of a concept to students for their first presentation. Use these examples to illustrate your point. Choose a, b, or c.

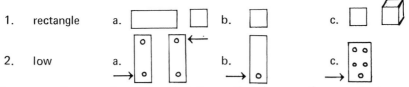

12.   The same colleague writes again. He tells you that these are the examples he used early in practice. Would you help choose an example to be used in advanced practice? Which of the examples listed under later examples would you choose: a or b?

Early Examples

Triangle   Not a Triangle

Later Examples

a.   b.

13. Imagine teaching a course on ethics. How would you have students practice to learn the concept *Christian?*

    a. Require students to define concepts.
    b. Give pairs of examples and nonexamples to discriminate.
    c. Ask the student to review examples used in the presentation.
    d. Present many examples to the student.
    e. Ask the student to state the concept name.

14. Your students have just demonstrated in practice that they are able to discriminate between difficult examples and nonexamples of the concept quartz. What kinds of examples would you use on the posttest? _____

15. Label these as true or false.   T   F

    a. You can teach a concept by definition when the student   ____   ____
       knows the prerequisite concepts nested in the definition.
    b. When using a discovery technique, examples should be   ____   ____
       made readily available for the students.
    c. One presentation approach useful in teaching concepts   ____   ____
       is definition-example-definition.
    d. In the course of a discovery approach, the teacher should ____   ____
       avoid checking the students' discoveries.

16. You are preparing to teach a task. Here are some statements a student must know. Check those which are *principles.*

    a. Reinforcement is the strengthening of a response.
    b. Two conditioned stimuli paired together are likely to elicit the same response.
    c. Present a reinforcing stimulus after the desired response to increase its strength.
    d. Pavlovian conditioning is synonymous with classical conditioning.
    e. Setting up electrical apparatus.

17. You want your students to make inferences using the principle: the fittest survive. Answer these questions regarding this objective: Given several species that survived, the student will be able to state reasons that they survived according to the survival principle.

    a. Conditions: Is the student given consequences?   YES   NO

    b. Terminal Behavior: Is the student required to state likely antecedent conditions?   YES   NO

    c. Criterion: Are the antecedent conditions measured according to the properties of the principle?   YES   NO

18. You are teaching teachers to increase the strength of students' behaviors. For this task they would have to learn the reinforcement principle. Consider this principle:

Reinforcement is a function of the immediacy, the intensity, and the valence of the reinforcing stimulus.

List the prerequisite concepts.

19.   Suppose you were assigned to teach students a basic principle of natural science. What steps would you follow to teach the students.

a.

b.

c.

d.

e.

Answers to this posttest can be found on page 336.

OVERVIEW OF LEARNING SYSTEM DESIGN • RECOGNIZING WELL-FORMULATED OBJECTIVES • DERIVING AND WRITING LEARNING OBJECTIVES • EVALUATING LEARNING SYSTEMS • TASK DESCRIPTIONS•TYPES OF LEARNING • ANALYZING TASKS, OBJECTIVES, AND LEARNER CHARACTERISTICS • GENERAL PRINCIPLES OF LEARNING AND MOTIVATION • THE LEARNING AND TEACHING OF CONCEPTS AND PRINCIPLES •**THE LEARNING AND TEACHING OF PROBLEM SOLVING** • PERCEPTUAL-MOTOR SKILLS • THE SYSTEM APPROACH TO INSTRUCTION • OVERVIEW OF LEARNING SYSTEM DESIGN • RECOGNIZING WELL-FORMULATED OBJECTIVES • DERIVING AND WRITING LEARNING OBJECTIVES • EVALUATING LEARNING SYSTEMS • TASK DESCRIPTIONS • TYPES OF LEARNING • ANALYZING TASKS, OBJECTIVES, AND LEARNER CHARACTERISTICS • GENERAL PRINCIPLES OF LEARNING AND MOTIVATION • THE LEARNING AND TEACHING OF CONCEPTS AND PRINCIPLES • **THE LEARNING AND TEACHING OF PROBLEM SOLVING** • PERCEPTUAL-MOTOR SKILLS • THE SYSTEM APPROACH TO INSTRUCTION • OVERVIEW OF LEARNING SYSTEM DESIGN•RECOGNIZING WELL-FORMULATED OBJECTIVES•DERIVING AND WRITING LEARNING OBJECTIVES • EVALUATING LEARNING SYSTEMS • TASK DESCRIPTIONS•TYPES OF LEARNING • ANALYZING TASKS, OBJECTIVES, AND LEARNER

10

CHAPTER OBJECTIVES

After reading this chapter, you should be able to:

- Correctly identify statements that describe problems.
- Choose realistic problem-solving conditions.
- Correctly name the steps in problem solving for a given example.
- Evaluate a problem-solving objective based on a given set of criteria.
- Choose the best strategy for assessing prerequisites for problem solving.
- Correctly identify three general rules for teaching problem solving.
- Distinguish among plans for teaching problem solving according to these procedures: programed procedure, simulated procedure, and on-the-job training.
- Match problem-solving heuristics to appropriate examples.

INTRODUCTION

Problem solving is an extremely complex process which involves many more basic psychological activities. We problem solve by applying principles and concepts. These three types of learning are, in a way, hierarchical. Concepts combine to form principles and principles are used to solve problems. Thus, everything we have said in the previous chapters about teaching concepts and principles applies to problem solving. Furthermore, learning in general, may be construed to be a form of problem solving. If, for example, a student is discovering (and learning) the properties of a concept inductively, he is, in a sense, solving a problem.

A problem is present when a desired goal cannot be reached. The situations listed below are problems because each involves a goal which, for the time being at least, cannot be achieved.

- A chimp's food is out of arm's reach outside of his cage. How can he get the food?
- A section of a farmer's land has eroded away. How can he replenish the land?
- An archeologist finds a small hole in his digging which might indicate that some artifact may have been buried there and rotted away. How can he find out what the artifact was?
- A truck is wedged under a low bridge. How can it be removed?
- A scientist considers how to counter a missile that cannot be detected on radar because it flies so low.
- A hunter tries to capture a monkey alive.
- A teacher would like to improve the way he asks questions.

- A homeowner is worried about his lawn turning yellow.
- An engineer is trying to figure out how to make a ball for blind children.

Tasks and problems are different. A problem involves a gap between what a person can do and what he would like to do, while there is no gap in a task.

A colleague of yours says that he is helping teaching assistants solve problems they have listed. You say you approve of what he is trying to do, but not all statements on the list are problems as they are stated. Check the ones that are statements describing problems.

F R A M E
10.1

_____ 1. We have to grade papers promptly.
_____ 2. We have to maintain office hours.
_____ 3. We have assertive students and we do not know how to deal with them.
_____ 4. We have to write task descriptions and no one has shown us how.
_____ 5. We do not know what to do to get students to pay attention in class.
_____ 6. We cannot figure out why some students do not learn.

Virtually any area or discipline may have specific problems associated with it. There are problems in mathematics, psychology, engineering, education, and so on. The homeowner faces many problems having to do with the repair and upkeep of his house. The businessman must solve financial problems daily. Even many leisure activities, such as chess and bridge, require problem solving. People have been solving problems in these areas for centuries, and in many cases, specific algorithms, formulae, or principles have been developed to help the novice solve them. If a beginner is taught principles, he can be saved the long and arduous task of discovering the solution for himself. In chess, for example, new players are taught to "develop their pieces" and "control the center of the board." Complex principles govern effective bidding in bridge. In the previous chapter, we discussed ways and means of teaching principles of this type. When important principles which can be useful for problem solving are known to a teacher, they should be taught to the student by using the procedures described in Chapter 9.

However, these principles are not always known before dealing with specific problems. For example, many of the problems of pollution and ecology remain unsolved. In addition, we cannot always anticipate what

---

FEEDBACK:
10.1 3, 4, 5, 6

particular problems a student will have to solve after he leaves the class-room, so that even when a solution to a problem exists, he may not know it and will have to discover it for himself. In these two cases, first, where no solution is known and, second, where the student is not aware of a so-lution, it is helpful for the problem solver to be aware of some general principles, to aid him in discovering the solution. In this latter case, in-struction is directed at general strategies of problem solving which can maximize transfer to specific types of problems in the future.

This chapter treats problem solving in general. In the next section, we will describe the steps a student should go through when the solution to a problem is not known to him (although it may be known to others). Later in the chapter, we will develop some general strategies and heuris-tics which a student may be able to use in the solution of any problem.

STEPS IN PROBLEM SOLVING

Problem solving often involves taking a series of well defined steps in order to arrive at a solution. A list of these steps constitutes what might be thought of as a generalized task description of problem solving. As we have observed repeatedly, a task description of this kind provides the basis for defining learning objectives and developing a training plan. Students should be able to describe the steps in problem solving and be helped to apply the process to different types of problems.

Five steps are involved in the process of problem solving:

1. Problem sensing
2. Formulation of the problem
3. Search for solutions
4. Trade-off among solutions and the selection of an approach
5. Implementation and evaluation

SENSING POTENTIAL PROBLEMS

What we seek and what we know determines which situations we perceive as problems. Consequently, each of us attends only to a few of the many potential problems that are present in situations we encounter. For ex-ample, as a man walks down a street, he may pay attention to a bewildered girl and ignore an overturned public litter basket. He senses one potential problem and ignores another, because at the time he is lonely and rela-tively unaware of the need for cleaning up the environment. The student must be taught to recognize a problem when he sees it.

Let's trace the following example through each step of the problem solving process.

Mr. Campbell, a teacher, has just finished reading a book about classroom interaction. The author convinced Campbell that students should ask many questions. Mr. Campbell's students do not ask questions, and he does not know how to get them to ask questions. Mr. Campbell has sensed a problem.

FORMULATING PROBLEMS

Once a problem is sensed, it is ready to be formulated; i.e., to have its nature and its elements described in the form of a question. Examples of this are: how can a fire be lit without matches? How can a fire be started with sticks, stones, and leaves?

People often neglect to state the problem. This deficiency can easily be demonstrated by an example. Write the number eight and three on the blackboard; then ask some students for the solution. Some will say five, others eleven, others twenty-four. But some students will recognize that all those answers are wrong because the problem was never completely stated. To continue with our example:

> Mr. Campbell formulated his problem by linking his goal and some of the elements of the problem. He asked, "How can I get a class full of students who do not ask questions now, to ask many questions?"

SEARCH FOR SOLUTIONS

Once the problem is formulated, the problem solver collects information from many sources to find a solution. By combining data and his own ideas, the problem solver formulates hypothetical solutions to try out.

> Mr. Campbell began to search for a solution. He asked his colleagues how they got students to ask questions. He also asked the school librarian what books provoke the most questions from students. Furthermore, he looked up books about the psychology of motivation.

TRADE-OFF AMONG SOLUTIONS AND INITIAL SELECTION

While many solutions to a problem may be conceivable, not all of them are necessarily feasible. There may be problems that can be solved by increasing available resources, but generally this turns out to be impractical because new money cannot be found. Another example is provided by the problem of improving undergraduate teaching. Since teaching style inevitably reflects the personality of the teacher, one way to improve teaching might be to change a teacher's personality—a potential solution to a serious problem that is fraught with difficulty and danger. The student should be taught to evaluate potential solutions and select from among them those that are apt to yield the greatest benefits for the investment of resources and those that are most likely to succeed.

> Mr. Campbell thought that his students might not really trust him and he felt it would be a good idea to spend a weekend with them. However, his class had over 300 students in it. No matter how much time he was willing to devote to building better rapport, there just weren't enough hours in the day to solve his problem by more interpersonal contact. Then he formulated some other tentative solutions for tryout. One of his colleagues suggested that he simply ask, "Any questions?"

IMPLEMENTATION AND EVALUATION

Subsequently, tryouts yield information regarding the acceptability of the most feasible solutions; i.e., how well each solution enables the problem solver to reach his goal. To conclude our example:

> Mr. Campbell tried asking if there were any questions and received no response; he discarded that solution. One of the books recommended the presentation of an ambiguous stimulus to provoke questions; so Mr. Campbell brought an unusual object into class, and the students asked many questions about the object. Mr. Campbell kept a record of the number of questions and continued to try other possible solutions. At the end of his tryouts, he chose the most effective solution, i.e., the solution that aided Mr. Campbell in getting his students to ask the most questions.

FRAME 10.2 Sherlock Holmes was a fine problem solver. Once Sherlock was called in on a case in which a woman was found dead near Thor Bridge. She had been shot at close range. A note telling of a meeting with a particular man was clutched in the dead woman's hand. The same man had been seen coming over Thor Bridge away from the scene of the murder before the shot was heard and a recently fired dueling pistol of the same caliber that killed the woman was found in his closet. The only other clue was a fresh chink out of the stone fence on the Thor Bridge.

Name the problem-solving steps Sherlock goes through.

1. Although most people felt the man who wrote the note had committed murder, Sherlock noted unexplained gaps: the fresh chink in the stone fence and the witness who saw the man return before the shot was heard.
   a. Problem formulation
   b. Problem sensing
   c. Solution
   d. Search

2. Sherlock explained that he had to account for all known facts in order to find the cause of death.

a. Problem formulation
b. Problem sensing
c. Solution
d. Search

3. He began by asking if the dueling pistol was one of a set. It was. The mate was missing. Sherlock inspected the chink in the stone, noting its position. He asked the inspector to dredge the water below. Just as Sherlock predicted, they found a dueling pistol attached to a stone by a long rope. Sherlock checked to see if the rope would stretch from the stone fence to the body. It did.
   a. Problem formulation
   b. Problem sensing
   c. Solution
   d. Search

4. Sherlock concluded that the death was suicide. After meeting with the man, the woman hung the rock over the stone fence, tied the pistol to the rope and shot herself. When she dropped the gun, the stone dragged it over the fence and into the water.
   a. Problem formulation
   b. Problem sensing
   c. Solution
   d. Search

TEACHING STUDENTS TO SOLVE SPECIFIC TYPES OF PROBLEMS

Assume that we wish to teach students how to solve interpersonal problems so as to minimize conflict in a group. This constitutes a specific type of problem. A number of known concepts and principles are potentially applicable to help the student reach a solution. If the teacher is aware of these concepts and principles and knows how to solve problems of this type, he can help the student to learn the process. The generalized model of problem solving just described may be applied by the student in this situation; that is, **the student** will need to know how to sense the problem, formulate it. etc. **The teacher,** however, will need to: (1) specify **objectives** for the student that relate the problem steps to the specific problem; (2) test for the students' **knowledge of prerequisite concepts and principles**; and (3) **arrange appropriate practice conditions** to give students the opportunity to sense the problem, formulate it, search for solutions, etc.

An example may help to clarify the role of the teacher in helping to solve specific types of problems. Assume that a student must discover how

FEEDBACK:
10.2   1 b   3 d
         2 a   4 c

to minimize conflict among conservatives and liberals in a social situation. From our previous discussion of steps in problem solving, the first objective would be to teach the student to recognize (or sense) that a problem exists. Accordingly, the teacher must specify this step in the form of a learning objective. Similarly, objectives should be written for the other steps in problem solving: formulation; search; trade-off and selection; and implementation and evaluation.

DEFINING PROBLEM SOLVING OBJECTIVES

How can an instructor assess a student's skill at problem solving? A hasty response to that question might be, "Obviously, give the student some problems and see if he can solve them." Although that answer is essentially correct, it is far more difficult to carry out than you might imagine. Problem solving is a complex process and it is often difficult to know precisely what to look for in a student's behavior when he is solving a problem. Therefore, to evaluate the learning of problem-solving skills, careful planning and preparation are required. Stating complete learning objectives in clear and unambiguous terms is an important part of that planning and can be very helpful in defining precisely what you wish to observe.

The steps in the problem-solving process, which we discussed in the last section, may each be translated into objectives. The key words used to describe the steps, i.e., **sense, formulate, search, select, implement,** and **evaluate,** are all action verbs which may be included in specific problem-solving objectives.

CONDITIONS FOR A PROBLEM-SOLVING OBJECTIVE To determine the conditions for a problem-solving objective, describe the type of problem to be given. In general, the problem should simulate encounters outside of the classroom. Equally important, the situation should exclude prompts which help the student to identify or sense a particular problem. In other words, to test for problem solving, an instructor must arrange a situation full of potential problems that remain **unrecognized** and **unformulated.** Although maximum uncertainty is desirable, the student may be given a goal. An example of a realistic problem situation is the typical candid camera vignette in which a person is told that he is supposed to box pies as they come down a conveyer belt, but the pies move down the conveyer belt much too fast for anyone to box them. This kind of situation is substantially different from a question used to assess knowledge of a principle such as "How would you use **division of labor** to box pies coming down a conveyer belt at the rate of one pie per ten seconds?"

Some examples of realistic problem conditions are:

- The student will be placed in the role of a foreign minister. A dossier will be presented containing at least one dozen potential problems.

- The student will be placed in a social situation that will contain arch-conservatives and arch-liberals who will argue their views. His role will be to minimize conflict.

- The student will be given a patient with a disease of unknown etiology.

- The student will be given an area of land to cultivate that has been badly eroded.

Suppose you were teaching high school students how to solve budgetary problems relating to grocery purchases. Which of these is the most realistic problem condition? The student will be given:

1. An anecdotal description of a grocery store problem.

2. A shelf full of imitation groceries to "purchase."

3. A drawing of a grocery store and verbal instructions.

F
R
A
M
E

10.3

TERMINAL BEHAVIOR FOR PROBLEM-SOLVING OBJECTIVES   Some aspects of the process of problem solving may be readily observed; other aspects may have to be artifically arranged. We may be able to view a student putting a solution to the test, but we may not be able to see him thinking about the information gathered. For this purpose, we might have to ask the student to say aloud what he is thinking.

In general, the problem solver does a lot of unobservable things, like thinking and imagining. Eventually he arranges conditions in the environment to achieve a previously unattainable goal. Consequently, some of the invisible processes must be inferred by observing the arrangement of the environment. Final arrangement of the environment is one criterion that can be used to judge the terminal behavior.

PRETESTING AND REVIEWING PREREQUISITES

After determining the instructional objective for problem solving, a teacher must consider his students' prerequisites. To derive prerequisites for problem solving, many types of learning which can contribute to the process must be considered. The types of learning have sometimes been assumed to fall into a hierarchy of less complex to the more complex categories. Problem solving is generally considered to be one of the most complex types of learning. Toward one end of a branch of the hierarchy we have concepts. Principles are composed of concepts and are at the next level. Finally, problem solving involves the use of both concepts and principles.

FEEDBACK:
10.3   2

On a pretest for teaching problem solving, the teacher should include immediate prerequisities, i.e., principles and concepts, in order to determine if a student understands some general principles of problem solving as well as specific subject matter principles. The teacher may wish to be certain that the student knows how to sense and formulate the problem or search for a solution. Prerequisites are assessed as described in Chapter 4. If students do not demonstrate a certain level of prerequisites, the teacher proceeds down the hierarchy to find their level of knowledge. Once the prerequisites are known, students can learn to solve problems more readily.

F R A M E 10.4

You are teaching students to solve engineering problems. You have a hetero-geneous class and are unsure of your students' abilities. What strategy do you suggest for assessing prerequisites?

1. Find their level of attainment by going from problems to principles to con-cepts, then work your way back up the hierarchy.

2. Assume they know nothing and talk about basic concepts.

3. Ask each one what they know about the subject, figure out where most of them fall, then teach from there on.

ARRANGING CONDITIONS FOR PRESENTATION AND PRACTICE

After prerequisites are assessed, an instructor should plan his teaching pro-cedures. However, some teachers say that problem solving cannot be taught. If the preceding statement means that one cannot learn to problem solve by listening to a lecture, the authors would agree. To teach problem solving, other methods should be used.

A large part of the research on problem solving has concentrated on fac-tors that interfere with problem solving rather than on methods to teach problem solving. Therefore, the methods in this section are in part, hypo-theses and in part, education assumptions.

GENERAL PRINCIPLES   There are three general principles for arranging con-ditions for learning problem solving.

   1. In your classroom presentation, include **specific ways** (strategies and techniques) for solving problems encountered in the environment outside of school. This will increase the probability that the strate-gies learned in class will transfer to the situation in which the student will use them.

FEEDBACK:
10.4   1

2. Provide **many** different **kinds** of problems for practice to maximize the probability of transfer to a wide range of problems.

3. **Model** the problem-solving approach in its entirety. It is a rare thing for a student to see an expert successfully perform the entire complex process of problem solving. To clarify each step, think aloud and label each step as it is performed. Label the antecedent conditions, relationships, and consequences of any principles used.

Which are general principles for teaching students to solve *specific types of problems?*

1. Show students specific ways to solve real problems.
2. Make students repeat unsolvable problems.
3. Allow practice on many problems.
4. Model problem-solving behavior.
5. Talk about general strategies.

F
R
A
M
E

10.5

THREE GENERAL METHODS FOR TEACHING PROBLEM SOLVING   There are three general methods that can be used for teaching problem solving.

Programed Approach   Of the three methods described, the programed approach provides the poorest representation of the real world. In this approach, the student is given parts of a contrived problem situation to which he is to react. For example, a real ecological problem may be presented as a written anecdote in a programed text. Once the student has responded, an instructor or instructional device provides feedback and directs him to the next step.

Programed procedures have the following characteristics.

- The student sees cues which precede his performance in an appropriate context, but often in an artificial way.

- The student is asked to perform one of a set of possible steps that make up a whole task. Each separate step is small enough to be done successfully, yet is complete by itself.

- The student receives feedback demonstrating the consequences of performance, often verbally.

- After the student receives feedback, he is required to retake certain steps until he is successful.

FEEDBACK:
10.5   1, 3, 4

- The student is given a set of cues for a subsequent step only when the previous step has been demonstrated successfully.

- The student first practices easy tasks and then graduates to more difficult ones.

To illustrate: using a nontext programed procedure, a student learning troubleshooting might be seated in front of an electric typewriter. A set of predetermined cues would be present in the situation, such as a note left by the secretary saying the typewriter doesn't type, a plug half out of the socket, and an old ribbon which needs replacing. The student might receive his initial instructions on a cassette tape recorder or from a live instructor. He might be required to respond to the cues that he detects. After responding, he might receive feedback directly from operating the typewriter or verbally by means of a cassette player. If the student responds correctly, he might be allowed to view the cues for the next step. (Criteria used for feedback are based upon a task description of an expert's procedures.)

Printed programed materials can be useful in teaching students problem solving. For example, an **In-Basket** technique has been used to study inquiry and problem solving. Specifically, a student learning to solve problems in business management might be given a prepared in-basket. The in-basket may contain bills, memos, receipts, phone messages, and assorted junk mail in a predetermined order. The student might take one or more of these items out of the basket at a time and write replies, make phone calls, fill out forms. At the completion of each response (or at the end of some series of responses) the learner might get oral or written feedback.

Computers sometimes use a programed format to teach problem solving. Using this technique, a doctor may learn to make diagnoses and prescriptions. The computer might print out the initial data on a patient. Then, the doctor may respond by asking for more information or by making a prescription. In either case, the computer may print out information to inform the doctor of the results of his prescription or to reveal the information he requested.

Simulation Procedures A simulation attempts to present problem conditions close to real life. The student is required to react to the conditions as he would in the real world. Usually the student gets feedback through natural channels as he would if he were in the real situation.

Simulation procedures have the following characteristics:

- Students see cues and consequences very much like those in the real environment.

- Students are placed in complex situations.

- Students act as they would in the real environment.

- Students receive feedback through natural channels.

- Fidelity (exact duplication) of a simulation is reduced in order to avoid danger or high cost.

Some problem solving can be simulated on a computer. School super-intendents might use this method in learning how to allocate budgets to schools to boost achievement scores. First, the computer might print out the total budget. Second, the superintendent may type the total budget allocations to all schools. A few seconds later the computer might give him year-end achievement test scores.

Expensive machines are used to simulate the cockpits of big jets to train pilots to solve in-flight problems. The cues are all represented with high fidelity, including visual cues coming from the windows, readings on the dials, and the pitching and yawing of the plane. Furthermore, the pilot receives consequences for his actions according to true flight logic.

Astronauts were trained for each moon shot in simulated settings. They were taught how to solve problems when in their rocket or when on the moon. They were made to feel relative weightlessness as they would in a rocket or on the moon. The simulation was made as realistic as possible based on the space administration's knowledge of what the real system was like, and based on knowledge of the surface and gravitational pull of the moon.

Students may be taught about social problems in a very dramatic and realistic way through simulation. To do this, students might be placed in the role of diplomats representing countries for which they must make treaties and decisions. They might act as community leaders in time of disaster. They might diagnose and prescribe medication for patients who have been trained to simulate certain disorders. They can plead a case in a mock trial.

On-the-Job Training For many years, on-the-job training has been very popular for teaching technical trades. However, it can be an efficient method to be used for other learning depending on the degree to which students possess necessary prerequisite concepts, principles, and skills.

The characteristics of on-the-job training are:

- Real work tasks are assigned to students while on the job.

- A supervisor is available to evaluate the student's performance and provide feedback.

On-the-job training does not necessarily imply the teaching of business tasks. It does mean that students perform in the environment for which they are being trained. For example, a teacher wanted to teach his students to adjust to a completely new environment. In this case, setting up a highly realistic simulated environment would have been very difficult. Instead, he made plans to drive his students to an unfamiliar rural town where they would be left for a day. They were given a limited amount of money and certain goals to accomplish.

There are training programs in some colleges that teach instructors how to teach while on the job. The authors of **Learning System Design** have developed such a program. The purpose of the program is to teach college teachers to recognize their own problems and follow a procedure to solve them. Specifically, each teacher is videotaped during a regular class. They then view the videotape of their class and select a short portion to illustrate a problem they have found. Next, this portion of videotape is shown to colleagues participating in the program. After that, the group discusses the problem and formulates solutions. Finally, the teacher tries out one of the solutions in his next class and brings in a videotape of that performance.

CRITERIA TO CHOOSE METHODS Here are some guidelines to help you choose among the three methods mentioned. The guidelines are based on four qualities: fidelity; cost; safety; and completeness. There are four general principles that govern the choice of method. First, the more realistic the practice, the more likely the learner is to be successful in applying his learning. Second, when methods are equally effective, a cheaper mode will do. Third, if methods are equally effective and costly but have about the same fidelity, the less dangerous one is preferable. Fourth, if methods are equal on all counts, the one which provides practice on events which occur rarely in the real world situation should be chosen.

TABLE 10.1   COMPARISON OF THREE METHODS AS TO THEIR FIDELITY, COST, SAFETY, AND COMPLETENESS

Quality	Programed Procedure	Simulated Procedure	On-the-Job Training
Fidelity	Moderate	Moderate to good	Excellent
Cost	Inexpensive	Expensive	Very expensive
Safety	Very safe	Safe	Possibly dangerous
Completeness	Quite complete	Complete	Incomplete

To read the table, let's first consider the rows. The four qualities represented by the rows answer these questions: Fidelity—How realistic are the cues, actions, and consequences in practice? Cost—How costly would the procedure be in time and money or equipment usage? Safety—Is there any danger to employer or to the student? Completeness—Will the student get a chance to practice all he needs to learn?

Next, consider one of the columns: On-the-job training. (The ratings in each cell are relative to the two other procedures.) The procedure with the most realistic situational cues, actions, and consequences is on-the-job training. However, this procedure has its disadvantages. In on-the-job training, instruction is likely to be a secondary purpose when compared to business purposes and is usually not pursued carefully. Consequently, apprentices may learn mistakes. Furthermore, their mistakes may be costly. They may cost the place of business money or time and worse yet, students may practice a mistaken procedure. In addition, on-the-job training may be physically dangerous as well, as in the case of a student who hurts himself while working on machinery. In addition, in the time provided for an apprenticeship, an instructor may be able to provide practice to students on rarely occurring critical events.

If you were teaching a student mechanic to solve engine problems, you could use any one of these three approaches. Match the name of the approach to the description below. Place the letter of the appropriate name next to the description.

F R A M E

10.6

    a. On-the-job training
    b. Simulated procedure
    c. Programed procedure

_____ 1. Set up a simple problem in an engine.
        Present the student an initial set of cues.
        Ask the student to respond.
        If he gives the right response, let him look further.
        If he makes another response, give him a prompt and ask him to respond again.
        Present problems in order of difficulty.

_____ 2. Find the student a position working at a gas station as an apprentice.
        Arrange for an employee to act as supervisor.
        Give the employee the objectives of the training so he can provide appropriate experiences for practice and evaluation.

_____ 3. Present an engine in class with particular sorts of problems planted for students to solve.

FEEDBACK:
10.6 1 c
      2 a
      3 b

GENERAL PRINCIPLES AND STRATEGIES OF PROBLEM SOLVING

INTRODUCTION

There are a number of general principles which may be useful to a student attempting to solve a problem in any area. These principles transfer to many types of problems. We divide these general problem solving principles into two broad categories: **heuristics** and **strategies**.

Heuristics are "rules of thumb" which serve to guide or reveal a solution to a problem. A heuristic helps the student solve a problem. However, empirical evidence for the heuristic may not be generally well established; heuristics may even be incapable of proof. Heuristics are operating rules and not a set of principles as a strategy might be; a strategy may employ many heuristics.

Heuristics are principles of a particular type. Strategies incorporate several principles. Therefore, both strategies and heuristics are taught using the same technique and methods as we use to teach principles.

A strategy is a systematic way of making a series of decisions. Most strategies are variations on the general scheme of problem sensing, problem formulation, search, and solution; however, some variations emphasize different parts of the process. For example, while the scientific method emphasizes the controlled, empirical testing of alternative solutions, the inquiry or discovery method emphasizes the problem-sensing and problem-formulation aspects.

HEURISTICS

If students are taught the following heuristics, it should help to improve their ability to solve problems in general.

RUNNING OVER ELEMENTS OF A PROBLEM Problem solvers should take into account all the elements affecting the situation at once. In fact, the problem solver should consider the system in which the problem is found and list as many of the factors acting on the system as he can find. This approach will reduce the possibility of gaps in the solution.

Inadequate problem solving is often due to ignoring some elements of the problem. To illustrate, Hawaii had a problem with rats that were coming off ships and reproducing at a rapid rate on the islands because they had no natural enemies. (The native wildlife were neither quick enough nor strong enough to kill the rats.) Then someone suggested importing the mongoose which is very quick and quite strong. Soon, hundreds of these animals were let loose on the island. However, someone neglected to take one important element into account: Rats are nocturnal, the mongoose is diurnal. Thus, the two species never saw one another. Now Hawaii has two problems, too many rats and too many mongooses.

HEURISTIC:
WHEN TRAINING STUDENTS TO PROBLEM SOLVE,
PROVIDE PRACTICE IN IDENTIFYING AND SCAN-
NING ALL OF THE ELEMENTS OF A PROBLEM.

VARYING RELATIONSHIPS OF ELEMENTS   The problem solver should place
the elements of a problem in different positions, either physically or sym-
bolically. Furthermore, students have to be able to ask questions such as:
How else can this object be used? How else can I relate these elements?
As an illustration, let us consider the problem of a huge airplane that has
rolled off a runway into the mud. How can we pull the plane back onto
the runway? If we vary some of the elements, we might change the question: How can we get the plane to use its own power to get back on the
runway? This suggests other questions: How can the plane's power be
utilized? How do we get something under the wheels? Lift the plane.
How do you lift a plane? You lift a plane the same way you jack up a car.
How do you jack up a plane so that it will not fall off the jack? Spread
the jacks all around and have them go up at an even rate. How can you do
that without the jack sinking in the mud? Use something that will spread
a wide base on the mud so it will not sink. What will do that and all the
other things? Several large balloons, like inflatable rafts. In summary,
this process involved changing the relationships of the elements of the
problem to arrive at an appropriate solution.

   A second example of how a solution may become more obvious when
elements are rearranged is the following problem. A student is given a
small box containing a thumbtack, a candle, and a match, and he is told to
mount the candle on the wall so that no wax drips on the floor and then
to light it. The solution to this problem requires that the student use the
thumbtack to mount the box on the wall. When the box is used as a container for the other articles, the solution is harder to arrive at because the
box may not be perceived as one of the elements in the problem-solving
task. If the student is trained to run over all the elements and vary the
relationships among them, he is more apt to "discover" the box as an element in the solution.

HEURISTIC:
WHEN TRAINING STUDENTS TO PROBLEM SOLVE,
PROVIDE PRACTICE IN VARYING THE RELATION-
SHIP AMONG THE ELEMENTS OF A PROBLEM.

PRODUCING MORE THAN ONE SOLUTION   When a student engages in problem solving, he is often tempted to stop after the first solution although there may be more effective and efficient approaches to the problem. For this reason, students should be trained to develop more than one solution to a problem and be forced to go beyond the first and most obvious example.

A good illustration of this is the tendency to immediately set out to find civilization whenever one is lost in the wilderness. Many times, it is best to simply remain where you are and wait for help.

HEURISTIC:
ENCOURAGE STUDENTS TO PRODUCE SEVERAL
SOLUTIONS TO A PROBLEM BEFORE ADOPTING ANY
ONE SOLUTION.

TALKING OVER THE PROBLEM   Talking over the problem, explaining the elements and the various relationships sometimes reveals hidden elements to the problem solver. By discussing the problem witn another person, the problem solver may become aware of new resources and new facets of the problem which had not occurred to him. As he discusses these things with his companion, the companion gains new insights and offers new suggestions. Our own studies verify this. Working with instructors, we have observed that they seldom perceive the student as a teaching resource. Students may work together in pairs, small groups, and other ways to teach one another. Once this is suggested as a possiblity to teachers with particular problems, they often go on to develop new ways of using students to teach.

HEURISTIC:
ENCOURAGE STUDENTS TO TALK OVER THEIR
PROBLEMS WITH OTHER PEOPLE.

USING GROUP RESOURCES   Talking with a group may help to solve a problem in certain situations. Using group resources is appropriate in the following situations:

- The problem is technical.
- There is a definite solution.
- A range of solutions are available.
- Each group member is involved in the problem.
- Consequences are given to the group as a whole.

- Information and skills necessary for the solution are additive.
- The task can be subdivided,
- Tasks include traps which an individual might miss.

An example of an exercise which demonstrates the usefulness of group problem solving is the moon survival problem. This problem is based on research done by the National Aeronautics and Space Administration. First, the group is told that they are a space crew scheduled to meet with the returning ship on the lighted surface of the moon; however, mechanical difficulties have forced them to land far from the meeting spot. Second, they are told that they must reach the returning ship. Third, they are given a list of items available for use. Because they cannot take all the items, they must rank them in order of priority for survival. Some of the items are: a box of matches; food concentrate; 50 feet of nylon rope; parachute silk; portable heating unit; two 45-caliber pistols; one case of dehydrated milk; two 100-lb tanks of oxygen. Finally, when the exercise is complete, the group participants can compare their rank ordering to the one researched and prepared by the National Aeronautics and Space Administration. If you will check the list of criteria above, you will note that this sort of problem is quite amenable to group problem solving; i.e., using the group as a resource is a definite advantage here.

HEURISTIC:
PROVIDE STUDENT PRACTICE IN GROUP SITUATIONS
SOLVING APPROPRIATE TYPES OF PROBLEMS AND
ENCOURAGE THEM TO UTILIZE THE RESOURCES OF
THE GROUP.

EVALUATING IDEAS   Problem solvers often tend to discard other people's solutions or discount evidence counter to their own beliefs. However, problem solvers should be highly critical of their own ideas and spend time considering other people's solutions, so that personal biases will not interfere with an objective solution to a problem.

HEURISTIC:
WHEN TRAINING STUDENTS TO PROBLEM SOLVE, PRO-
VIDE PRACTICE IN LISTENING SYMPATHETICALLY TO
OTHER PEOPLE'S IDEAS AND BEING CRITICAL OF ONE'S
OWN IDEAS.

DELAYING CHOICE OF THE SOLUTION   Effective problem solvers delay adopting solutions as long as it is practical. The longer one waits to select a solution, the more likely he is to see some new relationships, find additional solutions, or refine his present solution. One way to delay solutions is to proceed from broad solutions on an abstract level to several practical solutions on a very specific, concrete level, just as you go from a general goal to a specific instructional objective. This kind of systematic approach forces you to delay finalizing the solution. In addition, as you specify specific steps, you will see new facets of the problem and be forced to rework the solution.

HEURISTIC:
WHEN TEACHING STUDENTS TO PROBLEM SOLVE, RE-
QUIRE THEM TO DELAY IMPLEMENTING THE SOLUTION
UNTIL THE SITUATION DEMANDS IT.

STOPPING WHEN STUMPED   Problem solvers should not continue to pursue a course of action when it is no longer fruitful. Protracted and unproductive effort may only lead to frustration and perhaps capitulation. On the contrary, if a problem solver is blocked, he should stop and return to the problem later. Sometimes the fresh approach will help to break an established pattern. A period of "incubation" is often helpful to the problem solver.

HEURISTIC:
WHEN TEACHING STUDENTS TO PROBLEM SOLVE, EN-
COURAGE THEM TO STOP WHEN PROGRESS IS IM-
PEDED AND RETURN TO THE PROBLEM LATER.

PROBLEM-SOLVING STRATEGIES

In addition to the heuristics discussed in the previous section, students may also be taught how to use the following problem-solving strategies.

BRAINSTORMING AND POSTING   Brainstorming is the process of generating many possible solutions to a problem without imposing judgments based on stringent criteria. Specifically, problem solvers are told to state as many ideas as they are able, as if they had all the resources possible. In addition, no value judgments are made until the brainstorming session is over.

It is often helpful in group situations to **post** suggestions of the group. Posting may be used at all stages of problem solving: problem sensing and formulation, search for a solution and its implementation. When posting, the group leader uses a felt-tip pen, some masking tape, and a large desk pad of paper. He then states an objective for the students. In the problem formulation stage he might ask the group: "List the things that are wrong with the lecture method." "State some of the reasons that students cheat." "List some of the reasons students don't seem to be learning." After stating the objective, he asks the group to respond. All suggestions are accepted and posted. After posting the suggestions, they are categorized and discussed with the group.

MEANS-ENDS ANALYSIS This strategy incorporates three major steps. At first the problem solver compares his conception of his current state of affairs and the state of affairs he desires. Then he tries to reduce the differences between the two states. Based on an analysis of his tryout, he decides if he has made any progress toward the desired state and what course to pursue next in order to reduce the differences, if any are left. A physician exemplifies this strategy when he deals with a sick patient whom he would like to see in perfect health. The doctor analyzes the signs and symptoms present, prescribes a drug, and asks the patient to return. When the patient comes back, the physician looks for signs of progress and decides then whether to maintain the treatment, eliminate it, revise it, or substitute another. In this way, the physician is consistently looking at the relationship between the methods he uses and the ends he wishes to achieve.

PROGRESSIVE DEEPENING Progressive deepening is a strategy based on a **decision tree**. A decision tree is a representative drawing of a series of two choice decisions, such as yes-no, go-no go, on-off. Each branch of the tree leads to another binary decision; thus, it appears much like a stick-figure tree. The way most people use a decision tree is called **progressive deepening**. Specifically, they pursue a branch until a decision can be tested. Once it has been tested and found lacking, the problem solver returns to the base and pursues another branch. The following example illustrates this strategy.

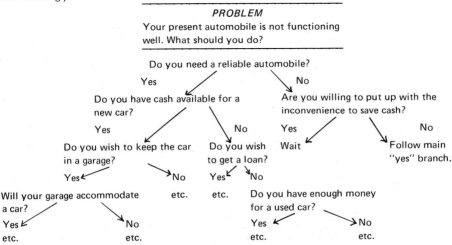

PROBLEM

Your present automobile is not functioning well. What should you do?

In this example, the owner of an unreliable automobile wonders what he should do. Does he need a car? Should it be new or used? What kind of a car should he buy? The strategy of progressive deepening requires him to develop a decision tree and follow it until he reaches a point of action or a block. If he meets a block, he must return to the last node and retest.

Normally people do not construct decision trees which reflect the full range of possibilities. Instead, they tend to consider bits and pieces of the problem in isolation or at random. Sometimes, people pursue a particular branch of a decision tree without considering others. The optimal approach is to consider a number of branches simultaneously.

TROUBLESHOOTING   Troubleshooting is a special form of problem solving used primarily in man-machine systems. Although troubleshooting is usually identified with man-machine systems, this approach can be extended to ecological and social systems. The job of the troubleshooter is to find the source of trouble within a system. The goal of the larger system is to keep the machine going so that it will continue to produce. If we were to label the role of the troubleshooter, we would call him primarily a problem sensor and formulator. Hence, he ends his job by pointing out the source of the trouble.

The steps in troubleshooting are as follows: First, the troubleshooter selects a test point; i.e., based on the initial cues, he picks a working point of the machine to check. For example, when the secretary complains the electric typewriter will not work, the troubleshooter might choose to check the plug first. Next, he recalls what signals should be present. Is the plug in a working socket? Then he locates the test point; that is, he crouches down and looks for the plug. Next he determines what signals are present and decides if the signal is as it is supposed to be. For instance, he sees that the plug is only halfway in the socket and realizes that this is not as it should be. Finally, he interprets the results and either selects another test point, makes repairs if they are minor, or he may call a more specialized repairman if the repairs are major. In this case, the troubleshooter would push the plug in and turn on the machine to see if the motor worked. If the motor does work, he leaves. If the motor does not work, he chooses another test point.

The troubleshooter's choices of test points will vary according to the system he works on. Here are some heuristics:

- Go from the most accessible, cheapest checkpoint to the least accessible, most costly checkpoint.
- Begin at the end of the system and work backward.
- Choose a test point that eliminates a whole subsystem.

Which are the first 5 steps you would take to troubleshoot a lamp that will not light? Choose 1 or 2 for the optimal sequence of steps.

1. a. Select a test point such as the plug.
    b. State what signals should be present (the plug should be in).
    c. Find the plug.
    d. Is the plug in?
    e. If it is out, fix it.

2. a. State what signals should be present.
    b. Find a test point, such as a plug.
    c. See if the plug is in.
    d. Fix plug.
    e. State if the plug is in.

Very often, troubleshooters do their work with a manual as a guide. Manuals usually include checklists and decision aids. Checklists and decision aids are outgrowths of the description of the troubleshooter's task. A checklist is a series of questions to be answered about steps a troubleshooter might take. For example, astronauts use checklists to verify the correctness of their dressing procedures. Each astronaut runs down a series of checkpoints to be sure his space suit is in order. As Fig. 10.1 illustrates, checklists are made from a series of decisions in a task description.

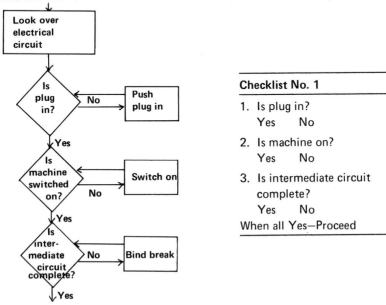

Figure 10.1 Derivation of a checklist from a flow diagram of a task description.

FEEDBACK:

10.7 1 is correct because it is in the proper sequence.

Decision aids are also used in troubleshooting manuals. The decision aid tells the troubleshooter what to do when a certain combination of cues is present. It is useful when many possible alternative steps depend on the presence of combinations of cues. Figure 10.2 is a diagram of this process.

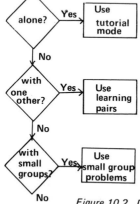

Are there students who wish to study:

Decision Aid No. 1

Cues present:	Appropriate action:
1. Study alone	Tutorial Step 17
2. Study with one other	Learning pairs Step 24
3. Study with small group	Small group problems Step 32

Figure 10.2   Derivation of a decision aid from a flow diagram of a task.

FRAME 10.8

A colleague shows you some of his task descriptions for some troubleshooting tasks. As you consider the flow diagram, you note sections that can be converted to checklists and decision aids. You say that he can save a lot of time by giving these aids to his students. Show him how to convert these two sections.

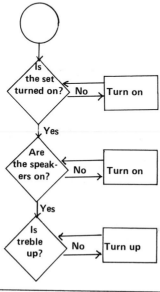

1. Should this be a
   a. Decision Aid
   b. Checklist

FEEDBACK:

10.8   b   Checklist

Is the set turned on?	Yes No	Is the treble up?	Yes No
Are the speakers on?	Yes No	When all yes—proceed.	

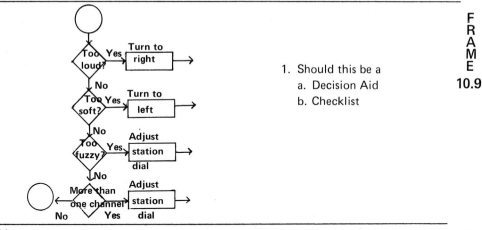

1. Should this be a
   a. Decision Aid
   b. Checklist

You are showing an observer the use of various strategies and heuristics. In column A are your observations. Label them by placing the letter associated with a strategy or heuristic in column B next to the observation.

A	B
_____ 1. Generated many ideas in a relaxed atmosphere and wrote them on a board.	a. Run over the elements
_____ 2. Checked all things affecting the problem.	b. Vary the relationship of elements
_____ 3. Discussed the problem with a layman and an expert.	c. Produce more than one solution
_____ 4. Put the problem down symbolically and manipulated the symbols in different ways.	d. Talk over the problem
_____ 5. Thought of as many answers as he could.	e. Use group resources
_____ 6. Found others who could contribute to parts of the solution in a group.	f. Evaluate ideas
_____ 7. Double-checked his own ideas and listened to others' ideas.	g. Delay solution choice
_____ 8. Waited until he had to put solution into practice to pick the best one.	h. Stopping when stumped

(continued on next page)

FEEDBACK:

10.9   a   Decision Aid

Signal:	Operation:
Too loud	Turn to right
Too soft	Turn to left
Too fuzzy	Adjust station dial
More than one channel	Adjust station dial

_____ 9. Looked for the cause of the problem in the machine by prescribed
steps.

i. Brainstorming and
posting

_____ 10. Made a series of logical decisions
to solve the problem.

j. Means-ends analysis

_____ 11. Tried to make progress by reducing
gap between his desire and his present state.

k. Progressive deepening

_____ 12. Took a break when problem seemed
too difficult to go on.

l. Troubleshooting

REMEDIATING PROBLEM SOLVING DIFFICULTIES

One of the most efficient ways to help students learn to solve specific problems is to locate the common weaknesses in present applications of previous learning and to provide remedial training. In using this approach, the teacher commonly asks, "What do most students do wrong?. . . Where do they commonly make their mistakes?" Training is then focused on remedying these errors.

The basic strategy for providing remedial training involves collecting data on student performance to identify common weaknesses in problem solving and designing an instructional plan for eliminating these weaknesses. A task description for teaching problem solving using this procedure would involve the following eight steps:

1. Assess student's prerequisite skills to determine whether or not he is capable of solving the problem.
2. Present the problem to a number of students.
3. Record all errors made in problem solving.
4. Identify the most common errors.
5. Analyze the errors for the types of learning involved.
6. Design an instructional plan for eliminating the error.
7. Teach students to avoid the error.
8. Retest and evaluate students' ability to solve the problem.

The following example illustrates how this procedure may be used to teach students to solve problems. Young mothers frequently complain about their children's unnecessary crying. Assuming that there is nothing

FEEDBACK:

10.10	1	i	4	b	7	f	10	k
	2	a	5	c	8	g	11	j
	3	d	6	e	9	l	12	h

physically wrong (hunger, thirst, sickness, or pain) and the children are able to talk, how can mothers reduce the crying? What common weakness exists in their problem-solving behavior?

Most mothers are not aware of a critical training principle in this regard, namely that behavior, which is followed by reinforcement, becomes more probable and is strengthened. Holding and cuddling a baby is reinforcing to the child. Therefore, when crying is followed by attention, the behavior is strengthened. If we were to observe a number of mothers with this problem, we would probably note that many of the mothers reinforce crying. An analysis of this error would indicate the need to teach the principle of reinforcement to the mothers. Using the techniques and methods discussed elsewhere in this book, we might design a system for teaching this principle and use it to remediate the weakness.

SUMMARY

Students may be taught how to solve problems of specific types or they may be taught general principles and strategies of problem solving which will transfer to problems of many different types. There are four major steps in teaching students to solve specific types of problems: (1) state an objective; (2) pretest and review prerequisites; (3) arrange conditions for learning by providing many kinds of problems, modeling the problem-solving approach, and teaching specific algorithms; (4) use procedures to provide practice such as simulation, on-the-job training, and programed instruction.

There are a number of heuristics or rules of thumb which can help to guide the students' efforts to solve problems. These heuristics deal with such topics as: running over elements of a problem; varying relationships of elements; producing more than one solution; talking over the problem; using group resources; evaluating ideas; delaying choice of solution; and stopping when stumped. In addition, the problem solver may utilize the following specific strategies to help him reach a solution: brainstorming and posting; means-ends analysis; progressive deepening; and troubleshooting. A useful approach to teaching problem solving is to help students identify and remedy common errors.

SUGGESTED READINGS

Guilford, J. P.: *The Nature of Human Intelligence*, (New York: McGraw Hill Book Company, 1967).

Johnson, D. M.: *Systematic Introduction to the Psychology of Thinking*, (New York: Harper and Row Publishers, 1972).

CHECKLIST FOR SPECIFIC TYPES OF PROBLEMS

Conditions for Learning Problem Solving

1. The objective

    a. State the class of problems to be solved.

    b. State the objective in this format.

1) Condition:	Given a new realistic problem situation, including an inaccessible desired goal whose solution is not evident, embedded among many extraneous cues
2) Terminal behavior:	Arrange conditions in the environment to require the student to sense the problem, formulate the problem, search for solutions, trade-off among solutions, and/or evaluate solutions
3) Criterion:	So that a final solution is achieved, i.e., the desired goal is reached. Specify the strategy or specific techniques to be followed if desired.

2. Pretest and review

    a. Pretest for the prerequisite principles, inquiry techniques, strategies, and skills required for solving the kind of problem specified in the objective.

    b. Review the prerequisites.

3. Presentation and practice

    a. General principles.

        1) Include specific ways to solve the problems.

        2) For more transfer, include a wide range of problems to practice upon.

        3) Model the entire problem-solving procedure.

POSTTEST

1. Suppose you were teaching students to solve problems in interior decoration. Check the ones which are statements describing problems.

    a. We will have to move a lot of furniture.

    b. We can't get the exact color of paint we need.

   c.   We need some tools from the hardware store.

   d.   These old appliances don't work.

   e.   We have $13.

William Moy was a community college teacher of psychology. Name the problem-solving steps he went through in the following four questions:

2. He noticed that his students were not paying attention to what was said in class. He worried because he felt if they didn't attend they would not reach the course objectives.

   a.   Search.

   b.   Problem formulation.

   c.   Problem sensing.

   d.   Solution.

3. He realized that he needed to find out how to get students to pay attention.

   a.   Search.

   b.   Problem formulation.

   c.   Problem sensing.

   d.   Solution.

4. He asked his colleagues. They told him to provide some novelty in presentation and content.

   a.   Search.

   b.   Problem formulation.

   c.   Problem sensing.

   d.   Solution.

5. So he did. After a few tryouts, it seemed as if students were attending to what was being said. Mr. Moy kept the procedure.

   a.   Search.

   b.   Problem formulation.

   c.   Problem sensing.

   d.   Solution.

6. Which of these is the most realistic problem in terms of its closeness to the real-world conditions to teach how to solve pollution problems?

   a.   Give students a sandbox where problems are represented and have them show what they would do.

   b.   Have City Hall loan the school a tract of eroded land to reclaim.

   c.   Give students written descriptions of problems and have them discuss solutions.

   d.   Have the students write essays on pollution problems.

Here is a set of questions (7-9) to use as criteria to judge objectives for problem solving: Answer them with regard to this objective:

The group of students will be given a financial problem within their own experience. The problem will be embedded in a task regarding stock market purchasing. They will use brainstorming and problem posting to arrive at a viable solution.

7. Are the conditions realistic?

        a. Yes.   b. No

8. Does the terminal behavior include desirable strategies or heuristics?

        a. Yes.   b. No.

9. Does the criterion include a solution?

        a. Yes.   b. No.

10. You are teaching medical students to solve problems dealing with allergic reactions. You are not sure of your students' knowledge. What strategy do you suggest for assessing prerequisites?

    a.   Assume they all have the prerequisites.
    b.   Find the students' level of attainment, then work up from there.
    c.   Assume no prerequisites and work up from the basics.
    d.   Teach to the middle ability students.

11. Which are general rules for teaching specific problem solving?

    a.   Use at least two heuristics for each problem.
    b.   Demonstrate how to solve problems.
    c.   Teach specific ways to solve real problems.
    d.   Give students many different problems to practice on.
    e.   Show students as few specific solutions as possible.

12. You are teaching your students to solve local governmental problems. Here are three procedures you could use. Label each one by placing the number of the name next to the approach.

    1. On-the-Job training
    2. Simulated procedure
    3. Programed procedure

_____   a. Find the student a position working with some local government official. Arrange for the official to be his supervisor. Give him the objectives of the training.

_____   b. Assign roles in class as if all the aspects of local government were represented and play out the consequences of decisions made.

_____   c. Give students a single problem in local government and ask them to respond. If they are correct, direct them on; if not, prompt their next response. Continue this until the most difficult problems are reached.

13. You have a colleague who is confused about the various choices he might make among general heuristics and strategies for problem solving. His confusion stems from his lack of ability to distinguish among the heuristics and strategies. Help him out by matching the examples listed in column A with the letter which represents a strategy or heuristic in column B.

A	B
____ 1. Went out for coffee when getting nowhere on problem.	a. Run over the elements
____ 2. Tried out methods to get closer and closer to goal.	b. Vary the relationship of elements
____ 3. Solved problem by considering a sequence of yes-no decisions.	c. Produce more than one solution
____ 4. Found out why car wouldn't start by working his way through system.	d. Talk over the problem
____ 5. Held out until last minute to choose best solution.	e. Use group resources
____ 6. Spent a lot of time on suggested solutions and was critical of his own.	f. Evaluate ideas
____ 7. Formed a team with complementary skills to solve the problem.	g. Delay solution choice
____ 8. Tried out many different solutions.	h. Stopping when stumped
____ 9. Made a model of the components of the problem and shifted them around.	i. Brainstorming and posting
____ 10. Explained the problem to a friend.	j. Means-ends analysis
____ 11. Looked for all things that could affect the problem.	k. Progressive deepening
____ 12. Put ideas down where people could see them initially without any value judgments.	l. Troubleshooting

Answers to this posttest can be found on page 337.

OVERVIEW OF LEARNING SYSTEM DESIGN • REC OGNIZING WELL-FORMULATED OBJECTIVES • DERIVING AND WRITING LEARNING OBJECTIVES • EVALUATING LEARNING SYSTEMS • TASK DE SCRIPTIONS•TYPES OF LEARNING • ANALYZING TASKS, OBJECTIVES, AND LEARNER CHARAC TERISTICS • GENERAL PRINCIPLES OF LEARNING AND MOTIVATION • THE LEARNING AND TEACH ING OF CONCEPTS AND PRINCIPLES •THE LEARN ING AND TEACHING OF PROBLEM SOLVING •

PERCEPTUAL-MOTOR SKILLS • THE SYSTEM APPROACH TO INSTRUCTION • OVERVIEW OF LEARNING SYSTEM DESIGN • RECOGNIZING WELL-FORMULATED OBJECTIVES • DERIVING AND WRITING LEARNING OBJECTIVES • EVALUAT ING LEARNING SYSTEMS • TASK DESCRIPTIONS • TYPES OF LEARNING • ANALYZING TASKS, OBJEC TIVES, AND LEARNER CHARACTERISTICS • GEN ERAL PRINCIPLES OF LEARNING AND MOTIVA TION • THE LEARNING AND TEACHING OF CON CEPTS AND PRINCIPLES • THE LEARNING AND TEACHING OF PROBLEM SOLVING • **PERCEPTUAL- MOTOR SKILLS** • THE SYSTEM APPROACH TO INSTRUCTION • OVERVIEW OF LEARNING SYS TEM DESIGN•RECOGNIZING WELL-FORMULATED OBJECTIVES•DERIVING AND WRITING LEARNING OBJECTIVES • EVALUATING LEARNING SYSTEMS • TASK DESCRIPTIONS•TYPES OF LEARNING • ANALYZING TASKS, OBJECTIVES, AND LEARNER

11

CHAPTER OBJECTIVES

- Define perceptual-motor skill.
- Define the term kinesthesis.
- Relate task descriptions and task analysis to perceptual-motor skills learning.
- State three of the five general rules governing information given before practicing perceptual-motor skills.
- State the one important principle concerning information given during practice of perceptual-motor skills.
- State three of the five general rules governing information given after practicing perceptual-motor skills.
- Decide whether skills should be taught using the whole or part method.
- Answer a series of true-false statements about kinesthesis, the conditions of practice, knowledge of results, and the debriefing in teaching perceptual-motor skills.

INTRODUCTION

From the moment of birth, a child begins to acquire skills involving coordinated muscular movements. The newborn child at first cannot even follow a moving object with his eyes, but he gradually learns to do this and countless other far more complex tasks as well. By the time he is ready for school, he will be able to walk, run, climb, feed himself, and do hundreds of other similar tasks, and he will continue to learn new perceptual-motor skills of equal or greater complexity until old age and death. In this chapter, we will develop some general principles for teaching and learning perceptual-motor skills.

DEFINITION:
A PERCEPTUAL-MOTOR SKILL IS DEFINED AS
A COORDINATED SERIES OF MUSCULAR MOVE-
MENTS TO SUCCESSFULLY COMPLETE A TASK.

The average adult has learned thousands of perceptual-motor skills in his lifetime and it would be impossible to list them all. Most perceptual-motor skills are so well learned and are performed so automatically that we are hardly aware of the fact that it was ever necessary to learn them. Only when we watch an infant, a child, or a beginner first try a new skill are we sometimes made aware of the fact that the skill had to be learned in the first place. Even then, we may grow impatient when it takes the novice so long to develop what seems to us to be such a simple skill. The fact of the matter is, many seemingly simple perceptual-motor skills are extremely complex and difficult to learn.

Perceptual-motor skills involve coordinated muscular movements to successfully complete a task. Generally speaking, these muscular movements are coordinated by our perceptions of **external** events. There are many muscular movements involved in driving a car: turning the steering wheel to round a corner, exerting foot pressure on the accelerator, braking sharply at the appearance of an obstacle in the road ahead. These are examples of muscular movements made in response to perceived events in the environment about you. However, not all perceptual information comes from outside the learner.

There is an important internal sense called **kinesthesis**. You know the position of your legs at this moment, even though they may be hidden beneath a desk, because you can "feel" where they are using muscular sense receptors. This ability to feel muscular tension and movement is called **kinesthesis**, and is an extremely important sense for learning perceptual-motor skills.

Close your eyes, extend your right arm, bring your forefinger toward you, and touch your nose with the tip of your finger. What sense did you use to accomplish this? Vision? Smell? Touch? Kinesthesis? Hearing?

FRAME

11.1

Obviously, we also use other senses such as vision and hearing to coordinate muscular movements. In psychology, the word **perception** refers to the way in which the individual organizes and interprets the information coming to him through the various senses. **Motor** refers to muscular movements. From these two concepts, we derive the term perceptual-motor skill.

Take a look at the following list of perceptual-motor skills and think about them for a few minutes. In what ways are they the same and how do they differ?

> Skeet shooting
> Swimming
> Playing basketball, football, or baseball

FEEDBACK:
11.1 Kinesthesis

Driving an automobile
Flying an airplane
Riding a bicycle
Operating a sewing machine
Playing the piano or any other musical instrument
Designing a poster or book jacket
Operating a lathe or another machine

All of them involve muscular coordination, but differ from one another in a number of ways. First of all, they are not equally complex. Some of the skills, such as swimming or sewing, involve relatively simple routine actions; one movement follows another in a tightly integrated sequence and each movement signals the next. Basketball and football, on the other hand, place a higher information load on the learner. As the skill is exercised, the learner's actions from moment to moment will depend on what happens in the external world so that he must make decisions while performing the skill. In other words, as we move from some relatively simple, automatic skills, like swimming, to very complicated skills like flying, the degree of decision-making complexity increases.

Then there are skills, such as flying an airplane or driving an automobile, which are so complex that they are actually made up of many component skills. Let us consider an example.

Here is a sequence of perceptual-motor skills in skeet shooting:

Perceive target (location, direction, speed)
Raise gun
Track target (aim, move gun)
Squeeze trigger
Perceive results

If you are out hunting, the above sequence is included in a larger sequence of perceptual-motor skills, involving more complex information processing and decision making.

Perceive movement of potential target
Perceive object
Decide if shooting is legal
Decide if your position is optimal
Shoot (above sequence)
If a hit, perceive fall
Retrieve

If you were training the skills in the above example, you might recognize that some of the components have to be learned; some are already in the repertoire of the learner and he has to learn when to use them.

If we were to break any of these skills down into their smallest components, we would discover that some involve relatively fine muscular movements, whereas others involve simply selecting from among responses already learned.

Skills also differ in terms of the critical cues which signal particular movements. Sometimes these cues are built in; that is the case with kinesthetic cues in swimming. Sometimes they are designed as is the case with warning lights in the pilot's compartment.

Thus, skills can differ in these four ways:

- Their information load or decision-making complexity
- The number of component skills involved and their integration
- The muscular actions involved, whether gross or fine
- The cues that signal particular movements

Rank the following skills 1 through 5 in order of their number of component skills (1 = most components), information load (1 = most decision making complexity), and muscular action (1 = finest).

FRAME
11.2

	Number of components	Information load or decision-making complexity	Fine/ gross
Landing an airplane	____	____	____
Operating a sewing machine	____	____	____
Bowling a ball	____	____	____
Swimming	____	____	____
Threading a needle	____	____	____

DESCRIBING AND ANALYZING PERCEPTUAL-MOTOR SKILLS

Many times when a perceptual-motor task is broken down, one discovers different types of learning within the task. For example, what are the types of learning involved in teaching perceptual-motor skills such as basketball? Is basketball entirely a matter of perceptual-motor skills? Is something else involved? What about the rules of the game? Scoring procedures? Obviously, most sports involve learning concepts and principles as well as perceptual-motor skills. In this chapter, we will focus our

---

FEEDBACK:

11.2	Airplane	1	1	2 - 3	Swimming	4	4	4
	Sewing maching	2	2	2 - 3	Needle	5	5	1
	Bowling	3	3	5				

attention primarily on the perceptual-motor aspect itself and ignore the concepts and principles involved in many tasks which seem, on the surface, to be only perceptual-motor tasks.

Now, let us look at a perceptual-motor task in greater detail. The task we will be describing is playing basketball; but as we take a hard look at basketball, you will soon discover that this task will have to be broken down. It is made up of many component skills, which can more or less arbitrarily be divided into individual and team skills:

Individual skills
    Handling and ball passing
    Goal throwing
    Dribbling
    Body movements and footwork
    Individual defense (man to man)
    Center and held ball jumping

Team skills
    Fast break attacks
    Defense against fast break attacks
    Slow break attacks
    Defense against slow break attacks
    Zone defense
    Defeating zone defense

Other information
    Rules
    Scoring

Any one of these can be broken down still further into a component set of skills. Take, for example, goal throwing, which has the following types: team shots, including the underhand loop shot, the poised chest shot, the push chest shot, and the one hand shot; carom shots; rebound shots; and free throwing. Any one of these shots could be described in greater detail and in describing them, the trainer might want to raise the following kinds of questions:

Under what conditions is the shot used?

    Example: Two hand shots are frequently impractical in the vicinity of the free throw circle.

What is the position of the head and eyes?

    Example: In the push chest shot, do not follow the ball after it leaves your hand until it hits the basket.

What is the sequence of actions the player must take?

Example: In the poised chest shot: relax before you shoot; point both feet toward the basket; hold the ball lightly; have thumbs 3 to 4 inches apart; move arms some before shooting.

What are some cautions?

Example: In the underarm loop shot, do not drop the ball below your waist or it will be blocked.

What prerequisite knowledge must the learner have?

Example: All shots require that the learner have some knowledge of the arch or path that the basketball follows when it leaves the hand from various positions and the effect of the arch on accuracy.

There are several things about the learner's entry state which should be considered in the task analysis. Age is one consideration. Young learners may find it difficult to concentrate for long periods. If they are very young, their coordination may not be too good, and consequently, performance standards may have to be lowered. Strength and endurance will inevitably affect the conditions for learning some perceptual-motor skills. The entry skills level, that is, what the student is already able to do when he comes into the learning situation, will also determine the approach to training.

Finally, the analysis should examine the task itself to determine whether or not it is intrinsically rewarding and keeps the learner interested, or whether it soon bores him; whether the task is approached eagerly or avoided altogether; whether the task is relatively light and can be carried on for hours at a time; or whether it quickly fatigues the learner. Again, all of these factors will influence the practice conditions. Often the effects on learning are obvious. If a task is boring or extremely fatiguing and the trainer detects that students are easily distracted or soon cease to attend to the task, he could remedy this by keeping practice sessions short and interspersed with frequent rest periods.

All of the things discussed in this section are preliminary to actually teaching the skill. Once the task and learner characteristics have been described, the learning system designer can turn his attention to the types of learning involved and the training methods to be used. As we have already noted, a skill may be predominantly perceptual-motor, but may also involve other types of learning. For example, the arch of the ball in basketball, which was mentioned above, is a concept, whose attributes might be taught in a classroom rather than on the floor of the basketball court. We might also teach the rules of the game in the classroom.

TRAINING PERCEPTUAL-MOTOR SKILLS

In the balance of this unit we will develop some general training principles for perceptual-motor skills. These principles fall into two categories: (1) information given to the learner and (2) the conditions under which a skill is practiced.

INFORMATION ABOUT THE TASK

Three kinds of information should be made available to the learner as he develops a skill. In general, these three types of information are given before, during, and after the task. Actually, this distinction is somewhat artificial, but adopting it will help us to organize and understand the material somewhat better.

Let us try to develop some general principles about information given to the learner, namely, how much and what kind of information should be provided to him before, during, and after the task? Later in the chapter we will consider the conditions of practice.

INFORMATION BEFORE PRACTICE   As in all learning situations, before the student begins he should know what his **objectives** are. It is important to set the performance criteria high enough to motivate the learner to work towards them but not so high as to discourage him. The objectives should be unambiguous. The learner should, in other words, know when he has reached an objective. You may want to begin with criteria of satisfactory performance set considerably lower than they would be for a more advanced student. As learning progresses these criteria should gradually be raised.

The student not only needs to know what his objectives are, but also needs to have an **overview** of the task; he needs to know how the task is performed by an expert. This knowledge serves two important functions. For one thing, it gives him the total picture. For another, it provides an explicit set of standards for evaluating his performance. The music teacher, who plays the melody properly, is giving the student a standard against which to evaluate his performance.

This overview can be provided in a number of ways. The instructor himself can show the student how the task is performed. He can have others demonstrate the task. He can use motion pictures or other visual aids to provide the overview. Whatever the method he uses, an overview is critical.

It is also important to keep the overview brief. Nothing turns a student off faster than a great deal of talk when he is anxious to learn how to **do** the skill—not just learn **about** it. So keep your comments and demonstrations direct and to the point.

Early in the training period, guidance can be helpful to the student. So

can imitation. But the nature of the guidance will depend on the task.
Sometimes, the overview itself is a form of verbal guidance. In effect,
when we guide a student, we try to minimize his errors early in the learning process by restricting his behavior in some way. How we restrict it depends on the task. Guidance is important because there is some evidence
to show that people actually learn the errors they commit and will tend to
repeat them on later trials. Once learned, these errors have to be un-
learned. Guidance helps to eliminate the learning of errors.

Again, just as with the overview, it is important to keep guidance to a
minimum and restrict it to the early trials. Guide the novice through a
correct golf swing, for example, only once or twice and then let him go
on his own. In addition, it helps if the novice is aware of the kinds of errors he might make, but he should not be allowed to practice them. Thus,
a swing or two of the golf club before guidance is given will help the student get the "feel" of an improper swing and allows him to put the guided
correct swing in context.

Now let us review these general principles regarding information given
to the learner early in the task.

1. Provide the student with precise, unambiguous objectives.

2. Begin with criteria the student will be able to meet and gradually
    raise the criteria of satisfactory performance.

3. Give the student an overview of the task by demonstration or audio-
    visual methods of presentation.

4. Avoid long, verbal descriptions and passive instruction before al-
    lowing the student to begin practicing.

5. If possible, early in the learning provide some form of brief guid-
    ance to minimize errors.

Look at the list below and insert the appropriate missing word in the principle.

1. Give the student precise unambiguous _____.

2. Gradually raise the _____ of satisfactory performance.

3. Provide an _____ to demonstrate the task.

4. Avoid long verbal descriptions and _____ instruction.

5. Provide _____ to minimize errors.

    a. Guidance   b. Passive   c. Criterion   d. Objective   e. Overview

F
R
A
M
E

11.3

FEEDBACK:

11.3 1 d   2 c   3 e   4 b   5 a

INFORMATION DURING PRACTICE   Now, what kinds of information should be provided during the performance of the task when the learner is on his own?

As the student responds, there are often critical cues available to him which he—being a novice—cannot discriminate out of the flood of information inundating him. His attention must be called to these cues. "Keep your head down. Do you feel your chin touching your collar? That's the way." Or, "Notice the V at your thumb. Is it pointing towards your right shoulder?" Or, "Do not try to follow the ball until you hear it hit the rim or backboard." The learner should be helped to discriminate these critical cues. They can provide him with useful information about the skill. These cues or prompts, as they are sometimes called, are a natural part of the event and are on occasion introduced by the trainer. High diving coaches may introduce a critical "Hup!" at just the right moment to signal a diver to perform a particular act, such as breaking out of a dive. But when these external cues are used, they will have to eventually be withdrawn; for the goal of most perceptual-motor training is to free the learner from his teacher.

Since these cues and prompts are introduced during the practice sessions, it is important that they not be allowed to interfere with the training. Be sure they are helpful and keep them to a minimum.

To review, there is probably just one important principle concerning information during the task: help the student to discover critical cues and prompts intrinsic to the task that will guide his behavior. Obviously, you cannot isolate cues for the learner unless you have first described and analyzed the task.

INFORMATION AFTER PRACTICE   Now what about information after an act has been performed? There are a number of useful principles of which the learning system designer should be aware. Before describing these principles, however, we need a framework within which to talk about them. A distinction is made in Fig. 11.1 between a task, an act, the information that follows tasks and acts, and a trial.

Take as an example the simplest sort of task: hammering a nail. The task involves several acts: holding the nail properly, raising the hammer, dropping the hammer, checking the nail, holding the nail, raising the hammer, etc. When a child is first learning to do a task of this kind, a trial might be defined as one attempt to coordinate the acts of holding the nail, raising the hammer, and dropping the hammer. Later the trial might be redefined to mean a complete attempt to drive a nail into a piece of wood.

In Fig. 11.1, the task (hammering a nail) is the largest block; it is made up of acts. Acts are shown as small discs within each block. Each act is followed by some kind of information. Often this information is intrinsic and provided by kinesthesis. But it may be extrinsic—something like a

TRIAL 2
HAMMER A NAIL

Act 1	F*1	Act 2	F*2	Act 3	F*3	Etc.
Hold nail		Raise hammer		Drop hammer		

Knowledge of results

*Feedback

F₁ = Visual and kinesthetic

F₂ = Kinesthetic

F₃ = Kinesthetic and visual

†Knowledge of Results

"That's a good job. But grip the hammer more firmly."

TRIAL 1
HAMMER A NAIL

Act 1	F*1	Act 2	F*2	Act 3	F*3
Hold nail		Raise hammer		Drop hammer	

*Feedback

F₁ = Visual and kinesthetic

F₂ = Kinesthetic

F₃ = Kinesthetic and visual

Figure 11.1 Relationship between tasks, acts, feedback, and knowledge of results.

bell, a light, or some other visual or auditory stimuli. In this case, extrinsic information is provided by both visual and auditory stimuli and possibly pain receptors as well. Feedback is symbolized by the small squares following each act.

A trial is one run of a task. A trail can also be followed by information. Thus, in operating a machine, a trainee could obtain feedback throughout the task after each act as well as obtaining some information after the task has been completed, which serves to summarize his performance. In this example, it is an adult's voice giving encouragement and direction.

Now, we will use the terms **feedback** for information a student gets after an **act,** and **knowledge of results** to describe the information that a trainee gets following the completion of a whole **task**. With this diagram in mind, let us now state some principles about feedback and knowledge of results.

First, feedback and knowledge of results are both extremely important. Arrange the learning situation so that both are provided. Knowledge of results, by the way, can have informational as well as motivational components; that is, it can give the learner information about his performance, for example, his accuracy and timing, as well as stimulate him to work harder or give up. Take the example of the hammering task. When the adult says, "That's a good job," he is emphasizing the motivational component of knowledge of results. When he says, "Grip the hammer more firmly," he is emphasizing the informational component. Keep the knowledge of results positive to avoid discouraging the learner. If you cannot encourage him, say nothing. Negative comments provide the learner with very little information. They do not tell him anything about how to perform the task correctly. Indeed, negative comments are often redundant in that the learner already knows that he is doing something wrong. Furthermore, they generate anxiety on the learner's part which only adds to the uneasiness he undoubtedly already feels. Excessive anxiety generally causes a deterioration of performance. So, once again, avoid negative comments and keep knowledge of results positive.

FRAME

11.4

Music teachers often rely almost exclusively on negative comments. Select the most positive statement (a or b) in each of the pairs below.

1. a. "That sounded terrible." b. "The first three or four notes sounded fine. Try it again." ____

2. a. "I like the way you are holding your wrists but bend the fingers a bit more." b. "How many times have I told you to bend your fingers?" ____

FEEDBACK:
11.4 1 b   2 a

If you inspect the diagram again, you will realize that it says nothing at all about time. We have said that feedback and knowledge of results should **follow** acts and tasks. They should be given as soon as possible, preferably within a minute. But, you should also note that knowledge of results not only follows a task, it precedes the next trial on that task (Fig. 11.1).

The time between trials should be kept as short as possible. Once a student has practiced a response, he should get knowledge of results. But as soon as possible thereafter, he should have the opportunity to practice the task again. (Example C in Fig. 11.2). How long is as soon as possible? Perhaps a minute or less. If longer time periods intervene between trials, reestablish the student's set by calling critical features of the last trial to his attention before beginning again. You might begin by saying, "Remember the last time you tried this task, you . . ."

When we talked about giving information early in the task, the point was made that the trainer should not set the criterion of satisfactory performance too high when the student is first starting out. In general, you should seek to **shape** the student's behavior by controlling feedback and knowledge of results. **Shaping** involves reinforcing behavior that approximates the final performance you want the student to achieve. As the student successfully approximates the desired behavior and improves in performance, you gradually increase the criterion before giving a reward. But the point is still the same. A teacher should praise or otherwise reinforce near approximations to the final behavior early in the learning process, gradually raising the standards of what is satisfactory.

In shaping, you gradually build desired terminal behavior by reinforcing successive approximations to it. Early in this process, you reinforce behaviors that later on would be considered less than completely satisfactory.

Assume you are training a beginner to shoot a rifle and you want to provide him with positive knowledge of results. You plan to praise him for satisfactory performance. Would you

1. Only praise him when he hits the bullseye?

2. Withhold all praise until after the session?

3. Praise almost all the things he does correctly?

F
R
A
M
E

11.5

There is one other kind of knowledge of results which is receiving more and more attention. At the end of a series of trails, the student and teach-

---

FEEDBACK:

11.5   3

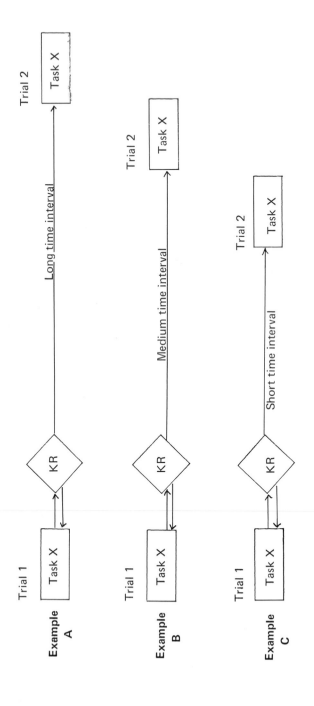

Figure 11.2 Knowledge of results both follows one trial and precedes the next. The time interval may vary.

er sometimes go back over the whole practice session. This is often called a **debriefing.** Sometimes the teacher uses special aids such as television tapes in the debriefing. At other times, the teacher may review some data he has collected about the student's performance over a series of trials. Debriefings often can be very helpful. Remember, however, to keep the tone of a debriefing positive. The object is to improve future performance—not criticize the past—so you should keep the debriefing oriented to doing things better next time. Try to keep it factual as well. That is one great value of video tapes, photographs, and other objective data; they add credibility to the debriefing. Obviously, some negative results may have to be presented—but again, keep it factual, not critical. Try to find evidence of improvement before criticizing, and avoid being personal. Help the student discriminate errors by pointing them out to him, but keep in mind that he may need some additional cues or prompts in the actual situation to help him recognize what he is doing wrong or when he is doing something right.

Debriefings are particularly valuable for crews and teams. The rules of the team debriefing are basically the same with two important additions. First, treat the team as a whole. Avoid concentrating on individuals as individuals. Analyze the interactions between the men and the machines (if there are any). Second, try to get everybody on the team involved in the analysis. Accept ideas from all members of the group at least as working hypotheses; you want free and open participation in the debriefing when teams are involved because each member of the team has information which may be vital and which is not necessarily available to **anyone** else, including the trainer.

Now, let us review the principles having to do with information given after a task.

1. Always provide feedback and knowledge of results for individuals and teams.
2. Avoid long delays before giving feedback or knowledge of results.
3. After feedback, give the student the opportunity to practice again as soon as practical.
4. Have a debriefing of the entire practice session. This applies to both individuals and teams.
5. Keep the tone of the of the debriefing positive and factual.

In teaching a perceptual-motor skill you should:

1. Provide _____ and _____ results.

2. Avoid long _____ before giving knowledge of results.

3. Give learners the opportunity to _____ after knowledge of results.

4. Have an individual or _____ debriefing.

5. Keep the tone of the debriefing _____ and _____.

CONDITIONS OF PRACTICE

Let us turn now to the conditions of practice. By conditions of practice, we mean how do you go about deciding **what** a student will practice and **how** he will practice it? There are three ways of looking at this problem and we will take them one at a time.

First, we are interested in **what** to practice: should the students practice the whole task or should it be broken down into parts which are practiced separately?

Second, we want to know **how** to practice: should the trials be massed or spaced?

And third, another **how** to practice issue is: will mental practices help?

WHOLE VERSUS PART PRACTICE From our discussion up to this point, it should be evident that tasks vary along a number of dimensions. Some tasks involve a highly organized sequence of acts. These tasks are generally simple and unitary. One act follows another in a routine, almost automatic fashion. As a matter of fact, one act often signals the next by kinesthesis. Examples of these highly organized, but simple tasks are swimming, driving a golf ball, high jumping, and many parlor games of skill, too numerous to describe. Other tasks are not so simple and unitary; they are often made up of many simple and unitary skills. These more complex tasks generally also have a major information processing component—that is to say, the learner must decide from moment to moment what to do next, sometimes under conditions of stress. In other words, the learner must **select** from among action sequences which are themselves simple unitary skills. Furthermore, improving these more complex tasks often requires a larger span of attention than any student is capable of giving in a single practice session. Some examples of more complex tasks are team sports, driving a car, and flying.

FEEDBACK:

11.6	1 feedback . . . knowledge of	4	team
	2 delays	5	positive . . . factual
	3 practice		

Tasks do not, of course, really divide up into any such neat dichotomy, as simple and complex. More realistically, they probably fall along a continuum from the simplest to the most complex, and it is up to the trainer to decide where along the continuum the task he is interested in falls.

With this distinction in mind, we can now formulate a general principle about whole versus part practice. In general, the more complex the task, (in the terms we have just described), the more profitable it will be for the trainer to divide it up into parts and teach the parts separately. If the task is simple and unitary, you should stick with the whole method. Although the research on this question is not entirely in agreement, one thing is clear; the part method takes longer. When it is possible, avoid it. On the other hand, once you have done a task analysis it should be clear whether the task must be divided up to be taught efficiently. Some concepts, such as the rules governing the use of the hands in football for offensive and defensive players, should be taught in the classroom because it can save valuable time during practice sessions. But again, one needs a task analysis to identify such concepts.

Individual differences among students can have an important bearing on your decision to use whole or part practice. Children of different ages, for example, have different spans of attention. Therefore, one would be more apt to break a task down into components for a child than for an adult.

If the task is complex and has a high information processing component, it should probably be taught by the _____ method.
1. whole
2. part

F
R
A
M
E

11.7

MASSED VERSUS SPACED PRACTICE   The question of massing trials or spacing them has been the subject of a great deal of research. Massing trials seems to have an **immediate** effect on performance and lowers it temporarily, but it does not seem to interfere with learning or long-term retention. Obviously, you can cram too much practice into a single session so that the student becomes fatigued or loses interest. As a general rule, one can say that more frequent practice sessions broken by rest periods is probably best and certainly the least apt to do harm, but the evidence is not overwhelming.

FEEDBACK:
11.7   2

**F
R
A
M
E**

11.8

In general, it is better to _____ trials.

   1. mass
   2. space

MENTAL PRACTICE Now, one final point about practice. There is some evidence to suggest that mental practice helps. In other words, just thinking over a task and rehearsing it in one's mind can improve performance. Mental practice has some real advantages. The learner can practice in his spare time; no special equipment is required; and, of course, it is not so fatiguing. Mental practice is not as good as really getting in there and swinging that old golf club, but it apparently helps.

Most illustrations used in this chapter come from the realm of physical education. The reason we have used illustrations from this area is that physical education provides a common reference point—we all know what swimming and basketball and football are. Therefore, it is easier for the reader to follow the examples. The principles we have developed, nevertheless, apply to all skills learning, whether in the factory, the home, the university, the trade school, or elsewhere.

SUMMARY

In this chapter, we have described a number of considerations which must be taken into account when teaching perceptual-motor skills. Perceptual-motor skills are defined as coordinated muscular movements to successfully complete a task. The period of instruction was artifically divided into three parts: before, during, and after practice. The types of information presented to the learner during each of these three periods were described and a series of general principles was developed. These principles are summarized in the checklist which follows. In addition, the problems of whole versus part practice, massed versus spaced practice, and mental practice were discussed.

SUGGESTED READINGS

Bilodeau, E. A.: *Acquisition of Skill*, (New York: Academic Press, 1966).

FEEDBACK:
11.8   2

Gagné, R. M. & Fleishman, E. A.: *Psychology and Human Performance*, (New York: Holt, Rinehart & Winston, 1959).

Holding, D. H.: *Principles of Training*, (Oxford: Pergammon Press, 1969).

Singer, R. N.: *Motor Learning and Human Performance*, (New York: The MacMillan Co., 1969).

CHECKLIST

Before practice, does the teacher:

		Yes	No
1.	Provide an overview	___	___
2.	Give objectives	___	___
3.	Avoid passive practice	___	___
4.	Provide guidance	___	___
5.	Start with lowered criteria for reinforcement and reward	___	___

During practice, does the teacher:

6.	Help the student to discover critical cues	___	___

After practice, does the teacher:

7.	Provide feedback and knowledge of results	___	___
8.	Avoid long delays before giving feedback	___	___
9.	Provide for practice after feedback	___	___
10.	Debrief the entire session	___	___
11.	Keep the tone positive and factual	___	___

POSTTEST

		T	F
1.	The term kinesthesis refers to a written record of perceptual-motor skills development.	___	___
2.	Guidance should never be used in teaching a perceptual-motor skill.	___	___
3.	Passive practice should be avoided in the case of perceptual-motor skills learning.	___	___

4. As a student learns a perceptual-motor skill, you should gradually raise the criterion of successful performance. ___ ___

5. It is best to delay knowledge of results until after a student has had a chance to get away from the learning situation and think over his mistakes. ___ ___

6. After feedback, the student should be given the opportunity to practice as quickly as possible. ___ ___

7. Perceptual-motor skills learning will probably be greatest if the tone of a debriefing after an athletic event is kept positive and factual. ___ ___

8. "Mental" practice helps improve perceptual-motor skills. ___ ___

9. In general, it is best to space practice sessions rather than mass them. ___ ___

10. A typical sport, such as basketball, involves only one type of learning, i.e., perceptual-motor skill. ___ ___

11. Define the term perceptual-motor skill.

12. Define the term kinesthesis.

13. Would you use the whole or part method to teach the following to an adult?

	Whole	Part
Drive a car	( )	( )
Golf swing	( )	( )
Fly an airplane	( )	( )
Breast stroke in swimming	( )	( )
Sew a seam	( )	( )

14. Give three general rules for providing information to learners before practice.

_____

_____

_____

15. What is the one important kind of information you may want to give a student for use during practice?

16. State three general rules about the kind of information you would give a student after practice.

_____

_____

_____

Answers to this posttest can be found on page 337.

OVERVIEW OF LEARNING SYSTEM DESIGN • REC
OGNIZING WELL-FORMULATED OBJECTIVES •
DERIVING AND WRITING LEARNING OBJECTIVES
• EVALUATING LEARNING SYSTEMS • TASK DE
SCRIPTIONS•TYPES OF LEARNING • ANALYZING
TASKS, OBJECTIVES, AND LEARNER CHARAC
TERISTICS • GENERAL PRINCIPLES OF LEARNING
AND MOTIVATION • THE LEARNING AND TEACH
ING OF CONCEPTS AND PRINCIPLES •THE LEARN
ING AND TEACHING OF PROBLEM SOLVING •
PERCEPTUAL-MOTOR SKILLS • **THE SYSTEM
APPROACH TO INSTRUCTION** • OVERVIEW OF
LEARNING SYSTEM DESIGN • RECOGNIZING
WELL-FORMULATED OBJECTIVES • DERIVING
AND WRITING LEARNING OBJECTIVES • EVALUAT
ING LEARNING SYSTEMS • TASK DESCRIPTIONS •
TYPES OF LEARNING • ANALYZING TASKS, OBJEC
TIVES, AND LEARNER CHARACTERISTICS • GEN
ERAL PRINCIPLES OF LEARNING AND MOTIVA
TION • THE LEARNING AND TEACHING OF CON
CEPTS AND PRINCIPLES • THE LEARNING AND
TEACHING OF PROBLEM SOLVING • PERCEPTUAL-
MOTOR SKILLS • **THE SYSTEM APPROACH TO
INSTRUCTION** • OVERVIEW OF LEARNING SYS
TEM DESIGN•RECOGNIZING WELL-FORMULATED
OBJECTIVES•DERIVING AND WRITING LEARNING
OBJECTIVES • EVALUATING LEARNING SYSTEMS
• TASK DESCRIPTIONS•TYPES OF LEARNING •
ANALYZING TASKS, OBJECTIVES, AND LEARNER

12

CHAPTER OBJECTIVES

After reading this chapter, you should be able to:

- Define a learning system and state its three fundamental characteristics.
- Name three phases of the system design process and two design procedures in each phase.
- Identify the design phase in which a learning design technique or procedure (e.g., deriving learning objectives or preparing a task description) is used.
- Identify four categories of information necessary to describe the current state of a learning system and give an example of each category.
- Identify the design principle exemplified by one or more system design techniques.

INTRODUCTION

There are two characteristics of the system approach to instruction. First, the system approach consists of a particular point of view toward the teaching-learning process. The teaching-learning process is an arrangement whereby a teacher and student can interact with one another. The specific purpose of this interaction is to facilitate student learning. The second characteristic of the system approach is the use of a specific methodology for designing learning systems. This methodology consists of systematic procedures for planning, designing, carrying out, and evaluating the total process of learning and teaching. It is directed at achieving specific objectives and is based on research in human learning and communication. Applying this methodology will produce a learning system which arranges human and nonhuman resources in an efficient manner to bring about effective student learning. Thus, because the system approach is both a point of view and a methodology, it provides a guide for planning instruction and for carrying out the plan.

These two characteristics of the system approach are analogous to other similar guides for human endeavor. The scientific approach also consists of a point of view and a methodology. The scientific point of view is characterized by a belief in the cause-and-effect relationship among events, by the concept of indestructibility of matter, and by the assumed orderliness of the physical universe. The scientific method is characterized by techniques for observing and recording natural events, procedures for experimentally manipulating and controlling variables, and methods for analyzing and interpreting data.

The preceding chapters of this book dealt with the procedures and techniques that comprise the methodology of learning system design. Using this methodology as a framework, this chapter will consider the system approach from a more general standpoint. It will explicate what is meant by the system approach as a particular point of view toward instruction and will develop general principles and guidelines for using the procedures and techniques of the learning system design method.

We shall proceed in the following manner. First, we shall define a learning system and discuss the characteristics an instructional unit must have in order to be considered a learning system. Second, we shall examine the entire design process as a whole and derive a basic strategy for designing learning systems.

WHAT IS A LEARNING SYSTEM?

DEFINITION:
A LEARNING SYSTEM IS AN ORGANIZED COMBINATION OF PEOPLE, MATERIALS, FACILITIES, EQUIPMENT, AND PROCEDURES WHICH INTERACT TO ACHIEVE A GOAL.

The people in learning systems are students, instructors, and teaching or laboratory assistants. Materials include books, chalkboards and chalk, photographic slides and motion pictures, audio- and video-tape. Facilities and equipment consist of classrooms, learning carrels, audio-visual equipment, and computers. Procedures include schedules and methods of sequencing information, providing practice, studying, testing, and grading.

The definition places no restrictions on the size or complexity of a learning system. A learning system may be one student reading a book or an entire school or college. We may even consider the educational establishment of an entire city as a learning system because its component elements are organized and interact with one another to educate students.

CHARACTERISTICS

The above definition contains three fundamental characteristics of a learning system. The first two are related to the concept of organization, and the third is conveyed by the concept of a goal.

When we say that a learning system is an organized combination of elements, we mean two things: first, that there is an intentional arrangement of people, materials, and procedures (the elements of a system are not arranged haphazardly, but according to a specific plan); and second, that the elements of a system are interdependent (the people, materials, and procedures are part of a coherent whole where each contributes something to the others and every part is essential). Two of the essential characteristics of a learning system are a **planned** and **interdependent** arrangement of its component elements.

The following example of a learning system illustrates a plan for arranging interaction among the elements of a learning system. The numbers in parentheses indicate planned sequence of events.

Element		Activity
Teacher	(1)	Specifies terminal and enabling objectives
	(2)	Sequences subject matter
	(4)	Assigns textbook reading
	(6)	Presents lecture to students
	(7)	Composes and distributes practice exercises
	(3)	Designs test for achievement of objectives
Teaching Assistant	(1)	Assists in specifying objectives and designing achievement test
	(8)	Conducts question and answer session with students
	(9)	Guides students through practice exercises and provides feedback
	(10)	Communicates students' questions to teacher
	(11)	Administers achievement test and provides feedback
Students	(5)	Read text and write questions for discussion
	(9)	Perform practice exercises and determine need for further practice
	(11)	Take achievement test
Media and Materials		List of objectives
		Text
		Slides and overhead projector transparencies for lecture
		Practice exercises and feedback sheet

The third essential characteristic of a learning system is that it have a **goal**. The goal is the purpose for which the system is designed. This characteristic distinguishes a learning system, and all other systems designed by men, from natural systems. Man-made systems, like transportation systems, communication systems, or governmental systems, all have goals. Natural systems, like the solar system, ecological systems, or the nervous system of animals, have interdependent elements arranged according to some plan, but they do not have a goal or purpose.

The system goal guides the system design process. For learning systems, the primary goal is, of course, student learning. The task of the system designer is to organize the people, materials, and procedures in such a way that student learning is achieved most efficiently. Consequently, throughout the entire system design process, the designer makes design decisions on the basis of whether or not they facilitate achieving the goal of the system.

The minimum elements of a learning system are a learner, a learning goal, and a procedural plan for achieving the goal. A learning system need not include a teacher in the traditional sense of someone who imparts information. There are many kinds of learning systems in which information is transmitted by some other medium than the teacher, such as a book, a motion picture, a set of photographic slides, or a programed text. A learning system may include administrators, equipment, and learning materials; but no matter how many elements are included in the system, there must be a procedural plan that describes how the elements function in achieving the system goal, which is student learning.

An instructor may perform two functions in a learning system. He may be the designer of the system as well as one of the system elements, performing the traditional teaching function. A learning system must have a designer, who is responsible for choosing the system goals and for developing the procedural plan of the system. Because of his knowledge of the subject matter and his experience with the students, the instructor should perform this function. But he can perform this function best only if he is acquainted with the principles and techniques of learning system design. As the instructor designs the system, he may decide that a teacher is needed for a particular purpose. For example, he may decide that certain information can best be imparted to the students by means of a verbal discussion. The instructor, as system designer, would therefore design himself into the system to perform the teaching function.

Three fundamental characteristics of learning systems are:

a. There is an intentional arrangement of people, materials, and procedures.

b. The system elements are interdependent.

c. There is a goal which guides the system design process.

Which of these system characteristics are the following design procedures directed at producing?

1. Writing objectives. _____

2. An instructor obtains feedback from students and uses it to modify course procedures. _____

3. An instructor plans a lesson that includes a lecture, visual aids, practice exercises for students, and a discussion session. _____

FRAME

12.1

FEEDBACK:

12.1 1 c

2 b

3 a

We have begun an analysis of the system approach to instruction by considering three characteristics of a learning system. In the following sections of the chapter, we shall discuss the process of designing systems that meet these characteristics. We shall begin by considering the design process as a whole.

THE STRATEGY OF LEARNING SYSTEM DESIGN

A strategy of learning system design is a plan for employing system design procedures most efficiently. The design procedures discussed in the previous chapters of this book describe how to select and organize components of a learning system. However, because the design process is so complex, having a design strategy helps the designer evaluate all important alternatives and arrive at solutions that most efficiently achieve the system goal.

BASIC DESIGN STRATEGY

A system design plan consists of three phases: (1) analyzing system requirements; (2) designing the system; and (3) evaluating system effectiveness. Particular design procedures are associated with each phase and will be discussed below.

In analyzing system requirements, the designer specifies two things about the system:

1. What must be accomplished.
2. What the current state of the system is.

The first describes the goal of the system; the second describes the available resources and the constraints that might interfere with achieving the goal. By considering goals, resources, and constraints together, the designer is in a position to evaluate all possible system components and methods of organizing them.

In the system design phase, the designer selects and organizes the particular components and procedures that will be employed in the system, and tries them out.

In the evaluation phase, the designer compares the actual performance of the system with the planned performance. The system may have to be redesigned, depending on the extent of discrepancy between planned and actual system performance.

Figure 12.1 illustrates the three phases of the system design strategy.

Procedures for two of the three phases of the system design plan were covered in previous chapters. Procedures in the **system design phase** were covered in Chapters 2 and 3 on objectives; task descriptions (Chapter 5); types of learning (Chapter 6); and task analysis (Chapter 7). Those chapters showed how to identify and select learning outcomes and how to choose and sequence subject matter. The chapters on learning and motivation (Chapter 8); concepts and principles (Chapter 9); problem solving, (Chapter 10); and perceptual-motor skills (Chapter 11) showed how to select and organize instruction to maximize student learning. The procedures in the phase of system design called evaluating system effectiveness were covered in Chapter 4 on evaluation.

In the next section, we shall discuss several procedures used in the phase of system design called **analyzing system requirements.** We shall outline the types of resources and constraints that a designer must consider when describing the current state of the system.

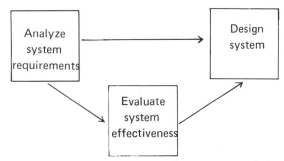

Figure 12.1   Basic strategy of learning system design

DESCRIBING THE CURRENT STATE OF THE SYSTEM

Learning system design is an orderly process. The designer must first specify the requirements of the system before he attempts to fulfill them. In specifying system requirements, the designer describes the beginning and the end of the design process. The beginning of the process is a description of the **current state of the system.** The end of the process is the **goal of the system.** After securely anchoring the two ends, the designer then proceeds to design a system to tie them together. The effectiveness of the system that is ultimately produced depends to a large extent upon how precisely the designer specifies the current state of the system and the system goals.

In the chapters on learning objectives, we described procedures for specifying system goals. Here we shall describe the procedures for specifying the current state of the system.

CURRENT STATE INFORMATION   In describing the current state of the system, the designer must collect information about all the variables that might affect the performance of the system. These variables fall into four categories:

1. The system environment
2. The resources the designer has at his disposal
3. The constraints that might be imposed on him
4. The characteristics of the learners

Unless the designer has collected and organized information of this sort, he will not be able to proceed rationally with the design process.

In most cases, much of the information about the current status of the system is known to the system designer. He is usually quite familiar with the environment of the system and has general knowledge of how things are done. However, unless the required information is written down and organized systematically, it will not be available when needed and cannot readily be communicated to others.

THE SYSTEM ENVIRONMENT   No learning system exists in isolation. Every system operates in a larger environment. The designer must consider the characteristics of the environment and design the system to function effectively within it. For example, if the learning system is to be a course which is part of a larger curriculum, the objectives and subject matter of each of the courses in the curriculum should be described. Thus, the gaps or areas of overlap may be identified and the objectives of each course will fit the objectives of the whole curriculum.

If the system has previously been in operation and is being redesigned, the designer should take careful note of possible changes in the system's environment. Before he proceeds to modify the system, he should consider whether or not changes in the environment require changes in the system's purpose. An example of this can be noted by the change in the curricula of many nursing schools in the past few years to fit the new role of nurses in hospitals.

AVAILABLE RESOURCES   The second category of variables in a system operating description are the resources available to the system designer. An inventory of such resources assists the designer in making decisions regarding the best choice of materials and procedures. Resources consist of instructional personnel, instructional materials and equipment, and facilities.

Instructional personnel include instructors and teaching assistants. When several sections of a course are to be taught by different instructors, agreements among them must be reached regarding common instructional goals and sharing of the instructional aids and materials. Agreements as to common goals are essential, especially if a common final exam is to be given. When instructional aids and materials are in short supply, it is necessary that they be shared. This usually involves setting up a schedule of use. Decisions regarding instructional goals and materials should be written down and included in the document describing the current state of the system. This document can then serve as a guide for each individual instructor.

Information concerning the functions of teaching assistants should also be specified in an account of the current state of the system. Such information is of value to the designer and to the assistants as well. Assistants are usually employed as discussion leaders, laboratory monitors, test scorers, or in some combination of these functions. When the assistants' functions are clearly described, the designer can estimate the skills they will need. He can use this information to select appropriate assistants or to specify the objectives of a training program. Specific information about the functions the teaching assistants are expected to perform is of value to the assistants themselves. In order to perform their functions efficiently, the assistants must clearly understand the goals of the course and how their functions contribute to achieving the goals. It is quite surprising how frequently this information is not made available.

Instructional materials and equipment are another kind of resource available to the system designer. Most instructors have, in the past, limited themselves to the use of the traditional chalkboard. However, modern educational technology is making available an increasingly greater variety of audio and visual aids including photographic slides, motion pictures, and viedotape recordings. In addition, instructors are learning to produce audio and visual aids for their own specific instructional uses. To make efficient use of these instructional materials, the designer must learn how to incorporate them in a learning system.

Physical facilities are sometimes overlooked by the system designer. While most instructors consider the library when they plan a course, there are several other facilities available which are often ignored. These include audiovisual media centers and learning consultative services. An audiovisual center is staffed by people who are experts in designing the kind of audiovisual aids for specific instructional purposes. Consultative services are staffed by experts in learning system design and evaluation. Consulting with these experts will assist the designer in planning a more efficient learning system. The system designer should inquire as to the availability of these facilities and plan to use the expertise they provide.

CONSTRAINTS Constraints are limitations placed on the system designer. There are generally two kinds of constraints to be considered in designing a learning system: (1) insufficient time to achieve instructional goals and (2) restricted freedom to innovate. By specifying the specific constraints he is likely to encounter, the system designer can seek ways to remove or alleviate them and then plan his objectives so that they can be realistically achieved.

The problem of insufficient time to achieve instructional goals occurs when the amount of subject matter to be covered in a course is not under the control of the system designer. For example, in some courses, the material to be covered is dictated by higher authority or simply by tradition, and thus the instructor must accept more instructional goals than can be effectively achieved in the period of time allotted to the course. Such a situation often results in the students not achieving all the goals or in superficial learning. When such a problem arises, the designer should rank the learning objectives that are to be achieved in order of importance. This will provide a framework for allocating time and designing instructional procedures.

A system designer may be restricted in his freedom to innovate because his learning system must be compatible with other systems. Such circumstances occur either when several instructors teach the same course or when the course is part of a larger sequence. In either case, the instructors should seek to reach a mutual understanding regarding the learning objectives to be achieved. Such an agreement will usually remove the constraint by permitting each instructor to develop his own instructional procedures.

STUDENT CHARACTERISTICS The final category of information about the current state of the system is the characteristics of the students. Although we take up this topic last, it is probably the most important information needed for system design. A learning system should be designed to accept students at the level they enter the system and assist them to achieve the system objectives. It is impossible to design an efficient learning system without information about student characteristics.

Four types of student information are required. First, the number of students may set an upper limit on the level of objectives and dictate the kind of instructional materials and procedures that may be used. For example, with large classes it may be impossible to achieve high-level problem-solving objectives unless plans are made to provide the appropriate individual practice. Although small classes permit the system designer to utilize a wider variety of instructional procedures, the limitations imposed by large classes may be overcome by careful use of appropriate audiovisual materials or independent learning units.

The second type of student information has to do with student entry skills. In Chapter 4 (Evaluating Learning Systems), procedures were described for obtaining specific data regarding entry skills and how to use this information for designing instruction.

The third type of student information deals with student academic background and aspirations. The system designer should be aware of the major areas of study of his students and how the system he is designing fits in. For example, he should know whether his course is required or is taken as an elective; he should know which courses students were required to take as prerequisites; and he should know how his course relates to students' professional goals. This information will help him choose relevant subject matter and learning objectives for the system.

The fourth type of student information is class heterogeneity. If the students differ widely from one another in their previous preparation, the designer must be prepared for a wide dispersion of entry skills. Consequently, he must be prepared to include remedial learning units in the learning system or consider instructional procedures which accommodate wide individual differences among students.

SUMMARY The learning system design process begins with a specification of system requirements which include a description of the system goal and the current state of the system.

There are four categories of information needed to describe the current state of the system:

1. The system environment
2. The resources available to the designer
3. The constraints on the system
4. The characteristics of the learners

With this information available to him, the system designer is better able to plan and design a learning system that accommodates the constraints and makes best use of the resources available.

A new instructor is assigned to teach one section of a course. The course is also taught by five other instructors. He is assigned one teaching assistant. He knows that he needs four categories of information in order to specify system requirements.

F
R
A
M
E

12.2

a. System environment
b. Resources available
c. Constraints
d. Learner characteristics

The following is a list of things the instructor does to gather the information he needs. In which category is each?

1. Checks to see how his learning objectives fit with related courses. _____
2. Makes a list of functions his teaching assistant will perform. _____
3. Plans to have students fill out a fact sheet listing previous courses taken. _____
4. Eliminates an irrelevant topic in order to allot more time to an important topic. _____
5. Checks to see what visual aids are available. _____
6. Checks learning objectives of other instructors. _____
7. Checks Media Center for cost of preparing new photographic slides. _____

FEEDBACK:

12.2 1 a   3 d   5 b   7 b
      2 b   4 c   6 a

PRINCIPLES OF LEARNING SYSTEM DESIGN

Figure 12.1 illustrates three phases of the learning system design process. It is also useful for illustrating several principles that characterize the design process. These principles are:

PRINCIPLE 1: SYSTEM GOALS AND RESOURCES ARE SPECIFIED BEFORE DESIGN DECISIONS ARE MADE.

PRINCIPLE 2: THE SYSTEM DESIGN PROCESS PROVIDES FOR PROGRESSIVE CORRECTION.

PRINCIPLE 3: THE SYSTEM DESIGN PROCESS IS ITERATIVE AND INTERACTIVE.

SYSTEM GOALS AND RESOURCES ARE SPECIFIED BEFORE THE DESIGN DECISIONS ARE MADE One of the primary characteristics of the system approach is that system requirements are specified before solutions are generated. This sequence of events ensures that the designer does not begin to work on the problem of **how** to design the system before he has clearly specified **what** the system is to accomplish and **what** resources and constraints he has to work with.

By considering goals, resources, and constraints together, the designer is able to generate many possible alternative solutions and judge the practicality of each one. In effect, he is considering, at the same time, the ends to be achieved and possible means for achieving these ends. Thus, when actual design decisions are made, he can be reasonably sure that no viable alternative will be neglected.

THE SYSTEM DESIGN PROCESS PROVIDES FOR PROGRESSIVE CORRECTION At all stages of the design process, the designer must check his work to determine whether the goal has been achieved. This rule is obvious when applied to the system as a whole. After designing and trying out the system, the designer determines the extent to which the objectives were achieved and what unforeseen problems developed. Then he redesigns the system to remove the indicated discrepancies.

However, the basic design strategy requires that the designer check his work at each stage of the design process as well as at the end. For example, after writing an objective, the designer writes a test item for the test that will eventually be used to assess student achievement of the objective. He does this to ensure that the terminal behavior of the objective has been written in operational terms and the conditions and standards of the objective have been met. If the objective and the test item are not compatible, one of the things he must do is review the objective.

THE DESIGN PROCESS IS ITERATIVE AND INTERACTIVE   Designing a learning system is a complex task because each component of the system must fit together with every other component. A designer does not put a system together as one would put beads on a string—starting at one end and preceding with each step until the end is reached. Instead, he characteristically begins with an overall plan consisting of general ideas about goals, resources, and constraints. Then, using the plan as a guide, he works on one part of the system at a time, putting in details, identifying problems that must be solved, and listing several alternative solutions for later consideration. He may return to the same step in the design process several times, each time adding more detail or correcting errors. For example, the designer first tries to specify all of his objectives as completely as possible. However, when he begins to work on his evaluation plan, he may find that he has omitted some objectives or that others do not include standards that are sufficiently precise to enable him to design a valid test. He must then return to the objectives and correct them. As more and more details are specified, he continually checks to see whether each part of the system fits with all the other parts. The diagram of the system design process (Fig. 12.1) illustrates the iterative characteristic of the design process; it has no beginning and no end.

Although the designer can only work on one phase of the design at a time, it is necessary for him to continually keep in mind the requirements of the other phases as well. All decisions made in one phase of the design process have implications for the decisions made in the other phases. We have discussed several examples of such interaction: relating goals to resources; relating objectives to test items; relating constraints to design alternatives. The designer must continually look back to what he has already done and ahead to what remains to be done in order to consider the impact of each decision on the decisions he made previously and on the decisions he will have to make in the future.

To illustrate in more detail the interactive nature of the system design process, we have redrawn the design diagram in more complicated form. The two-way arrows between and within the blocks signify the interrelatedness of the various phases of the design process. The reader should try to remember the names of blocks to assist him in developing an overall plan for designing his learning system.

The system design procedures and techniques you have learned in this book are tools for obtaining and utilizing information in making design decisions. Table 12.1 summarizes these design procedures and illustrates how they are interrelated. The procedures are listed in the first column of the table. The second column tells what information is required to perform the procedure. The third column tells where else in the system design process the results of the design procedure are used.

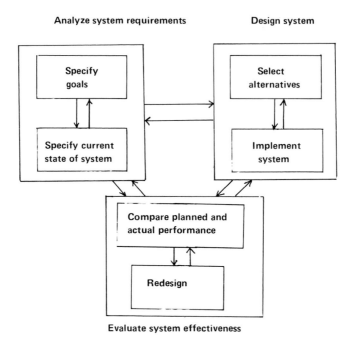

Figure 12.2 The interrelations among the phases in the learning system design process.

F
R
A
M
E

12.3

Three principles that characterize the strategy of learning system design are:

a. System goals and resources are specified before design decisions are made.

b. The system design process is self-correcting.

c. The system design process is iterative and interactive.

What principle does each of the following design activities illustrate?

1. The designer checks an instructional unit to determine if all the _____ enabling objectives have been covered.

2. The designer selects a movie from the school film library because _____ a learning objective requires students to make visual discrimations.

3. The designer eliminates an objective from one of his instruction- _____ al units when he finds that students have achieved the corres- ponding entry skill.

FEEDBACK:
12.3   1 b
        2 a
        3 c

TABLE 12.1   INFORMATION RELATIONSHIPS AMONG LEARNING SYSTEM DESIGN PROCEDURES

Design Procedure	Information Required for Practice	Where Information Is Used
1. Describe current status of system.	What resources do I need? What resources do I have to work with? What limitations and constraints must I consider? (Examples: time; student entry skills; administrative rules; space)	Deriving and writing objectives. Designing instructional procedures. Formulating and implementing evaluation plan.
2. Derive and write learning objectives.	Goals. Referent situation analysis. Subject matter areas. Resources and limitations.	Formulate evaluation plans. Describe and analyze tasks. Instructional procedures. Feedback to referent situation and learning system description.
3. Formulate evaluation plans.	Objectives. Resources and limitations.	Implement evaluation plan, e.g. assessment of student achievement. Redesign of learning system. Feedback to objectives.
4. Describe and analyze tasks.	Objectives. Referent situation analysis.	Design and implement instructional procedures. Feedback to objectives and evaluation.
5. Design and implement instructional procedures.	Learning principles. Task description and analysis.	Implement evaluation plan (i.e., analysis of what was planned, what was done, what resulted).
6. Implement evaluation plan.	Evaluation plan. Instructional procedures design plan.	Assess student achievement. Identify instructional problems for redesign.
7. Redesign.	Evaluation data. Learning principles. Instructional procedures design plan. Learning system description.	Redesigned system.

SUMMARY In this section of the chapter, we have presented a strategy for designing a learning system. This strategy consists of three phases: (1) analyzing system requirements in terms of system goals and the current state of the system; (2) designing the system by selecting from among available alternative procedures, equipment, and materials; and (3) evaluating system effectiveness by comparing planned performance with actual performance. All the procedures covered in previous chapters apply to one or more of these three phases of the design strategy.

We also presented three principles that guide the system design process. The first principle states that system goals and resources should be specified before design decisions are made. Applying this principle will enable the designer to use available resources to achieve the system goal and stay within the imposed constraints.

The second principle states that the system design process includes procedures for progressive self-correction. Application of this principle enables the designer to identify and remedy design errors or omissions throughout the entire design process.

The third principle states that the design process is iterative and interactive. Application of this principle enables the designer to plan the entire system and interrelate the various component parts.

The following section of the chapter deals with the question of how to design a system so as to increase the effectiveness with which the system components interact. Three further principles of design will be developed.

SYSTEM INTERACTION

One of the most important distinguishing characteristics of an effective learning system is that the system elements are interdependent and thus must interact to achieve the system goal. A teacher and a group of students in a classroom do not necessarily constitute a learning system. However, if they were engaging in a question-and-answer session to clarify some assigned reading material, the interdependency criterion would be met.

No learning system exists in isolation. Every learning system is related to some other learning system. It is both part of a larger learning system and it contains component parts which themselves are learning systems. A typical school course is a learning system. It is a component part of a curriculum, which is another learning system. The curriculum is, in turn, part of a larger learning system, a field of study. The course itself contains learning systems. It is composed of subject matter units which, in turn, are composed of still smaller units having to do with individual learning objectives. Every learning system is composed of learning subsystems and is itself part of a larger learning system.

Sometimes it is difficult to think of some system components, such as a book or an overhead projector, a classroom or the students and teacher, as subsystems. However, when we consider that a book or a projector can be used in different ways to facilitate or hinder student learning, or that the temperature or size of a room may have a similar effect, it is reasonable to think of all the components of a system as subsystems that do interact with one another in their effect on student learning. When we get into the habit of thinking this way, we realize that when we design a system, we must pay attention to how its subsystems interact.

The effectivenss and efficiency of a learning system usually depend upon how compatibly the system components interact. Compatible interaction means that the components assist one another in achieving the system goal. It is achieved by selecting the right components for the job to be done and arranging conditions so that the components can work together. Consequently, in designing a learning system, the designer must take into account all possible interaction among system components and organize the system so that the components interact in a compatible manner.

In this section, we will consider system interaction in more detail. First, we will show how interaction is related to system performance and to the system design process. Then we will state three principles of effective system interaction and show how these principles apply to learning system design.

An instructor is designing a course in psychology. He knows he must consider interactions outside the course (larger system) and inside the course (among system components). The following is a list of the instructor's design activities. Label **O**, those activities that illustrate interactions outside the course; label **W**, those that illustrate interactions within the course.

F
R
A
M
E

12.4

1. Sequence course topics.   _____

2. Checks course objectives with requirements of state certification exam.   _____

3. Plans discussion sessions to be conducted by teaching assistants.   _____

4. Discusses student rating reports with teaching assistants.   _____

5. Prepares visual aids to accompany lectures.   _____

6. Checks what other departments expect their students to get from the course.   _____

7. Schedules question and answer session at end of each lecture.   _____

8. Checks with Media Center on availability of demonstration film.   _____

FEEDBACK:

12.4	1 W	3 W	5 W	7 W
	2 O	4 W	6 O	8 O

DESIGNING A LEARNING SYSTEM FOR EFFECTIVE INTERACTIONS

We have been discussing two ideas about systems: (1) that the components (subsystems) of a system interact to achieve a goal; and (2) that every system is both embedded in and includes other systems. These ideas suggest three more principles that characterize the system design process.

PRINCIPLE 4:	A LEARNING SYSTEM OPERATES MOST EFFICIENTLY WHEN ALL THE COMPONENTS ASSIST ONE ANOTHER IN ACHIEVING THE SYSTEM GOAL.
PRINCIPLE 5:	A LEARNING SYSTEM MUST BE DESIGNED TO OPERATE COMPATIBLY WITH OTHER SYSTEMS.
PRINCIPLE 6:	NO SYSTEM COMPONENT OR PROCEDURE CAN BE MODIFIED WITHOUT HAVING AN EFFECT ON OTHER COMPONENTS OR PROCEDURES.

COMPATIBLE INTERACTION AMONG SYSTEM COMPONENTS   No system can operate efficiently unless we design it so that the components (subsystems) work well together to achieve the system goal. When we design our teaching methods and procedures, we select the system components and specify how these components will work together; that is, how they will interact to achieve the system goal.

The following examples illustrate some of the factors that must be considered in designing a system so that the components work well together to achieve the system goal.

1. The teacher whose course consists solely of a series of lectures has designed a learning system with a particular relationship between him and his students. He is the purveyor of information and they are the recipients. He is active, they are passive. What type of learning goal will this kind of interaction effectively achieve? Presumably, an instructor who designs this kind of interaction has as his goal the ability of the students to reproduce what he said.

2. Chapter 9 on how to teach principles indicates that one of the first requirements is to communicate the learning objectives to the students. How should this aspect of the learning system be designed so as to facilitate compatible interactions? One alternative is for the teacher to present them verbally to the students; another is for the teacher to write down the objectives, together with some illustrative test items, and distribute them in written form to the students. There are two advantages to the latter procedure. First, it insures that all the students have the objectives in their notes. If the teacher communicates them

verbally, some of the students may not write them down. Second, having the objectives in written form means that the students can use them continuously as a guide in their own learning.

3. Consider the conditions of providing practice. The teacher may ask questions which the students answer. He may assign homework problems for the students to solve. The students might work together in small groups where one student presents a problem which another student solves by applying the principle. Whichever procedure the designer selects, he must consider that a wide variety of examples will be needed and the students must be provided with feedback regarding the correctness of their efforts.

These examples elucidate the fact that when a learning system is designed, attention must be paid not only to choosing the right components for the task, but also to the interactions among the components. The system must be designed so that the components work together toward achieving the goal. The designer should consider a variety of ways the components can interact so that he will not limit himself to traditional modes. He should also consider the advantages and disadvantages of each alternative from the standpoint of how the components can aid one another in achieving the system goal.

COMPATIBILITY WITH OTHER LEARNING SYSTEMS The designer must ensure that the learning system he designs is compatible with other systems in achieving the goal of the larger system to which it belongs. We all are familiar with instances of leraning systems that are ineffective because this guide is ignored. One example is the instructor who teaches what is of interest to him, excluding topics that will help his students in the other courses. Another example is the college service course which is taught as if the students were all majoring in the subject. An instructor who designs a learning system with no thought for the goals of the larger system may easily interfere with achieving those goals.

DESIGN CHECKLIST The following checklist summarizes the procedures a system designer should follow to apply the principles we have been discussing:

- Consider one learning objective at a time. For each objective, write a plan of the procedures to be followed in achieving the objective. State the purpose of all instructional media, materials, and equipment that will be used and the activities of teacher, students, and teaching assistants.

- Check your plan to ensure that: (1) all persons and important equipment are included; and (2) that the components aid, or at least do not interfere with, one another.

- Write procedures to ensure that equipment will be available when needed and in good working order.
- Write procedures to inform each person of what he is to do, and how he is to do it and what is expected of him
- Write procedures for determining whether or not each person has the prerequisite knowledge and skill to perform his function.
- Write procedures for providing the necessary training.

An instructor should follow this checklist point by point until he gains enough experience in designing learning systems so that he automatically considers interactions among components.

The larger the system, the greater the number of components it contains. Consequently, there will be many more possible ways the components may interact. The above checklist will help in identifying and planning for these interactions. Incorrect design decisions and omissions will inevitably occur because of the complexity of the system design process. Undoubtedly it was an experienced system designer who coined the famous saying that has come to be known as **Murphy's Law.** Murphy's Law states (ruefully): Anything that can go wrong, will go wrong.

F R A M E

12.5

Two principles of learning system interaction are:

a. A learning system works best when the components all assist one another in achieving the goal of the system.

b. No system component or procedure can be changed without having an effect on other components or procedures.

For each of the following design activities; indicate whether it is a correct or incorrect application of these principles.

1. A designer writes objectives for all instructional units but does not tell the students what they are.   _____

2. A designer plans to conduct a large group lecture followed by student discussions in small groups. The small group discussions will be conducted by graduate teaching assistants. The designer provides the teaching assistants and the students with a list of objectives for each lecture.   _____

3. An instructor substitutes videotaped lectures for "live" lectures. In addition, he plans weekly discussion sessions in which students can ask questions.   _____

4. At the beginning of each laboratory period, an instructor gives the students a short test to determine whether or not they know how to operate the lab equipment.   _____

FEEDBACK:

12.5 1 Incorrect   2 Correct   3 Correct   4 Correct

EVALUATING THE DESIGN

After providing the initial design plan, the system designer should check his work to determine whether the materials and procedures chosen assist or interfere with the learners in achieving the objective. Three factors should be considered in evaluating the interactions among components. These are: (1) duplicate activities; (2) adequate instructions; (3) and feedback information.

DUPLICATE ACTIVITIES If any of the activities overlap; that is, if the same activity is performed by more than one component, the duplication should be necessary in order to achieve the objective. For example, many instructors assign a chapter of reading for homework and then lecture on the same material the next day. This duplication can only be justified if the students are not able to learn the material from the book. In that case, the instructor's lecture should be directed at integrating the materials or providing a different viewpoint from that presented in the book. On the other hand, giving practice problems in class and then assigning practice problems for homework may be considered a justifiable duplication of activities. Solving problems in the class is a group problem-solving technique in which the students mutually assist one another, whereas solving problems at home is an individual learning procedure.

ADEQUATE INSTRUCTIONS Each person in the system should be informed of what he is to do and what is expected of him; otherwise, there will probably be misunderstandings and interference. One method of providing such information is to distribute a course prospectus at the beginning of a term describing the content and procedures of the course. This example should be followed, at least at an information level, for each learning unit of the course. In formulating instructions, the designer usually gets a clearer picture of how the various components interact and whether or not the interaction among them contributes to or impedes achieving the objective.

FEEDBACK INFORMATION The instructor should insure that each person has enough information and guidance to work with other students efficiently. This is especially important when students are working together using procedures and equipment that are unfamiliar to them. If students are to work together in providing each other practice and problem-solving, it would be desirable to give each of them a checklist or a set of questions to guide their activities.

TRAINING All persons should be trained to use the equipment and procedures of the system. Teachers have planned to use an overhead projector without learning how to focus it and without knowing how to design a lecture so that the visual material supports, rather than interferes with, what they were saying. Teachers have designed auto-tutorial learning units involving slide projectors and audio tape recorders without providing instructions to the students on how to operate the equipment.

FRAME 12.6

In evaluating the interactions in a system, the designer should use the following guidelines:

1. If any activities are performed by more than one component, the duplication in effort should _____ achieving the system goal.

2. Each person in the system should be informed of his _____ in the system.

3. The designer should ensure that all persons in the system have sufficient _____ and _____ to work together efficiently.

4. All persons should be _____ to use equipment and procedures of the system.

INTERACTIONS IN SYSTEM REDESIGN

We have been discussing how principles dealing with interactions among components or subsystems should be applied in designing a learning system. These principles, and one more which we shall discuss in this section, also apply in revising or redesigning the system. Having tried out the system, the designer is in the position to evaluate how well the system goals have been achieved and to identify problems that arose. At that point, he is prepared to revise or redesign the system to alleviate these problems and make the system more efficient.

One important reason that problems arise in the designing of learning systems is that the designer does not anticipate and prepare for the wide variety of interactions that may occur. After the system has operated and evaluation data are available, the designer can determine whether everything went according to plan. For example, he may discover that a needed component or procedure was inadvertently omitted, or that subsystems did not work together as they were supposed to. He may find that there was a breakdown in communications causing interference, conflict, or friction among the components.

The design checklist on pages 319 - 320 can help to identify such interaction problems. It focuses the designer's attention on interactions among components as a possible cause of system problems and guides him in making redesign decisions.

FEEDBACK:

12.6 1 assist or contribute to   3 information . . . guidance
         2 function   4 trained

In redesigning a system, it is particularly important to follow the sixth principle stated on page 318. This principle states that no system component or procedure can be modified without having an effect on other components or procedures. Consequently, during the redesign process, when the designer considers modifying one aspect of the system, he must analyze the possible effects of the proposed modification and determine other changes in the system that are required.

The designer should be particularly sensitive to interactions among system components when considering the following types of design modifications:

- When adding a component to perform a function previously omitted. Examples: employing a new evaluation instrument or adding a new visual aid.

- When substituting one component or subsystem for another to accomplish a particular goal. A typical example is a teacher substituting an auto-tutorial unit for a classroom lecture.

- When changing a procedure. The following anecdote illustrates the necessity for considering interactions when modifying an instructional procedure. A teacher of our acquaintance was concerned about the lack of student participation in his discussion classes. After some discussion of the problem, he accepted the suggestion that one of the reasons his students were not volunteering answers to questions was that he habitually answered his own questions himself. He asked a question and, without giving the students sufficient time to formulate and volunteer a reply, he immediately launched into an explanatory discussion. When the teacher became aware of this habit, he firmly resolved to remain silent after asking a question; however, nothing changed; his students still did not volunteer answers nor did they participate in the discussion. Further analysis revealed that by modifying the question-and-answer procedure, he had changed the behavior of one component of the system (the teacher) without considering the effect on the other components (the students). The students, having been conditioned to regarding the teacher's questions as rhetorical, did not perceive that any change in the system had occurred. They did not realize that a consequent change in their own behavior was expected. When the teacher informed them of the new procedure and what was now expected of them, there was an immediate increase in responsiveness and participation.

Many efforts to modify and improve educational systems have floundered because they were directed at changing one component of the system without considering the effects of that change on the other components. Consider the examples on the next page:

- Teachers learn to lecture better, but students are not taught how to take notes better.
- Grading procedures are changed, but teachers do not learn how to plan adequate evaluation procedures.
- Teachers are trained better and then are assigned to schools where administrators do not know how to take advantage of the teachers' improved teaching skills.
- Instructors use graduate teaching assistants in courses, but the assistants are given no training in teaching.
- New audiovisual equipment is purchased, but teachers are not instructed in its use.
- Plans are made to provide tutors for disadvantaged students, but no provision is made to insure their compatibility.

The list could go on, and the reader can probably supply many examples of his own. The implication is clear. A learning system cannot be redesigned efficiently, without taking interactions among the components into account.

In summary, we have stressed that sensitivity to and concern for interactions among components and subsystems is a particularly important characteristic of the system approach to instruction. We have stated three principles dealing with system interactions and provided a checklist to guide the system designer in applying the principle.

INTERACTION AND SYSTEM BOUNDARIES

The first few times a designer attempts to apply the principles of system design, he usually becomes lost in a morass of interactions. Every aspect of the system seems to be related to everything else, and every decision he faces seems to require that he make ten more. The designer begins to see implications extending far beyond the system he is designing. Surely, he thinks, his choice of objectives affects the objectives of other courses, of other curricula, perhaps of the entire school. How far shall he go in considering the impact of his design decisions on other systems? Where are the boundaries of the system he is designing?

There is no simple answer to these questions. When dealing with such complex phenomena as learning systems, the answer is bound to be provisional. However, there is a rule that will focus the designer's attention on the most important interactions of the learning system he is designing.

The instructor should place an arbitrary boundary on his learning system and consider only the interactions among the subsystems that fall within the boundary. Where should the boundary be placed? The boundary should include only those components or subsystems that: (1) relate to achieving the objectives of the system; and (2) the designer can do something about. If a course is one of a sequence of courses in a curriculum, the other courses would be within the system boundary since the instructor must consider them in writing his objectives. On the other hand, if an instructor wishes to include audiovisual aids in his course, but the policy of his department is to provide no funds for such aids, it is useless for him to try to include these aids in his design unless he can influence department policy. Departmental policy regarding audiovisual equipment is outside the boundary of his instructional system.

An instructor can always improve his own course since it is within his power to do so. However, he must recognize that if he succeeds, the increase in student learning and in positive student attitudes that result are likely to produce a considerable impact on other courses in his department. Even by setting arbitrary boundaries, one cannot escape system interactions.

Which of the following system modifications require the designer to consider interactions?

1. Adding a component _____
2. Substituting one component for another _____
3. Changing a procedure _____
4. All of the above _____

F
R
A
M
E

12.7

SUMMARY CHECKLIST

Principles of Learning System Design and Redesign

1. System goals and resources should be specified before design decisions are made.
2. The system design process provides for progressive correction.
3. The system design process is iterative and interactive.
4. A learning system operates most efficiently when all component assist one another in achieving the system goal.
5. A learning system must be designed to operate compatibly with other systems.
6. No system component or procedure can be modified without having an effect on other system components or procedures.

Strategy of Learning System Design

1. Analyze system requirements.
   a. Specify system goal(s).
   b. Specify the current state of the system.

FEEDBACK:
12.7 4

    1)   List materials, procedures, and facilities that are available for incorporation in the system.

    2)   Specify constraints that might prevent achieving goal of the system.

    3)   Specify alternative materials and procedures that might overcome constraints.

    4)   For each design procedure, specify other design procedures in which the information will be used.

2. Design and implement system.

    a.   Select materials and procedures with reference to learning principles.

    b.   Specify and sequence instructional units. For each objective specify:

        1)   What teacher and students will do.

        2)   How learning materials and procedures that are selected contribute to achieving objective.

        3)   Instructions and aids to inform each person in the system what he is to do and how he is to do it.

        4)   Procedures for determining entry skills of student.

        5)   Materials and procedures for evaluating system performance.

        6)   Check and justify duplication of functions among components.

    c.   Operate system according to design plan.

3. Evaluate system effectiveness.

    a.   Compare planned and actual system performance.

        1)   Specify discrepancies between goals and actual system performance.

        2)   Check interactions among components.

            a. Was a needed component or procedure inadvertently omitted?

            b. Was there a breakdown in communications among components?

            c. Did components interact as planned?

            d. Was there conflict or interference among components?

    b.   Redesign.

        1)   Should goals or objectives be changed?

        2)   If redesign involves

            a. adding a component or procedures;

            b. substituting one component for another; or

            c. changing a procedure;

            check effect on other design decisions, components, and procedures.

        3)   Consider the possible effects changes might have outside the system.

POSTTEST

1. An instructor was scheduled to teach a course for which he was assigned one teaching assistant. He prepared a plan which included the topics to be covered and two achievement tests. Which essential characteristic(s) of a learning system did he omit.

    a. Goals

    b. Procedures the teaching assistant was to follow

    c. Materials and media to be used

    d. All of the above

2. The following diagram illustrates the learning system design process. Write the name of the correct design procedure in each blank.

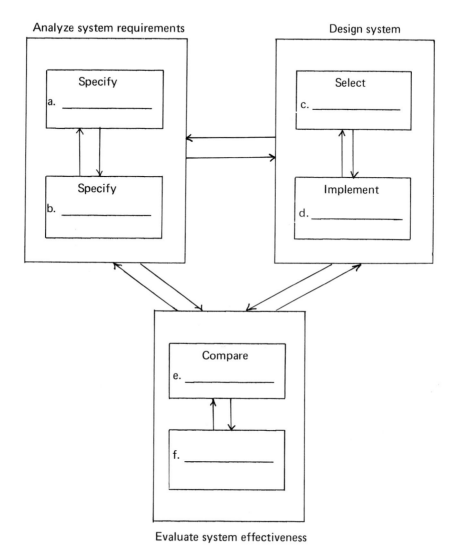

Analyze system requirements

Design system

Specify

a. _____

Select

c. _____

Specify

b. _____

Implement

d. _____

Compare

e. _____

f. _____

Evaluate system effectiveness

3. The three basic system design phases are:

    A.   Analyze system requirements

    B.   Design system

    C.   Evaluate system

To which of these phases does each of the following examples of design procedures belong?

a. Write objectives. _____

b. Assess student achievement. _____

c. Obtain information about student entry skills. _____

d. Select instructional materials. _____

e. Provide students practice in problem solving. _____

4. An instructor is planning to teach a new course. He is assigned three teaching assistants. He knows that in order to specify system requirements he needs four categories of information.

    A.   System environment

    B.   Resources available

    C.   Constraints

    D.   Learner characteristics

The instructor does the following things to gather the information he needs. In which category is each?

a. Checks to see if requirements of the next course in the curriculum have changed. _____

b. On the first day of class, he gives an entry skill test. _____

c. Checks teaching experience of his teaching assistants. _____

d. Lists objectives in order of importance and allocates instructional time according to list. _____

e. Checks his preliminary design plans with university learning service. _____

5. When a designer analyzes the requirements of a learning system, he specifies the system goal(s) and the current state of the system. Which of the following categories of information is usually *NOT* included in specifying the current state of the system? _____

a. The subject matter to be covered

b. Available facilities

c. Instructional procedures he cannot modify

d. Select a slide-tape unit

e. Previous courses taken by students

6. Three principles that characterize the strategy of learning system design are:

    A.   System goals and resources are specified before design decisions are made.

    B.   The system design process is self-correcting.

    C.   The system design process is iterative and interactive.

Which principle does each of the following design activities illustrate?

a. The designer checks behavioral objectives by _____ writing test items.

b. The designer designs several independent study _____ units after determining that students have a wide range of entry skills.

c. The designer prepares a general evaluation plan and _____ then specifies the test instruments and procedures.

d. The designer specifies the terminal objectives for _____ each unit of a learning system and then uses task description and task analysis procedures to specify the enabling objectives.

7. Two principles of learning system interaction are:

    A.   A learning system works best when the components all assist one another in achieving the goal of the system.

    B.   No system component or procedure can be changed without having an effect on other components or procedures.

For each of the following design activities, indicate whether it is a correct or incorrect application of these principles.

a. After writing the learning objectives for an instruc- _____ tional unit of a course, the designer lists the follow-ing information: what the teacher does; what the students do; how visual aids will be used.

b. An instructor is assigned a new graduate teaching _____ assistant. He asks him to conduct a discussion session for the students.

c. An instructor introduces a new procedure where- _____ by students work together in groups. The instruc-tor distributes a list of directions describing the new procedure.

d. An instructor shows the learning objectives for _____ his course to other instructors to determine whether gaps or overlaps exist.

Answers to this posttest can be found on page 338.

SUPPLEMENTAL READINGS IN LEARNING SYSTEM DESIGN

Baker, R. L. and Shutz, R. E. (Ed.): *Instructional Product Development,* (New York: Van Nostrand Reinhold Co., 1971).

Briggs, L. J.: *Handbook of Procedures for the Design of Instruction,* (Pittsburgh, Pa.: American Institutes for Research, 1970).

Briggs, L. J., Campeau, P. L., Gagné, R. M., and May, M. A.: *Instructional Media,* (Pittsburgh, Pa.: American Institutes for Research, 1967).

Buckley, W. (Ed.): *Modern Systems Research for the Behavioral Scientist: A Sourcebook,* (Chicago: Aldine Publishing Co., 1968).

Churchman, C. W.: *The Systems Approach,* (New York: Dell Publishing Co., 1968).

Crawford, J. (Ed.): *National Research Training Manual,* (Monmouth: Teaching Research Divsion of the Oregon State System of Higher Education, 1969).

Davies, I. K.: *The Management of Learning,* (New York: McGraw-Hill, 1971).

Edling, J.(Ed.): *The Contribution of Behavioral Science to Instructional Technology,* (Monmouth: Teaching Research Divsion of the Oregon State System of Higher Education, 1968).

Heinich, R.: *Systems Engineering of Education II: Application of Systems Thinking to Instruction,* (Los Angeles: Education and Training Consultants, 1968).

Hunkins, F. P.: *Questioning Strategies and Techniques,* (Boston: Allyn and Bacon, 1972).

Kaufman, R. A.: *Educational Systems Planning,* (Englewood Cliffs, N. J.: Prentice-Hall, Inc., 1972).

Kemp, J. E.: *Instructional Design,* (Belmont, Calif.: Fearon Publishers/Lear Siegler, Inc., 1971).

Knirk, F. G. and Childs, J. W. (Ed.): *Instructional Technology: A Book of Readings,* (New York: Holt, Rinehart, and Winston, 1968).

MacKenzie, N., Eraut, M., and Jones, H. C.: *Teaching and Learning: An Introduction to New Methods and Resources in Higher Education,* (Paris: United Nations Educational, Scientific, and Cultural Organization, 1970).

Mager, R. F.: *Goal Analysis,* (Belmont, Calif.: Fearon Publishers/Lear Siegler, Inc., 1972).

Merrill, M. D. (Ed.): *Instructional Design: Readings,* (Englewood Cliffs, N. J.: Prentice-Hall, Inc., 1971).

Popham, W. J. and Baker, E. L.: *Systematic Instruction,* (Englewood Cliffs, N. J.: Prentice-Hall, Inc., 1970).

Siegel, L.(Ed.): *Instruction: Some Contemporary Viewpoints,* (San Francisco: Chandler Publishing Co., 1967).

Silvern, L. C.: *System Engineering of Education I: The Evolution of Systems Thinking in Education,* (Los Angeles: Education and Training Consultants Co., 1968).

Smith, R. G.: *The Design of Instructional Systems,* (Alexandria: The George Washington University Human Resources Research Office, 1966).

Taylor, G. (Ed.): *The Teacher as Manager: A Symposium,* (London: The Camelot Press (National Council for Educational Technology), 1970).

Weisgerber, R. A. (Ed.): *Developmental Efforts in Individualized Learning,* (Itasca, Ill.: F. E. Peacock Publishers, 1971).

Wittich, W. A. and Schuller, C. F.: *Instructional Technology: Its Nature and Use,* (New York: Harper and Row, 1973).

SUPPLEMENTAL OBJECTIVES

A series of slide-tape presentations is available from the *Instructional Media Center, Michigan State University, East Lansing, Michigan 48824.* These slide-tape units were designed to aid the reader in practicing the skills described in this book.

There are a total of eleven such slide-tape presentations to accompany the text. In order to help the reader evaluate the potential value of these slide-tapes as a part of his learning experience, we have listed below the supplemental objectives that can be achieved through interaction of the text with these audiovisual presentations.

Chapter 1: Overview of Learning System Design

After reading the chapter, you will be given a slide-tape presentation which illustrates a well-designed learning system. After the slide-tape presentation, and in accordance with the discussion in the text, show that you recognize: (1) a description of the current state of the system; (2) a learning objective; (3) a task description; and (4) an evaluation plan.

Chapter 2: Recognizing Well-Formulated Learning Objectives

After completing Chapters 2 and 3, you will see a slide-tape presentation depicting a teacher developing a learning objective for a course. You will also be given an aid called the Guide for Writing Learning Objectives, which lists the correct sequence of steps to follow in writing objectives. Using this guide, decide whether or not the teacher has written a well-formulated learning objective.

Chapter 3: Deriving and Writing Learning Objectives

(See Chapter 2.)

Chapter 4: Evaluating Learning Systems

You will see a slide-tape presentation depicting a teacher developing an evaluation plan for a learning system by using an Evaluation Decision Aid which has been included in this chapter. You will be asked questions regarding the teacher's decisions which you should answer according to the principles discussed in the chapter.

Chapter 5: Task Descriptions

Given a simple fixed sequence action task, describe the task. Include all relevant steps.

Chapter 7: Analyzing Tasks, Objectives, and Learner Characteristics

Given a simple task and a flow diagram describing it, analyze the task for the types of learning involved and suggest some special conditions and constraints which might influence the learning.

Chapter 8: General Principles of Learning and Motivation

Given a slide and tape demonstration of an instructional sequence, rate the teacher's performance according to the nine general principles of learning and motivation included in this chapter.

Chapter 9: The Learning and Teaching of Concepts and Principles

After reading the chapter and watching a slide-tape presentation in which concepts and principles of social distance are taught, evaluate the teacher in accordance with the guidelines described in the text. You should be able to do this with 100 percent accuracy.

Chapter 10: The Learning and Teaching of Problem Solving

After viewing a slide-tape presentation which illustrates the five steps in problem solving, indicate that you recognize all the steps and name them.

Chapter 11: Perceptual-Motor Skills

Identify the things an instructor you observe does correctly and incorrectly in teaching a perceptual-motor skill.

Chapter 12: The System Approach to Instruction

You will see a slide-tape presentation in which a teacher describes how he designed a learning system. You will also be given a list of the principles of learning system design discussed in the chapter and will be asked questions regarding events in the design process. Identify the principle illustrated by each event.

ANSWERS TO POSTTESTS

CHAPTER 1

1. a. T
   b. F
   c. T
   d. F
   e. F
   f. F

2. Direction __b__
   Method __a__
   Content and Sequence __c__
   Evaluation __e__
   Constraints __d__

3. a. F
   b. T
   c. F
   d. F
   e. T
   f. T
   g. F
   h. T
   i. T
   j. F

CHAPTER 2

1. All T
2. b
3. b
4. b

5. a. Condition
   b. Condition
   c. Performance
   d. Standard and stability limit

CHAPTER 3

ITEM I

1. F
2. F
3. T
4. T
5. T
6. T
7. T
8. T

ITEM II

1. a
2. b
3. b
4. d
5. d

CHAPTER 4

1. a
2. d
3. d
4. b
5. d
6. c

7. e
8. d
9. d
10. d
11. e

CHAPTER 5

1. F
2. T
3. T
4. F
5. F
6. T
7. F
8. F

9. T
10. F
11. Cue or sign
12. Action
13. Person or object
14. Feedback
15. b

16. c
17. a
18. d
19. Narrative or outline
20. Flow diagram
21. Narrative or outline
22. No description

CHAPTER 6

1. F
2. F
3. F
4. T
5. Operant
6. Classical
7. Operant
8. Classical
9. Classical

10. Concept learning
    Principle learning
    Problem solving
    Perceptual-Motor skills
11. e
12. f
13. a
14. d
15. b
16. c

CHAPTER 7

1. F
2. T
3. T
4. T
5. T
6. F
7. T
8. T
9. T
10. T

11. A
12. B
13. B
14. A
15. Not an output
16. Output
17. Not an output
18. Output
19. Output
20. Not an output

CHAPTER 8

1. b, d
2. The teacher assumed the students could perform the basic skills.
3. b
4. The picture was a poor example of a train.
   No objectives were stated.
   The introduction was vague.
5. d, e
6. b, c
7. d, e
8. Students don't work by themselves in practice.
   The teacher helps them most of the time.
9. a, c
10. b, c, d, e

CHAPTER 9

1. a
2. c
3. d
4. d
5. b
6. b

7. a
8. b
9. Inductive
10. Deductive
11. (1) a
    (2) a

12. a
13. b
14. New ones—ones he has not practiced on
15. a. T
    b. T
    c. T
    d. F
16. b, c
17. a. Yes
    b. Yes
    c. Yes
18. *Reinforcement* is a *function of immediacy* of *reinforcing stimulus, intensity of reinforcing stimulus, valence of reinforcing stimulus.*
19. a. State an objective—explanation, control, prediction, inference, or problem solving.
    b. Derive and test for prerequisite concepts embedded in the principle.
    c. Compose the principle—question, tell or demonstrate.
    d. Require practice according to the objective.
    e. Give a posttest.

CHAPTER 10

1. b, d
2. c
3. b
4. a
5. d
6. b
7. a
8. a
9. a
10. b
11. b, c, d
12. a. 1
    b. 2
    c. 3

13. 1. h
    2. j
    3. k
    4. l
    5. g
    6. f
    7. e
    8. c
    9. b
    10. d
    11. a
    12. i

CHAPTER 11

1. F
2. F
3. T
4. T
5. F

6. T
7. T
8. T
9. T
10. F

11. A perceptual-motor skill is a series of coordinated muscular movements to successfully complete a task.
12. Kinesthesis is the sense which provides information as the result of the movement or position of muscles, joints and tendons.

13. Drive a car   Part
    Golf swing   Whole
    Fly an airplane   Part
    Breast stroke in swimming   Whole
    Sew a seam   Whole

14. Any three of the following:

    Give precise objectives.
    Gradually raise the criterion.
    Provide guidance.
    Avoid passive instruction.
    Provide an overview to demonstrate task.

15. Help students discover critical cues.

16. Any three of the following:

    Provide feedback and knowledge of results.
    Avoid long delays before providing feedback.
    Give opportunity for practice after feedback.
    Hold an individual and/or group debriefing.
    Keep the tone of the debriefing positive and factual.

CHAPTER 12

1. d

2. a. Specify goals
   b. Specify current state of system
   c. Select alternatives
   d. Implement system
   e. Compare planned and actual performance
   f. Redesign

3. a. A
   b. C
   c. A
   d. B
   e. B

4. a. A
   b. D
   c. B
   d. C
   e. B

5. d

6. a. B
   b. B
   c. A
   d. C

7. a. Correct
   b. Incorrect
   c. Correct
   d. Correct

Index